The White Deer
Ecospirituality & the Mythic

Melinda Reidinger

Advance Praise for *The White Deer*

This is a unique and important new book, that like the best of its kind is neither cumbersome nor difficult, but a delight. As one follows the track of the white deer back through our shared human and animal past, Reidinger's work takes us on a journey in search of both the origins of our modern ecological crisis, and for its solution. This is more than the analysis of an archetype, it is a wide-ranging exploration through history, prehistory, psychology, and philosophy of our profound connection to nature. It is a book about loss, estrangement, yet also re-enchantment and hope. Reidinger is a polymath, whose excursions into a tapestry of disciplines is as delightful as Joseph Campbell at his best; in this volume Reidinger has joined the ranks of the storytellers her work seeks to praise—it is a lyrical tour-de-force.

—**Dr. John Grigsby**, archaeologist, author and lecturer

Reidinger's mythic sense is sharp and she finds a way to line up mythical insight in the bone marrow of modern quandaries and problems. Spiritual problems ultimately beg for spiritual guidance to their solutions or transformations. It takes mythicists and poets to reveal these sorts of things- and when such a soul can also wield the power of the academic world like Reidinger, the entire world might be a bit more hopeful.

Reidinger's work reminds me much of the works of David Abram, and several others that have been completely critical to my own understanding, in the way that nearly every paragraph is seeded with fertile ideas that can make you stop and ponder them for hours or days. This book is a well-balanced and conversation-provoking joy.

—**Robin Artisson**, author of *An Carow Gwyn* and *The Clovenstone Workings*

The White Deer is perhaps the most thorough and complete examination ever published of the worldviews and attitudes that support and justify humanity's ongoing exploitation of the earth. Yet Reidinger's conclusions follow nobody's party line: her thought is original as much as it is deep. If the solution to our climate crisis lies in the re-enchantment of the world, Reidinger shows us what that motto really means, and how it is so much more than what most people believe. Re-enchantment happens in our languages, our oldest stories, our customs and symbols, even our ways of seeing and thinking. Re-enchantment is a story about us. The White Deer is a brilliant book. Everyone who wants to think deeply about how to face the changing climate of the world and its increasingly-rare occasions for enchantment, should read it.

—**Prof. Brendan Myers**, author of *Reclaiming Civilization* and *The Circle Of Life Is Broken*

Melinda Reidinger's The White Deer is a gorgeous exploration of two of my favorite subjects: place informed spirituality and myth. Working with the story and motifs of the White Deer and its meaning throughout Arthurian legend, Melinda takes us on a journey that weaves ancient tradition with modern science and delivers us into a realm full of sovereignty and possibility—a realm we might just call home. For those who wish to take their magic and spiritual understanding into the deep wild, this book is a true gift!

—**Briana Saussy**, author of *Making Magic: Weaving Together the Everyday and the Extraordinary* and *Star Child: Joyful Parenting Through Astrology*

The White Deer
Ecospirituality & the Mythic

Melinda Reidinger

The White Deer: Eco-Spirituality and the Mythic, by Melinda Reidinger

Text of this work CC-BY-NC-SA 2023 Melinda Reidinger
Images within this work Copyright 2023 James Hutton.

Paperback edition ISBN: 979-8-9852028-7-8
Hardcover edition ISBN: 979-8-9852028-5-4

First Published 1 March, 2023, by RITONA
3 Rue de Wormeldange, Rodenbourg, LUXEMBOURG

Editing by RITONA
Images by James Hutton: instagram: @stitching_a_laugh_to_darkness

Ordering, distribution, and information about RITONA available at abeautifulresistance.org

De te fabula narratur
(The story is told about you)
—Karl Marx, after Horace

I sat upon the shore
Fishing, with the arid plain behind me
Shall I at least set my lands in order?
—T.S. Eliot, The Wasteland

Within

Eight of Batons—7
Acknowledgments—11
The Challenge—13
The Nature of Myth, the Myth of Nature—17
Sir Gawain and Lady Ragnelle—27
Is it Wyrd, Is it White, It it Promised to the Night?—41
The White Deer in the Grove of Symbols—53
All-Devouring Appetites—95
We Didn't Start The Fire—113
Unheimlich Maneuvers—133
The Hart-Breaking Work of Erring Stag Genes—145
Loathly Ladies and the Men Who Love Them—153
Hubris and the Green Wall—185
Sophrosyne and the Extended Mind—195
At Last Setting Our Lands In Order—213
Songs of Sovereignty—235
Works Cited—251
Index—263
About the Author—267

Eight of Batons

The first tarot deck I ever owned had the White Hart as its Eight of Batons. Not a bad association as these things go. Forward momentum. A rapidly approaching opportunity. A gathering speed. A harbinger. Even growing up in regional Australia—a place not exactly known for its white deer—I implicitly understood this signification at the age of thirteen. The card began to intrigue me, whether I was playing with my tarot or not. Omens. Signs and wonders. I was taken with the idea that the appearance of some animals might "mean" something. I had just purchased a fortune telling oracle, after all. In for a penny, in for a pound.

Why was it that some animals carried more meaning than others? The owl. The snake. In comparison to, say, the guppy or the plover. As for the hart, was it just the rarity of finding a white one that gave it more semantic heft? Or was there something else? Years later, I pondered this while drinking at the White Hart on Drury Lane—London's oldest licensed premises. This creature has been bounding through the English unconscious for centuries.

But what is it? Is it a physical deer? Is it the idea of a deer? A deer spirit? Some kind of pagan survival (as if that were in any way a differentiator)? Plainly, how we encounter and how we experience an "animal" is contingent on the cosmovision in which such an encounter takes place. During the creation of the Fifth Sun at Tenochtitlan—now Mexico City—the Gods convened and set a great fire. Tēcciztēcatl had volunteered to immolate himself in the fire and become the new sun, but at the last moment his resolve failed. Nanāhuātzin, who had also volunteered but was deemed too old, stepped into the flames and became the sun. Seeing this, the younger Tēcciztēcatl discovered his resolve and followed him into the fire. Two suns begin to rise, but the Gods, angered by his cowardice, throw a rabbit at

Tēcciztēcatl, dimming his brightness and turning him into the moon. (Which is why the moon has a rabbit-shaped mark on his face, incidentally.) Two animals threw themselves in after: Jaguar and Eagle. Note this is not the Jaguar God, this is not the Eagle Spirit. It is Jaguar and Eagle.

In the Wiradjuri Dreaming of eastern Australia, the task of creating the sun belongs to Emu. All was darkness and Emu was the only being in existence. She flies up and lays an egg that hatches the sun. Again, this is not the Emu Goddess. This is Emu.

We derive the word "spirit" ultimately from the word for "breath." So it is an essence that can enter and leave a physical form. And to be the Emu Goddess is to be above "mere" emus, or at least to be somehow bigger than an emu one might encounter in the wild. How we conceptualise our non-human brothers and sisters under the fifth sun tells us everything about our cosmovision. If the White Hart is, to you, some kind of deer spirit then you are operating inside at least a partial dualism. There is a special "deer-ness" that can enter and leave the otherwise base or lower matter of the physical deer. If you conceive of the White Hart as some sort of God then perhaps you are closer, as divinity does not necessary preclude the physical or material encounter.

Those cosmovisions around the world that never had the life drained out of them can say "deer" and allow that term to carry the complexity of spirit, god, food, friend, teacher and guide. In Amazonia, there is the notion of the Beast Master or Beast Mother, where every animal in the jungle has a mother or lord in the spirit world that the various human groups must negotiate with, especially if they plan to hunt her children. This Beast Master is, is not, and can enter the form of any of her children. This is not imprecision. This is precisely the best framework for managing the complexity of being in relation to the rest of the living cosmos.

Deer comes to bring us this message, also. As described later in these pages, the first lesson in the Mabinogion story is one of interrelation, of a decentring of the human, of humanity in its true and much wider context. Pwyll, out hunting with his hounds, sees another pack of dogs bring down a stag. These turn out to belong to an Otherworld prince, also out on his hunt. The story shows us that humans are not the only game in town, and we are not the only beings to have agency. The cosmos is not our backdrop. The world is out there worlding. Our failure to see this has and will continue to lead to disaster.

In the form of White Deer, the hart returns to share this message once again. Melinda Reidinger first catches sight of her quarry deep in the thicket of the European imagination. From there, she tracks it through history and then out into the wild uplands of some future scenarios, many of which we would do well to avoid. This is a journey that asks us to consider firstly what these beings are. And, contingent on our conclusion, what they will say when we allow ourselves to hear them.

Gordon White, 2023
lutruwita/Tasmania

Acknowledgements

I would like to express my most sincere thanks to those who have helped bring this book into being. The first two are Robin Artisson and Briana Saussy. Robin inspired me to write the very first version of my reflections on the white deer in essay form, and Briana taught me to apply the profound power of myths and other stories to my life. She also first introduced me to the tale of Sir Gawain and Lady Ragnelle. Thirdly, at a deep level, I am also indebted to the mentorship provided by my academic advisor, Richard Handler, at the University of Virginia.

Several friends have read drafts of this work in various stages and provided encouragement and feedback: in particular I would like to mention Amy Smith Muise, Seán Pádraig O'Donoghue, Kyle Downey, and John Grigsby. John also generously provided me with a copy of his thesis and supplied one of the stories I cite. Brendan Myers not only read the manuscript, but also sent me a very timely and much appreciated gift of Glenn Albrecht's *Earth Emotions*. Mark Fitzpatrick has given me abundant moral support for my nonfiction and fiction writing, and he suggested that I show the early essay version of this work to Rhyd Wildermuth. Mark also read and proofread the last draft, and shared some of his expertise in Irish language and lore. I owe my deepest gratitude to Rhyd for seeing the potential in the essay, having faith that it could be developed into a full-length book, and doing everything necessary to make it happen. I would like to thank all the women, men, and institutions whose work I have relied on to help build my own text. And finally, I would like to thank whoever or whatever it was that sent a vision that saved me, my family, and a magnificent wild animal from danger on a dark November evening.

The Challenge

In the winter of 2016, I was preparing to start a new semester teaching at a small private university in Prague. My two courses, an Introduction to Sociology and a seminar on Subcultures, were ready to go. Then, my dean presented me with my dream come true, but also a daunting challenge. He asked me to substitute for a colleague who was suddenly unable to teach her class in Environmental Anthropology. I was thrilled—but I was being given only one week to get ready before the first day of class. How was I going to face the students? I had nothing prepared. I wished I'd had a year to design the course, but I had been given only seven days.

Before sketching out the topics we'd cover in the coming semester, I began thinking about the ways we relate to the land. How do we see and understand it? What is our place within it? How does this understanding guide the ways we interact with it? How do we perceive and then talk about harm we have done to it? How do cultures warn people against acts that would damage it?

I wanted to show the students some examples of land which had been profoundly altered, and then I'd situate these in folk conceptions of the web of relationships between people, animals, and the land itself. So, on the day of our first session, I projected the visual panorama of horrors displayed in Jennifer Baichwal and Edward Burtynsky's 2006 documentary project *Manufactured Landscapes*.

This film depicts places drastically altered by human activity, as captured by Burtynsky on Super 16 millimeter film. From above and from the ground level, his images show the devastation wrought by mining and other extractive industries, and he examines the ongoing construction work that was then taking place to create the world's largest dam: the Three Gorges Dam on the Yangtze River. However, *Manufactured Landscapes* also illustrates the stark interiors of factories upon which the West relies for consumer goods and the extremely regimented life of their workers—who seem to resemble ants. These interventions in the land and in human lives are painful to witness, and it is clear the fate of the people and the land are connected. The land is scraped bare and used as a dumping ground, and the people are exploited to extract the maximum labor value. What viewers see are wastelands and degraded human conditions—all in the service of industrial production.

With the question hanging in the air of how this type of devastation—which is happening worldwide—might be critically analyzed or even perhaps halted, I then read them the Arthurian tale of Sir Gawain and Lady Ragnelle.

The book you are reading had its first beginnings in that seminar, when I started thinking through how myths and folklore can lead to understanding of present crises. Another influence was a suggestion by Robin Artisson that I choose an aspect of his book *An Carow Gwyn* on which to write an essay. The title of his work means "The White Deer" in Kernowek (Cornish), and when I had learned some of the lore associated with white deer, I wanted to research more. I discovered many tales and legends that were new to me, and I began to recall the appearance of white deer in literature I'd read before. I then started to connect this figure with much older stories.

The connections between the uncanny appearance of a deer that was usually white, the way people were treating the land, women's self-determination, and a fateful warning to a ruler kept repeating in the source materials I studied. While we cannot know exactly how these tales were received by those who heard them in the distant past, it is significant that they kept retelling them. Clearly, the deer was bearing a message that we ignore at our peril.

I am a cultural anthropologist by training and an omnivorous reader by inclination. In this book, I take you on a wild ride through a range of academic disciplines. Besides anthropology, they include: history, various genres of literature, ecology, psychology, philosophy, philology, religious history, climate science, Celtic and Medieval studies, zoology, neuroscience, archaeology, and art history. In addition to deer, you'll also find bats, unicorns, aurochs, horseshoe crabs, cephalophores, fairy godmothers, screaming skulls, and enchanted forest maidens in these pages. You'll find out why some unicorns have beards, why ghosts wear sheets, and what Venus puts in her morning beverage. There are sublime poems and terrible puns, and a story about a royal foot fetish; and it's not just about all of that, but as Karl Marx often said (after Horace), *de te fabula narratur*: the story is told about you.

At the end of the journey I will bring you back home, hopefully feeling both challenged and inspired. You will have tracked the white deer to the quiet heart of the wilds within, where she can guide you to apply some of her evergreen wisdom where it is most needful: right where you are.

The Nature of Myth, the Myth of Nature

One of the clichéd ways we talk about human-inflicted damage to a landscape, especially damage to its fertile, creative powers, is with the metaphor of rape. The story I chose as a companion to *Manufactured Landscapes* and which we'll look at later in depth—Sir Gawain and Lady Ragnelle—explicitly deals with this theme. Yet, the idea rankles: where does this association come from? Google Ngrams[1] reveals that forms of phrases referring to rape or raping of the earth or land first came into more common use in published works in the 1930s. These proliferated the most during the the mid-1960s to late 1990s, years during which second wave feminism's anti-rape movement was beginning to push back against engrained patterns of violence against women. These are also the years when concepts of "the environment" as something that needs our awareness and protection rose to prominence.

At the same time, there are also many reasons why such language is unclear and problematic. First, "raped" is not an end state. What in nature

---

[1] The Google Ngram Viewer is an increasingly popular research tool launched in 2010. It generates plotted line charts that illustrate the frequency of single or multiple "search strings" (generally, words and phrases) over time. This enables a quick visual comparison of the changing prevalence of the terms and allows their comparison with other terms.

even has an end state? Surely it is arrogant—hubristic even—for humans to believe they have caused or have the power to predict an end state for the planet they inhabit. Patriarchal ideologies that prize chastity in the "vessels" that grow a man's progeny may promote this view; but outside of such frameworks, why would "raped" need to be a final status ascribed to a woman?[2] Even if one's body were somehow physically tainted by an assault, it changes all of its cells many times over a lifetime: the raped body gradually fades out of physical coherence. What happened in the past was done to another body, just as what has been done to a landscape in the past happened to a different ecosystem. In both cases, there is the possibility to re-tell the tale and bring about healing.

Also, a subtle grammatical issue in discussions of rape sets it apart from discussions of other crimes. Passive formulations that focus on the victim's state do nothing to advance understanding of why the perpetrators acted this way. If the motivations are misunderstood or ignored, there is little reason to press for redress or for corrective action to prevent more instances in the future. As Jackson Katz explained in an influential TED talk titled "Violence Against Women—It's a Men's Issue,"

> We talk about how many women were raped last year, but not about how many men raped women. We talk about how many girls in a school district were harassed last year, not about how many boys harassed girls. We talk about how many teenage girls in the state of Vermont got pregnant last year, rather than how many men and boys impregnated teenage girls ... So you can see how the use of the passive voice has a political effect. [It] shifts the focus off of men and boys and onto girls and women. Even the term "violence against women" is problematic. It's a passive construction; there's no active agent in the sentence. It's a bad thing that happens to women, but when you look at that term "violence against women," nobody is doing it to them. It just happens to them ... Men aren't even a part of it![3]

---

[2] One might also keep in mind the widely-cited statistic that roughly one third of all women older than 15 (worldwide) have experienced sexual or physical violence at the hands of men. So it is hardly an unusual ordeal.

[3] The quote from the hour-long presentation by Jackson Katz is cited in the text of an article written by Robert Keren, which can be accessed on the home page of Katz's personal web site: jacksonkatz.com.

Our common language minimizes and even erases the perpetrators of these crimes. One result of this focus on the victim's state (which is perceived as shameful) is that, in criminal justice systems around the world, only a vanishingly small number of sexual assaults are successfully prosecuted. Cases are hushed up before being brought to trial, or at some point the prosecution simply halts before a verdict and sentence can be pronounced. The woman thus remains "raped," living under stigma, and the man who perpetrated the crime moves on, either discreetly or perhaps swaggering among his peers.

Those who cause damage to the Earth are likewise usually neither named nor held to account in our culture. Some of them, such as corporate functionaries who approve the release of chemicals into rivers, remain forever anonymous, while others—a small handful of those who live in industrial countries and perpetrate the worst ecocidal crimes—dream of moving on to other celestial bodies. This is celebrated in some circles and decried in others, but nothing is done to make them more accountable to—or for— the planet that supplied them with all these resources. Then, there are generations upon generations of more ordinary people whose actions have cumulatively brought ecosystems to and over crucial tipping points. Thus, it is often unclear who should be held responsible and who should remedy the damage.

When humans assault each other, reflexive assumptions often arise that this is a "natural" aspect of behavior. Such actions are then believed to appear only when certain inherently hypocritical and unstable civilized norms are not enforced vigorously enough. If the best we can hope for is to apply checks to a violent "natural instinct," what sort of society could ever be built on this understanding? It's a quick slip from there to where it seems "natural" for *Homo economicus* to maximize gain while offloading the damage and cost onto animals, plants, ecosystems, and others.

I don't see any of this as natural at all, but rather the outcome of many ages of pernicious ideologies which poison our relationship with the world that sustains us.

Roland Barthes famously quipped in his *Mythologies* that "myth transforms history into nature." This may seem counterintuitive; after all, many of us have heard that myths or fables mostly provide cultural explanations for natural phenomena such as seasons or weather. The more subtle view, however, is that the highly communicable narrative form of myth actually conceals political motives, ideology, values, and expectations, ensuring their circulation in public spheres and discourses.[4] Let's now look at what kinds of myths might drive some of our ideas about human and divine nature, and about rape and domination of the earth.

The Great Chain of Being

The motif of rape and social stigma was certainly present in the Classical world; however, these cultures were not connecting it with a concept of the Earth being composed of "resources" awaiting exploitation. This link was later forged with the introduction of the theological model of the Great Chain of Being. At the top of this chain is a transcendent deity who suffuses all of his "creation," while also standing apart from it. Humans are tasked with trying to understand his arrangements: just as God is set apart from his creation, human beings are set apart from the rest of nature, which they enjoy the prerogative of using as they will.

The Great Chain of Being proposes a hierarchy that begins with God, who has supremacy over angels and demons. Then, there are beings who want to teach and interact with humans; beneath those supernatural beings are the celestial bodies of the stars and moon. In the human hierarchy, kings are placed over princes; princes stand over nobles; nobles over commoners; and men over women. All humans enjoy dominion over animals; wild animals over domesticated ones; animals over plants; and plants over the minerals and soil.

Why are they ranked in this order? It's because the entire framework is founded upon a conception in which spirit is considered superior to changeable and "corruptible" matter. God was said not to have been created by anything else, but he created all the rest. He and the angels exist wholly in spirit form and are eternal, and spirit is a higher emanation of divinity than matter. The "lesser" earthly flesh of humans and animals is subject to disease and death; animals have motion and appetite; plants possess life; and minerals merely exist. We still retain the memory of this

---

[4] Warner, *Six Myths of our Time*, xx; 19.

hierarchy when we use phrases such as "we're not animals!" or even "he treated me like dirt!" when people are not granted fitting levels of dignity.[5,6]

Nature as Resource, Nature as Machine

In his essay "The Rape of Mother Earth: The Rise and Fall of Western Dominance," Pierre Madl draws the logical conclusion that this view of nature's instrumental value has been cemented in certain strains of Christian theology by a teleology that represents nature as a "support system for rational human beings." Unfortunately, coldly utilitarian (and, under the influence of scientific modernism, also mechanistic) views persisted in European thought into the Enlightenment, with or without explicit religious underpinnings.

Francis Bacon may not have actually said some of the very worst things attributed to him, such as Leibniz's suggestion that Bacon advocated "torturing nature on the rack" to "reveal her secrets,"[7] but he did organize his discussion of nature into three states that it might exist in: free, erring (creating "wonders" and "monsters"), and "constrained by human art and labor." His explicitly stated aim—quite in keeping with the theology of his times—was "so that man can recover that right over nature that belongs to it by divine bequest" after Adam and Eve's expulsion from Eden. As though that were not immodest enough, this should be pursued in order to "establish the power and dominion of the human race over the entire universe."[8]

---

[5] The hierarchy of humans in medieval Great Chains of Being deals with social estates, not with the later concept of human "races." It served as a prototype for later taxonomic classifications by scientists, because both the medieval and the early modern schemes propose that all living beings and nonliving substances were created by God with various virtues and weaknesses. This, then, puts them into certain natural hierarchical relations. Only in the 18th century did human phenotypes became a topic of scientific interest in Europe. Such research and concepts arose in a broader context of conquest and colonialism, putting the natural sciences into the service of imperial expansion. The gold gained from conquered lands supported the growth of learning and improvements in technology in a very tidy feedback loop.

With the old Great Chain of Being was set aside, human racial "varieties" were proposed on the basis of prejudiced ideas about non-Europeans. These were shaped by Christian theology and bestiaries inherited from the classical antiquity, and by feudal notions about how "natural" hierarchies work. In service to God and empire, the most desirable features and prerogatives were always assigned to the white, European race, with others placed along a continuum of progressively more undesirable attributes and lower levels of access to power, dignity, and self-determination. Further, the early modern taxonomic racial scheme inherited the medieval arrangement where any being has the right to use, command, or kill those located beneath it. Thus, just as God commands the angels, angels can command or kill people; people have dominion over animals; wild animals eat domestic ones, and animals consume plants, Europeans had the right to conquer, enslave, or kill those they believed "below" them.

(This is adapted from my unpublished lecture notes for the Introduction to Sociology course I taught between 2012 and 2019, which drew inspiration from the graduate seminar in cultural anthropology taught by Richard Handler at UVA in the late 1990s).

[6] See the collectively-authored *Muséum Manifesto: Humans and Other Animals*.

[7] Pesic, 81-2.

[8] Francis Bacon in *Novum Organum* (1620), cited by Merchant, 748.

21

In Bacon's time, a great proliferation of proto-industrial activities—ranging from mining and refining ores, working with metals, constructing wind and water mills, and designing machines to do labor—took place all across Europe. The famous formulation "knowledge is power" (*scientia potentia est*) is correctly attributed to Thomas Hobbes, who had served as a secretary to Bacon when he was a young man, but the idea was incipient in Bacon's work when he wrote "knowledge itself is power"(*ipsa scientia potestas est*). This view was inherent throughout this period's research and manufacturing activities. The practical application of understanding of physical and chemical processes to inventions, mechanics, crafts, medicine, and so on facilitated their further development. When nature was understood as a complex machine, it became possible to analyze its constituent parts, which could then be reassembled and set to tasks that would serve humankind.[9]

The same coldly utilitarian logic was also applied by prominent thinkers to animals. René Descartes claimed that animals do not think or suffer because they lacked souls: essentially, he saw them as machines. Animals were still described mechanistically by philosophers well into the twentieth century; for example, Martin Heidegger set man into the role of world-former and impoverished the animals by denying them this faculty. Like the medieval Scholastics, Heidegger proposed that (non-human) animals can only interact with what is immediately available to them, and that they suffer from a poverty of attunement to broader contexts.[10] He said: "the

---

[9] ibid, 735. Scholars argue over subtleties of translating Bacon's aphorisms in *Novum Organum* from the Latin. One translator renders Aphorism 3 as "The *Knowledge* and *Power* of Man are coincident: for whilst ignorant of the Causes, he can produce no *Effects*: Nor is Nature to be conquer'd but by Submission," and explains that "the only method by which Men can rule Nature, must depend upon learning her Ways," and "Man himself being necessarily subject to the laws of nature; tho' within the compass of these laws he has a very extensive Power, that will always be commensurate to knowledge." Another translation offers the variant "subdued by submission": "... For nature is only subdued by submission, and that which in contemplative philosophy corresponds with the cause, in practical science becomes the rule." A third English translation suggests "conquered only by obedience": " ... For Nature is conquered only by obedience; and that which in thought is a cause, is like a rule in practice"(Merchant 737, fn 17).

Philosopher of environmental ethics Carolyn Merchant points out that the applications of the theory of conquering/subduing to experimental contexts "range from the study of reptiles, birds, and dogs in evacuated bell jars to creating new species through genetic engineering; the study of caged monkeys deprived of their mothers; the Tuskegee syphilis experiments; Depo-Provera trials on fertile women; underground nuclear tests; DDT tests conducted on whole ecosystems; the act of laying out transects and counting species within grids; testing the responses of dogs, birds, and plants to spaceflight; abstracting away friction and air resistance in inclined-plane experiments; and calculating momentum/energy transfers among colliding balls. Although not all of these experiments administer pain to a living thing, all reflect the confinement of nature by technology. Although not all raise equal moral issues, all reflect human 'power over nature.'" (Merchant 738-39, fn 22).

[10] To prove his point about animals missing the "bigger picture" he cites experiments in which bees are provided with honey, which they suck. Under normal circumstances, they would stop ingesting it when full, but when scientists cut away their abdomens they continue sucking, because the sensation of satiety never arrives. This is an odd (and extremely cruel) example to extrapolate to the entire animal kingdom, and it represents the worst of the Baconian tradition. See Kuperus.

stone is worldless; the animal is poor in world, man is world forming."[11] Pierre Madl argues those who accept this logic are not constrained to treat the Earth or other creatures with consideration for their welfare. Wielding a theological or philosophical license that allows one to dump chemical, radioactive, or bio-hazardous pollution, or to harvest old-growth forest, or drive animal or plant species to extinction, is part of the "bulldozer mentality of developers."[12]

This kind of logic (or teleology) has sometimes been considered to be specifically "capitalist." It would be more accurate to call it by other names, such as modernist or mechanistic, because a coldly anthropocentric logic also dominated communist thinking and planning. We see this in V.I. Lenin's 1909 *Materialism and Empirio-criticism*, where humanity seems to have a stark choice between being enslaved by nature, or becoming its "master" by learning about the working of natural laws.[13] In 1930, under Stalin, a brutal volume called *New Russia's Primer: The Story of the Five-Year Plan* was written as a children's primer and translated the next year into English. In a section titled "We Will Force the Dead to Work" it declares: "the remains of the swamp grass, the ferns, the horsetails rotted under the layers of sand and clay, become black, and turned into coal. And to this cemetery we intend to go, drag the dead out of their tombs, and force them to work for us." This language, Rebecca Solnit comments, "frames it as a zombie movie, a horror story, the dead come back to haunt us, in this case with their carbon."[14]

Similar framing also appears in Chinese communist theory and practice. In his article "On the Persistence of the Non-Modern" the contemporary philosopher of technology Yuk Hui shares the lyrics written by Hu Shi for the "Song of the Chinese Science Society":

---

[11] The lectures Heidegger delivered in 1929-1930, which include this quote, were collected in *The Fundamental Concepts of Metaphysics*.

[12] See Madl. Timothy Morton notes the anthropocentric concept of "world" is only useful when some beings are believed to have it and others aren't. "When, like Jakob von Uexkill, you start to realize that at least all lifeforms have world, you have begun to cheapen the concept almost to worthlessness. The concept reaches zero when humans realize that there is no 'away,' that there is no background to their foreground" (46). This is not an infinite regress where the human mind is trapped in solipsistic nihilism, but rather where it reaches out into an expansive inter-animistic mode of intelligence sharing.

[13] "For until we know a law of nature, it, existing and acting independently of and outside our mind, makes us slaves of 'blind necessity'. But once we come to know this law, which acts (as Marx repeated a thousand times) independently of our will and our mind, we become the masters of nature. The mastery of nature manifested in human practice is a result of an objectively correct reflection within the human head of the phenomena and processes of nature, and is proof of the fact that this reflection (within the limits of what is revealed by practice) is objective, absolute, eternal truth." See Lenin, 196.

[14] Solnit, 61.

> We do not worship nature. He is a [sic] tricky and weird;
> We have to beat him, boil him, and tell him to listen
> to our assignments.
> We want him to push wagons; we want him to deliver
> letters for us.
> We need to expose his secrets so that he can serve us.
> We sing that heavens act perpetually, and that we dare
> knowing the truth.
> We know that truth is infinite, still feel joyful when
> moving every inch forward.

Hui comments: "What we can see in this lyric is the idea that meaning is no longer to be deducted from nature, as was central to ancient Confucian and Daoist thought, but rather that nature is something to be explored and exploited."

De Te Fabula Narratur

Nonplussed by any civilization's claims to master nature, Sigmund Freud wrote in 1927 that, while civilizations arose to defend us against nature,

> the aim of achieving total control over either our inner nature or the outer world was a dangerous illusion, an illusion of control and mastery to protect us from feelings of helplessness and fear in the face of the awesome power of mother nature, our fear of acknowledging dependency on this largest of "holding environments," the ultimate "environment mother."[15]

Out of fear, people undertook to do unto Nature before nature did unto them—but, of course, Nature has the last say.

What do classical myths, medieval theology, and industrial worldviews have to do with us and the ever more ominous problems we face today? Taking hints from Freud, and from Timothy Morton's *Dark Ecology*, as well as from Horace and Marx who remind us that the tale is about us, we are going to take a trip into some unfamiliar and uncanny territory, where we will discover wondrous and monstrous things.

---

[15] See Joseph Dodds' chapter titled "The Ecology of Phantasy," 120-121. The inset quote was cited from Donald Winnicott.

What we find in these dark areas is sometimes disconcerting, and it may take on forms that arouse dread. But we have to take heart and keep exploring. Leigh Bardugo wrote in *King of Scars*: "I am the monster, and the monster is me."[16] As in *noir* novels or films, or legends of mystical quests, the seeker believes she is examining a situation external to herself, but the further she progresses in her inquiries, the deeper her realization she is deeply implicated in it. Increasingly, captive to morbid curiosity and also desire, she discovers that neutral standpoints, such as those proposed by many traditional Western forms of science and philosophy, are illusory.

We who seek discover that we are both victims and perpetrators of crimes against our *oikos*[17] (that is, our home), and our extended families. Yet, in this delve into a dark thicket, just like in all the oldest and best tales, and often in dreams and visions, we will meet a guide: the white deer. It is a bright form shining in a darkness, as close to us as our own repressed thoughts and desires

That darkness has nothing to do with evil or depression, but is instead a place of potential, shimmering with hidden symbols, waiting to give birth to new associations. The hidden pleasures of the "dark sweet" can be tasted when we step aside from the glaring light of causal reasoning, let ourselves breathe deeply, perceive the land where we live more sensitively, and ask how we can be of service.

---

[16] Monster derives from Latin *monstrum*: "divine omen (especially one indicating misfortune), portent, sign." The association came about because abnormal or prodigious animals—such as those with unusual coloring—were generally regarded as signs or omens. They de*monst*rate (yes, another derivation from the same root) that a message is being conveyed from or to our minds. The connection becomes even more explicit when we dig back farther to the Proto Indo-European root **moneie-* "to make think of, remind," which is the causative form of the root **men-* "to think." Here is the explicit suggestion that the omen, the strange animal, is sending us an important message, a warning.

Yet another scion stemming from **men-* is **moneō* (which carried the meaning of "to warn" or "to advise," as seen in the forms *admoneō* and *praemoneō*). And even more curious is that this was carried over to Moneta (a name for the goddess Juno, who had a temple in the center of Rome where coins were minted), and then finally to "money." That's quite a lot to contemplate.

[17] *Oikos* (οἶκος) is an ancient Greek word meaning household, home, dwelling place, family, or property. The scientific discipline of ecology, which was to focus on how organisms interact and relate with each other and their environment, was given its name by the German zoologist Ernst Haeckel in 1866. If *oikos* is "house" and *logia* (λόγια) is "discourse," "doctrine," or sometimes "divine communications" or "oracles" (messages from deities obtained by divination), then ecology is a discussion—or perhaps a series of oracles—that describes or prescribes the condition of our broader household or family.

Sir Gawain and Lady Ragnelle

Returning to the paradoxical character of myths about rape, it seems strange to associate it with death and infertility, as people do when they talk about "raping the Earth." After all, "a god's embrace is never fruitless."[18] Classical myths involving rape almost always seemed to result in the conception of a son, not a daughter: it was the male overcoming the female and imposing his dominant imprint over both men and women when the heir grew up and began to rule.[19] To avoid rape, a nymph would have to become a plant or animal—something lesser than her previous state of being—and she would be reabsorbed back into the generative forces of the landscape. However, this paradox starts to unwind if you look at other lore, such as the tale of the Wedding of Sir Gawain and Lady Ragnelle, where the outcome of a rape has broader significance than just a pregnancy, and more—and deeper—impacts than just a reconfiguration of the positions of men and women.

At first glance, the legend of Sir Gawain and Lady Ragnelle might look like a variation of the better-known tale of Beauty and the Beast, featuring an attractive man and an "ugly" woman. One of my first approaches to it was as a kind of gender-inverted version of the Fisher King (or Wounded

---

[18] From Homer's *Odyssey*, trans. E.V. Rieu [1946] (Hammondsworth, 1982), Book XI, lines 177-8; quoted in Warner, 98.
[19] Helen and Clytemnestra are a notable exception of female progeny who resulted from a rape, in some—though not all—versions of their myth.

King) legends in the Arthurian cycle. In those legends, a king who is the last in a line of rulers—who are the keepers of the Holy Grail—suffers a painful wounding in the thigh or groin, a polite symbol for impotence.[20] The land that he should be stewarding becomes dry, blasted, and infertile, and human and animal populations collapse. When this is styled as a divine punishment for sin against sexual taboos, we are seeing later Christian accretions on much older myths. In any case, a king in this condition is unable to father an heir, and the fate of his kingdom—reduced to a wasteland—hangs in the balance while the king languishes, waiting for someone to heal him. In the older versions, the one who manages the task is Percival, and later he is alternated by Galahad and Bors.

In the story of Sir Gawain and Lady Ragnelle, however, it is a female of noble status with otherworldly powers who is wounded in her soul after a grave violation of her bodily autonomy. In Briana Saussy's modern retelling of the tale,[21] after a double crime (a rape and the killing of a white stag), "the land itself languished in a death spiral as pestilence and famine spread from town to town. It was evident to everyone now that the crime had infected the land's soul and body. True justice had not yet been served..."

Here is the tale as Briana Saussy tells it:

---

[20] The genteel mention of a "thigh" when a grievous wound to the genitals—or even castration—is tradition in Biblical, Egyptian, and Ancient Greek myths as well as in Celtic legends. The intention is not merely euphemism, but derives from ancient beliefs held in many cultures that semen was produced in various places in the body, and especially in the marrow of men's thigh bones. The testes were considered mere reservoirs for the fluid.

Neil Godfrey explains: "But why the thigh? We believe that we are dealing here with a literal translation of a West Semitic idiom which euphemistically designated begetting: 'sprung from one's thigh' (yōṣeʾ yᵉrēkó, inaccurately translated in English Bibles by 'loins') merely meant 'begotten by one,' his child ... In the literature of ancient Greek myths thigh wounds are often euphemisms for castration. So ... Classical scholars are generally aware of the trope that *in literature from around the world thigh wounds are often euphemistic for castration, or at least for impotence. But classicists have not noted how thigh wounds frequently symbolize not only physical impotence but political or spiritual impotence, and how such wounds also represent a temporary or permanent loss of heroic status for the wounded individual as well as a crisis for the group of people represented by that individual*. This association apparently has its roots in a belief, held by many cultures, that semen was produced in several places in the body, including in the marrow of the thigh bone, and the thighs' proximity to the testicles resulted in a close association that was nearly an interchange between the thighs and the male genitalia. Consequently, any kind of wound to the thigh, whether a wrenching, piercing, crushing, or other injury or mutilation, could represent a blow to a man's physical and spiritual virility." (Emphasis added by me.)

To wit: the thigh was considered a male womb: "The Greeks shared in this cultural association of the thighs with organs of regeneration. Hence, Zeus can incubate the infant Dionysus in his thigh, which becomes the male equivalent of the womb. Aristotle was among those who believed that veins ran from the genitals through the thigh to the heel." Ibid.

[21] The retelling of this story I am using was part of the course materials for Saussy's Spinning Gold course. The course can be found online at: brianasaussy.com/spinning-gold.

The Tale of Sir Gawain and Lady Ragnelle

Some say it all started with the deer. A white stag, to be exact. A well-placed arrow had pierced its heart. Red blood streaming over thick white fur. And I believe it. But I also know that wasn't all. I know how the man leered at my sister. How he pushed her down onto the hard ground, deaf to her pleas. He tore at her skirts. And—oh, violation! Oh, violence: it cannot be told. He took what should only be freely given. An inmost part of her not only changed forever, but died on that day.

Now, the criminal was found, and he was tried and executed. But to what end? The swift sword of justice fell either too late, or it wasn't enough. All we know is that the land itself began to die. It languished in a death spiral as pestilence and famine spread from town to town and village to village. It was evident to everyone, to all of us, now, that the crime had infected the land's soul and body. And that true justice had not yet been served.

Not knowing what else to do, the people soon laid the crime at the feet of the king, whose name was Arthur. Some blamed him for the crime, while others did not, but still sought his help. All of us divined correctly that there was a deep relationship between the health of the land and the health of the people and their political leaders. There was only one place to go under these most unusual circumstances, to someone—or something—Arthur was loathe to come into contact with. But necessity demanded that he seek her out anyway, and so she did. She lived under the lake, and was known as the one who weaves.[22]

The great king, mighty, shining, stood before the weaver, trembling. Back and forth her shuttle moved, forming color and image on her loom. And to him, she said only: "Wait for a while, and you shall see." So he returned to his castle, head hanging, bereft of hope, but he did as she commanded—for what else could he do? He waited.

At Yuletide, when the Sun came back to the people once more, a strange knight appeared in the hall. He gave no name. He was broad of shoulder and long of leg, and he wore bright, burnished armor that changed colors

---

[22] Recall the ancient motif of the weavers of *wyrd*, of fate.

depending on how he moved in the flickering flames. Without waiting for a "by your leave" from our king, the knight spoke, with a deep voice that rumbled and trembled like an oncoming storm:

> Blood was shed and tears were cried
> Land once living now has died
> To men heal and make right
> Solve a riddle, else we fight.
> Solve then, this question fair:
> Wanted more than earth or air, water or fire:
> Tell me what women most desire.
> A year and a day to find it—no more!
> With proper answer, your life assure.
> Otherwise, no kingdom, no wealth
> Will keep you from certain death.

Now, as I heard it, after the king listened to these words, he closed his eyes in fear and his step faltered. He trembled—and the strange knight simply vanished, as quickly as he had first appeared and with as little explanation. Standing alone at his great hearth, Arthur looked out over his men, and fair Sir Gawain stepped forward, and held him, strongly, so that his king might stand. Gawain was young and fair and beloved by all of us throughout the kingdom. And though he was tried in battle, he possessed a sweet innocence. He promised that day to accompany his king on a great journey to solve the riddle and win the prize of his liege lord's life.

So the very next day the two set off, leaving the golden-roofed castles, departing from the fresh flowing springs and fountains, moving through the heavy orchards covered in frost and snow, and making their way into the woods. Here, the trees were huge and they grew so that the sun was all but blotted out. Because it was deep winter, snow and frost lay heavy on the ground. The wood was unusually, unearthly silent—because all the animals and the creatures were tucked safely into their nests. The famine and the plague that cursed our lands around the kingdom seemed not to have touched this place. But, then, that was to be expected. For with Merlin living here as a protector, with Lady Nimue running from branch to branch, this was a blessed land.

While on his journey, Arthur thought much of his kingdom: the warm hearth and spiced wine, the white round arms of his beloved queen, the rosy cheeks of his people, and how they had changed before his eyes, becoming pale, and drawn, and sallow as the crops under the hot August sun all dying one by one. Gawain, though, was different. Gawain had his mind on adventure.

Thinking that perhaps there would be a great conquest: an evil knight to slay, and a beautiful maiden to rescue. He liked maidens, especially, and contented himself riding through the snow-covered woods thinking on his ideal maiden's fair face and lovely graceful form. She would be sweet and innocent as a dove. Beautiful, of course. Fragile, pure, glowing like a luminous pearl. Thoughts of her and the cruel knight from whom he must rescue her occupied him throughout the journey, so that the days turned to weeks and the weeks turned to months. The two comrades traveled farther and farther into the depths of the great forest. The snow and ice began to melt. A breath of fresh warmth exhaled through the green wood. Flowers began to bloom once more, and birdsong filled the air that had been heavy and quiet with winter. On their journey, the two men spoke little, as men tend to do—each lost in their own thoughts and concerns. They hunted when they needed to, but always made sure to keep away from the white stags. They had at least learned *that* lesson.

At midsummer, they came to the end and to the edge of the great forest. Jagged foothills leading up to high and tall mountains took over the terrain. Both men knew that it was time to turn back, to take a different path through the wild wood and return to Camelot. But they still did not have an answer to the strange knight's riddle.

Winds changed once more, and seasons fell one into another. From gentle spring to high summer with trees heavy with fruit and babies of all creatures running through the woods. Then, to autumn once more. Moons before this point, Arthur had secretly given up on the mission.

"A woman's desire—ha! Everyone knew that women were fickle creatures, and that meant their desire was fickle too. One day it would a fine gown, the next a strong pair of thighs wrapped around them in the dead of night, while on the next day it would be a bright-eyed child, and never mind anything else. Who could know the heart of a woman?" They would return; he would die.

Truly, it was that simple. His heart swelled at the unjustness of it. He had not shot the deer! He had not harmed the woman, whoever she was! And yet. And still. He was king. If one of his subjects did it, then he might as well have done it himself. The land was not a gentle mistress.

Sir Gawain sensed that time was now against them too. The year had turned, and each day brought them closer to Yuletide. Moreover, there had been no ladies. No evil knights to defeat. Only trees and rain and green wood, all around. Cold air blew through the wooded corridors once more, and Gawain imagined that he felt the cold steel of a sword against his skin. Just as he was shaking off the sensation, he heard a strange snuffling sound. Arthur heard it, too, and put a hand up in warning. Both men were silent. The snuffling became louder and was accompanied by shrieks, and squeals, and the occasional growl. The bushes around them trembled violently, and Gawain got a glance of torn white lace and bristly hair. Drawing their swords, the men stood at attention. It was only the hideousness of the creature who tumbled through the bushes that froze them in place.

Not exactly a wild boar, not exactly a bear, not exactly a wolf, but somehow all three and more. The figure stood before them, hugely tall with runny yellow eyes and sharp white tusks, pointed teeth, red lips, and a long pink tongue that lolled out to one side of her mouth—a bit comically. She was some kind of ... lady ... maybe, dressed in rags of what had once been a lovely lace gown. Gawain had never seen such a sight in all of his years as a knight, and Arthur had dropped his sword in surprise. At a loss for what to do, the king recovered first:

"My ... lady. We are but poor knights on a quest in this wild, inhospitable wood. Please, do not eat us—and let us know if we may be of assistance to you."

A thin line of drool fell from the creature's maw onto her hairy bosom, and she snuffled, snorted, and spoke with some difficulty through her tusks and teeth.

> I know you, Arthur, and the gallant one by your side.
> I know, too, the riddle you must solve or die.
> The answer is simple, and I'll give it thee now.
> If you will first accede to one small vow.
> Whatever it is, I first ask of you: promise me to give it true.
> Then the answer you shall gain,
> And free yourself from death's cold pain.

Gawain spoke immediately: "Do it, sire! For this lady is no ordinary woman, and no doubt she knows of more mysteries than you or I."

So Arthur agreed, and then demanded with curtness: "The answer, if you please!" The beastly woman sat down on her haunches, and sighed, looking down at the ground.

> The thing it is a woman most desires
> Sweeter than earth, or air, water, or fire
> Some say is wealth, fame, love,
> Some say is favors from above
> I say, none of these things for me.
> Like all women, I treasure most
> My Sovereignty.

Arthur bowed before the hideous creature and took her hairy hand in his own. "Good lady, a thousand thanks for saving this poor man's life. And now, what is your request, so that I might fulfill it? The beast-lady licked her lips somewhat lasciviously, and breathed loudly through her ursine nose. Then with her hairy and clawed left hand, she pointed straight to Sir Gawain:

"The young and handsome man's hand in marriage shall please me most. And with haste, too, for I am not getting any younger!"

Arthur stood agape: what had he done? What had he consigned young, handsome, noble, and true Gawain to? What misery? Whatever response he might have uttered was cut off by his faithful knight.

The young knight saw that his liege lord was about to speak to deny the lady her request. But to do so would forfeit his life. Of this, Gawain was sure. And so, although she was as far from a luminous pearl as a castle is from a cave, he turned away from Arthur and placed his hand in her own large claw. "Good lady, I am honored by your attention and your request. Our vow to you shall be fulfilled. Let us wed on the morrow."

What I have heard is that there was in that moment a shift and a glimmer in the lady's eyes. But whether it was so or not, I cannot say. I can only tell what happened next. The rest of the short journey back to Camelot was like a dream. It sped by so quickly. The strange and shimmering knight was waiting for both king and Gawain, and as soon as they arrived, Arthur whispered the hard-won knowledge into his ear. So the old knight vanished, and was never seen again. The land came back to life. Though it was the dead of winter, small buds here and there, and tiny green shoots of crops, could be seen stirring themselves up, reaching towards the sky through the snow. Roses flowered, and looked all the more stunning covered in ice and frost. New mothers had milk and then some for their babies. And grandparents walked with a spring in their step.

Our story might end there, except wait—there is a wedding, and, of course, a wedding night. Now Gawain found that he faced the most difficult trial he had ever experienced as a knight. No fierce and evil foe. No impossible monster to slay. But his bones turned to liquid and his blood turned to water at the thought, the very thought, of binding himself forever to the hideous woman-beast, and he felt his courage take flight. Thoughts of rescuing a maiden, any maiden, were far, far from his mind—and he laughed at his fancies. Simply to be joined to a human woman would have been a treasure.

Still and yet, a promise had been made. Though she was foul with the stink and slavering of a beast, the lady, whose name was Ragnelle, had proven to be true in her bearing and intention. The king was saved. The kingdom thrived. The land lived. What more could he, a simple knight, ask for? So his servants dressed him in fine linen and brocade, and his sword was polished and glowed warm silver for the ceremony. The priest had been summoned. The wedding party guests had all arrived, and the entire kingdom turned out for the event. A marriage! What better way to celebrate the new life across the land? And a marriage to one of the most handsome and beloved knights.

Lady Ragnelle had been secreted away, but he had seen the quick and worried glances and the hesitation as the maidservants screamed in silent horror at their charge. Arthur had given precise orders about her dress. She would be heavily gowned and veiled so that the most hideous features were not be seen by the entire kingdom. He could not do much for his loyal retainer—but that, at least that, he could do.

Incense swirled in the stone chapel, and the prayers were said and the vows were made. For a moment in the glow of the candlelight, Gawain saw his lady's form as something else. Something that was perhaps beautiful and quite lovely. But then, light glinted off one white tusk, and it was all he could do not to pull his hand away in revulsion.

After the wedding, there was the feast. Trestled tables laden with the finest fruits and savories ran throughout the great hall. All the lords and ladies in their finery gathered to congratulate the beloved knight and his mysterious bride. Quite a few ladies bewailed the fact that one of the choicest men was no longer theirs for the taking.

At first, all went well. Gawain gallantly held his lady's hand and guided her through the unfamiliar room, introducing her to a sea of strange faces. But as the night went on and the music played and the wine flowed, Ragnelle removed her hand from Gawain's and made her way to the largest table, all laid out in white and gold. At the center stood a beautiful cake made of honey and spun sugar, glistening in the flames from a thousand silver candlesticks. Then, there was a crash and a bang—and a shudder of horror moved over the guests like a wave.

Gawain looked over to the table, already knowing what he would find. His bride's true colors, so carefully hidden until this point, had been revealed. She dove into the cake, and as she did so, her veil went askew, the ill-fitting gown tore at the shoulder, and black bristly hairs, hard claws, and those damnable tusks were there for the entire banquet to see. Women screamed in horror, and men took up an immediately defensive posture, with swords drawn, ready to attack. But Gawain went to the side of his bride, and though he was as red as the apple that had been stuffed into a poor pig's snout, he said: "Be not afraid, good sirs and ladies. Though my bride's appearance is somewhat unusual, what she lacks in physical grace she more than makes up for in wisdom and kindness." Gawain did not see

Ragnelle blinking at him curiously from beneath her crooked veil. He was too busy meeting the eyes of his peers and resting in the small consolation that at least his words had been true—if not the whole truth.

Well, it wasn't soon after this that the wedding and the feast was over. As was the tradition, bride and groom were escorted into their wedding bower, which had been especially prepared and was lovely in every way. Now, typically, sniggers and jests were made during this part of the evening, but tonight everyone was stone silent. No one knew why, exactly, Gawain married such a hideous and strange beast. But one thing was for certain: never would the handsome knight have agreed to such a union freely and willingly. He was cursed! He was tricked! He was trapped! It was a tragedy on so many levels. So the unhappy couple was placed in their chamber. The door was slowly shut, and the wedding guests tiptoed from the rooms, grateful that they could finally flee the unhappy occasion.

In the room, more candles glowed, turning the cream and gold embroidered coverlets into enchanting pools of shadow and light. Sweet scents floated in the air because flowers had been strewn all about. Ragnelle, who had been unusually quiet, moved to her bouquet and pulled a single rose in her clawed hand, and turned, offering it to her bridegroom.

> You have kept your word to me, good sir
> And wedded me rightly where many would flee.
> And so now I will reveal a truth I have long hid:
> For it will cause no peace, comfort, or harmony.
> For this form you see is but one,
> And in its place I could become
> Bonny of figure and fair of face.
> But should you choose the fairer flower,
> Know I will cuckold you in this bower.
> And shall never be honest, never be true, never treat you as a good wife ought to do.
> Or choose the form you see before you now: sharp of tusk, claw, and bristled brow.
> And in me, you shall find a wife worth keeping: one who is true, kind, and wise, awake and sleeping.
> I await your word—the choice is yours.
> But the decision once made will never change course.

As she spoke, she showed Gawain her other form, which was indeed pleasing in every way. Such beauty that he almost fell to his knees, with long shining locks, skin as smooth as honey and silk, and eyes full of forest wisdom shining forth from her perfect face. In this form, she was all Gawain had ever wanted—and more. But he remembered her words, and after a few moments which felt like years, he hung his head and took her hands in his own, and said:

> Lady Ragnelle, my bride and wife:
> The choice is yours, as is your life.
> For you told me once among the forest trees
> That what every woman most desires is Sovereignty.
> The choice was never mine to give:
> Tell me how *you* wish to live.
> By your choice I will abide
> And ever and always call you bride.

Sure that he had sealed his fate with those words more surely than any wedding oath might ever do, Gawain continued to look at the floor, and was somewhat surprised when a pair of very soft hands that had a tiny bit of dirt under their fingernails took his own hands. The arms connected to the hands were lovely, and rounded with youth, without a sign of bristly hair. The bosom was heavenly and smooth. There was no claw, no tusk, to be seen. He raised his head and saw his bride transformed into the most radiant woman in the kingdom, looking at him with wide and wise eyes. Even her voice had changed:

> You are a kind man, brave and true,
> To do these things that I've asked you to.
> And now the truth to thee I'll tell:
> A terrible curse upon me fell.
> One knight took away my liberty, my free will.
> Leaving me for dead, ruined, and ill.
>
> After the rape, the crime was done.
> No one listened and no one would come
> To aid me in my time of need and harm.
> And so the curse caused me to transform.
> Turning me into this lately beast
> Whom you found and took to feast.

> The only way of breaking it was to try to find a way
> To become a bride, and to give my new husband a choice
> That would in turn give me back my voice.
> These things you've done, and done in love
> Of country, king, and the heavens above.
> And so informed, I will be fine and free
> In heart true, kind, and with deep fidelity.
> I will love you deeply and fill our home with laughter
> And we shall live most happily ever after.

Then they embraced. What I heard from my sister is that their mutual life was long and blessed. Her words did ring true throughout her life and Gawain's.

An Inverted Fisher-King

This story inverts some of the Fisher King's motifs. The Fisher King had first sinned against social expectations, which results in him receiving a wound that doesn't heal, with consequences that spill over into deadly plagues on the living world. Here, however, the first crime was committed by a commoner rather than a king, and he had committed it against an animal.. The slaughter of the white deer sets the stage for the crime against Ragnelle, and the consequences spill back into the social world via environmental devastation. Yet, even when the events run "backwards" like this, they still reveal the depravity of the monarch's subjects and his unfitness to rule, unless or until he set things right. His failure to protect the holy deer and the women of his kingdom had raised the ire of the supernatural forces that lie beneath the land's surface, causing its regenerative powers to shut down. Arthur was well aware of having failed in his sworn duty.

Trying and executing the rapist was not a sufficient remedy: it was too little, too late. As Arthur mused on his ride in search of an answer to the strange knight's challenge: "He had not shot the deer! He had not harmed the woman, whoever she was! And yet. And still. He was king. If one of his subjects did it, then he might as well have done it himself. The land was not a gentle mistress." The land itself was holding Arthur accountable.

In this tale, the king's failure to be more perceptive about the ways these things are connected became everyone's problem, and soon it would also have been his problem, too. If the king was responsible for the actions of each or any of his subjects, the subjects were also responsible for the morals of the king, because in the world of King Arthur, kingship was not hereditary. A candidate for kingship had to be selected prudently, and after coronation he needed repeatedly to confirm his worthiness through tests of virtue.[23] Any failing could call his mandate and divine contracts into question.

There was a deep lore that connected the sacred body of the wild woman with the mystical deer, and it seemed that it was just on the verge of being forgotten when this tale was being told. Something had to be restored before the land could be healed from its condition as a desolate wasteland incapable of supporting life. The white deer had been a messenger of some kind, bearing very fey[24] tidings, and its slaughter was a baneful act indeed.

---

[23] Primogeniture (the right of succession by the firstborn son) wasn't introduced until the Norman conquest in the 11th century. Previous to this period, kingship was elective, with potential successors nominated from within a royal clan claiming a common ancestor. A candidate had to be of full age, and free of deformities or blemishes of any kind that could affect his abilities or the people's respect for him. He had to embody physical beauty and spiritual virtue. One of the proofs of a king's virtue and of his bond to Sovereignty (a female divinity who, among other functions, granted the right to rule) was accepting *geasa*—personal prohibitions or obligations that bind him on pain of the loss to his honor if he does not uphold them. Violating a *geas* not only diminishes his authority, but also "mystically" causes harm to the land. See Matthews, 17-18.

[24] The word fey is derived from the Old English *fæge* (which means "fated to die soon"). In poetic modern English it retains this sense of something that is doomed, particularly to a sudden or violent death, or of something that is strange, otherworldly, or perhaps enchanted. In Scottish, "fey" may have an additional connotation of second sight or other psychic senses, such as clairaudience.

Is it Wyrd, Is it White, Is it Promised to the Night?

The modern English *weird* is derived from the Old Norse *urth*, which means twisted, or perhaps looped. There are many layers to the word weird, and they keep getting stranger the further back and sideways you explore. Urðr is the name of one of the Norns—mysterious female beings who nourish the roots of the tree of the cosmos with water and white clay, and who shape the destinies of humans and gods alike.[25] Whether they are one or three (doubling, tripling, and multiplication of supernatural figures is a theme that will also come up later in the book), the fateful weaver(s) "entwine the web of fate with itself. The term *weird* can mean *causal*: the winding of the spool of fate. The less-known noun sense of *weird* means *destiny*

---

[25] According to the folklorist Claude Lecouteaux, Urðr is probably the only one of the three Norns who is truly ancient and authentic, and the others two, Skuld and Verðandi, were introduced later so that the three figures could be considered an equivalent trio to the Parcae/Fates/Moirai. Lecouteaux (2016), 209-210.

"Fae" in the sense of subtle, tricky spirits is derived from the Latin *fatum*. These "Good Neighbors" have variously been associated with the souls of ancestors or other dead people; with the souls of the unbaptized who cannot enter either Heaven or Hell; with prophetic spirits that herald an approaching death; and with animating powers that indwell the land. The late medieval term "fairy" was a catchall that also included banished Pagan gods.

or *magical power* and, by extension, the wielders of that power, the Fates or Norns. Yet *weird* can also mean *strange of appearance*," in the sense of the prodigious animals or "monsters" that convey omens or warnings.[26]

These fateful weavers of our destinies are sending messages along dark, obscure pathways. Karen Bek-Pedersen has proposed that the word *norn* is related to a Swedish dialect term *norna* (*nyrna*), which means to inform or communicate secretly.[27] Thus, in the term weird, "there flickers a dark pathway between causality and the aesthetic dimension, between doing and appearing, a pathway that dominant Western philosophy has blocked and suppressed ... the thing about seeming, is that seeming is never quite as it seems."[28]

The key to understanding fateful messages is that they are conveyed in symbols rather than in lexical terms, and there is a feedback process. As the poet Charles Baudelaire expressed it:

> Nature is a temple, where the living
> Columns sometimes breathe confusing speech;
> Man walks within these groves of symbols each
> Of which regards him as a kindred thing.[29]

That is: the message and the messenger both have perceptual intelligence, and the recipient is being *regarded*: observed, evaluated, perhaps considered fondly.

Sometimes, an animal is more than just a living organism going about its business. This is the case when we are able to interpret it and to act upon the message we have received. As Freudian ecopsychologist Joseph Dodds asserts, "as an expression of our inner space, these creatures stalk

---

[26] Morton, 5-6. All emphases in his cited text are in the original.
[27] Bek-Pedersen, 191.
[28] Morton, 5-6.
[29] This translation of the first stanza of the poem "Correspondances" from Baudelaire's *Flowers of Evil* is by James McGowan. An alternate rendering that is much more frequently quoted online is: Nature is a temple in which living columns/ Sometimes emit confused words./ Man approaches it through forests of symbols/ Which observe him with familiar glances. However, I prefer McGowan's version for several reasons, including the more human-made sense of "grove" versus "forest" and the resonances of "regard" that go deeper than "glances," which are implied to be superficial. I have therefore selected this phrase for the title of my review of myths and literature.

our dreams, our stories, our myths, our fairy tales, our films, and our nightmares, and they influence the way we deal with the nature around us."[30]

This is not to say that they have no reality or meaning outside of our perceptions or conceptions. Instead, this places emphasis on the way the ecology of inner worlds of experience guides our behavior. Real animals that we interpret as symbols or omens and those that appear in our dreams shape the ways we interact with the ones in our ecosystems, and they help us shape the lives and fates of the communities of beings we share space with. Ideally, we receive warnings in time, and make adjustments when our relationships are starting to fall out of balance.[31]

Why White Deer?

The white deer has very specific sets of associations which make it into an omen of potential ecological collapse, and it differs from the symbolism of other white animals. Indo-European cultures have long regarded white cows and horses as sacred, and they developed numerous rituals to imbue themselves with these creatures' ascribed powers of blessedness and fertility.[32] But why white *deer*?

The wild, antlered beast of the forest was of an entirely different category than domestic creatures, such as cattle and horses. Outside of the steppes and subarctic regions where reindeer are herded, deer did not contribute

---

[30] Dodds (2012), 2.

[31] I will further expand on the ways animals are interwoven in our unconscious and dreaming minds in the "Unheimlich Maneuvers" chapter.

[32] For instance, Julius Caesar used to import white cattle for the purpose of sacrifices. According to folklorist Dee Dee Chainey, they were believed to have the best meat, and were bred by tenant farmers for the tables of high-ranking clergy and to help them perform the "oblation of the white bull," a rite in which the churchmen attempted to relieve women of their barrenness (45-6). And there was the very elaborate and costly Indian *Ashvamedha* sacrifice in which a king earned glory by asserting his right to rule over neighboring provinces. A white stallion with black spots was given freedom to wander, and the rulers of any lands it entered could choose to either fight the king who had loosed it or submit to his rule. At the end of the specified period (a year or a year and a half), there was a lot of public feasting and the stallion was killed as the most prominent victim among many animals offered. Then that night, the queen was required to engage in symbolic (feigned) sexual intercourse with its corpse.

to the rural domestic economy. On the contrary, they were pests who ate crops, fruits, vegetables, and other garden plants.³³

More importantly, before and also after the Neolithic Revolution, deer have primarily been regarded as the prize of the chase. For millennia, Europeans have believed their ancestors consumed more venison than people of the present generation. However, at least in historical times and more recent prehistory, this is more myth than fact. As archaeologist and art historian Miranda Green writes, despite its ubiquity in artistic representations, evidence in faunal remains indicates that wild game made up a minimal part of the Iron Age Celtic diet. She provides evidence that the average across all the sites comprises less than five percent of all animal bones, and the largest number of the bones of wild animals were from hares. Hunting large game such as deer was an activity generally limited to an elite who owned the rights to the land and had the means to finance expeditions with horses, hounds, and servants. The accoutrements were more or less the same as those required for warfare, and it was considered a form of training or a substitute activity in peacetime—but again, mainly for the wealthy.

There was always a numinosity suffusing hunting tales, because, as Green puts it, "the relationship of the hunter to his prey is equivocal and ambiguous." The elite who were able to engage in this activity faced trials of their luck and courage that would prove their fitness as leaders. "There is no doubt about the desire of the hunter to overcome and kill his quarry. But there is also respect and the animal must in some manner consent to its death," just as the gods also had to consent to it being killed by this hunter at this time. There was also always the chance that some misadven-

---

³³ Several types of animals, and various names for them—both current and archaic—are used by the authors I cite, as well as in my discussion of "deer." In modern English, a hooved ungulate called a deer may be from either the *Cervinae* or *Capreolinae* branches of the *Cervidae* family. In most smaller species the male is a stag or buck, the female is a doe, and their offspring are fawns. In larger species such as elk and reindeer, the terminology is borrowed from cattle, so there are bulls, cows, and calves. In more archaic usage, a hart is a male red deer, and a hind is a female. Sometimes, there is poetic play with the homophones "hart" and "heart" in works of literature. Until recently, debates were still raging over whether red deer are, in fact, elk, but the matter was settled with DNA tests that show they are different species. The reindeer (*Rangifer tarandus*) is a different animal entirely, but they will also enter the conversation at times because there has been slippage between the categories of deer and reindeer in some ancient cultures and lore, and even some overlap in their range. Some of the confusion has been caused by female reindeer having antlers.

Use of the word "deer" to refer to these various creatures is a refinement that occurred around 1500 CE from original root words that referred to any kind of wild animal. The Proto-Indo-European **dʰewsóm* ("living thing"), came from **dʰéws* ("breath"). This primitive root can be traced through the Proto-Germanic **deuza*, the Proto-West Germanic **deuR*, to the Old English *dēor* (which originally referred to all quadruped animals). *Fia* is one of the Irish words for deer, and it also means "wild." The modern German *Tier* and Norwegian *dyr* mean animal in general; modern Czech, however, distinguishes between *zvíře* (any animal) and *zvěř*, which specifies a wild animal hunted as game. Both are derived from the same PIE root.

ture would result in the wounding or death of the hunters, so there were rituals, taboos, and protocols for creating weapons in the correct ways. And there was the sense of debts incurred: life was being taken, so it ought to be repaid later.

This is why ancient artwork depicting hunters often shows them tenderly cradling the animals they hunt,[34] rather than, for instance, slinging them over their shoulders or leaving them slumped on the ground (in the manner of photographs shared by modern trophy hunters on social media). Hunting large wild game was fraught in many ways, which made it an attractive subject in stories. The very prevalence of stories that relate the deeds of gods, heroes, and kings engaging in the chase likely led to later people believing it was more typical in the misty past than in the present time.

Finally, let's recall two majestic species that once stalked the European continent, Britain, and Ireland: the Irish "elk" and the aurochs. Until 20,000 years ago, Irish elk (*Megaloceros giganteus*) ranged from Ireland to east of Lake Baikal. Bulls were about the size of a modern Alaskan moose, and they bore the mightiest antlers ever to crown an animal's head: their racks measured 12 feet (more than 3.5 meters) across, weighed 90 pounds (40 kg), and were shed and regrown annually.[35] Sometimes, bones and antlers must have surfaced, for example in peat bogs, which would have been a source of wonder when people came upon them later.

Aurochs (*Bos primigenius*) were the direct ancestors of modern domesticated cattle, and they grazed in plains and woodland regions. Their curved horns were each almost a meter long (more than 3 feet), and they also grew to a very impressive stature: mature bulls were taller at their shoulders (up to six feet) than most of the people who saw them alive. Aurochs are a prominent motif in Paleolithic cave paintings, engravings, and carvings. The Celts associated the imposing bulls with the forest and the god Cernunnos, and the Romans sent them into rings to fight with their best gladiators. "These are a little below the elephant in size, and of the appearance, color, and shape of a bull," Julius Caesar noted in

---

[34] See Green, 60.

[35] See Grant. For the record, the name "Irish elk" is a double misnomer, as it was neither exclusively nor predominantly Irish, and it also wasn't related to European or North American elk. Modern taxonomists classify it as a giant deer.

Commentarii de bello Gallico. "Their strength and speed are extraordinary; they spare neither man nor wild beast which they have espied."[36]

Unfortunately, despite the hype, aurochs never stood a chance against humans. Some of them were domesticated and founded lineages of domestic cattle; those living in the wild were hunted to extinction. Aurochs were extinct in Britain by the late Bronze Age, and their extirpation in European regions proceeded apace with the clearcutting of forests. The last known herd dwindled down to its final few members in Jaktorów Forest in Poland in the early 17th century: the last aurochs bull died in 1620, and the last cow in 1627.[37] Their legacy has been immortalized in cave art, artifacts (including blowing and drinking horns), in myths and legends, and even, it is theorized, in the choice of the site for the Stonehenge complex.[38] Both of these extinct species left the impression that wild game was bigger and better in the past, and this probably served to bolster the reputations of the heroic figures whose hunting tales were told. It is easy to see how the ancient hunters must have seemed like giants or other supernatural beings to later audiences.

Why White Deer?

Let us now look at why, rather than being a harbinger of good fortune, a wild white animal conveys a warning. Like all good taboos, the white deer is associated with danger and with death—primarily because of its color. The color white is associated with death[39] for a variety of reasons: firstly, because an unusual lightening of skin and mucous membranes is a symptom of pathological conditions such as anemia, infection, frostbite, hypothyroidism, disorders of the circulatory system, and massive bleeding, among many others. Most significantly, when a person or animal dies, one

---

[36] See Hubbell.

[37] Doubt exists as to whether this herd was of pure aurochs stock—they may have been hybrid with domestic cattle to a certain extent, though not enough to cause significant morphological changes. Moreover, some of the Scandinavian drinking horns that were thought to have been sourced from aurochs bulls were actually made from the horns of domestic cattle. See Masterson.

[38] See Tia Ghose's summary of archaeological research in *Live Science*. Evidence indicates that a place continually occupied by a population of hunters for 3000 years was strategically sited near an aurochs migration route and a freshwater spring. Perhaps this became a feasting site, "drawing people together from across different cultures in the region." There is much more that can be said about Stonehenge, and I will discuss a few other aspects of the monument later. This is an intriguing primordial layer to its history.

[39] The color white also has other associations unrelated to death, such as hygienic sterility, angels, infants, and virginity. I am not attempting an exhaustive discourse on the symbolism of this color. Readers can explore further correspondences themselves. I owe the initial inspiration for my own list of associations to Robin Artisson's discussion in *An Carow Gwyn*.

of the first signs of death is *pallor mortis*, an ashen discoloration of the corpse's complexion that sets in within about 20 minutes of death, following the collapse of capillary circulation.

White is the color of the hairs eventually growing on people's heads, faces, and bodies, betraying their advancing age: a very poignant *memento mori* (reminder of one's mortality) that nearly every human being who doesn't die young must reckon with. The appearance of that whiteness is as if something were treacherously emerging from within: after our lives have ended, white is the color of the clean bones we'll leave behind. It is also the color of our teeth, the only bones that are normally visible while we are alive, a symbolically potent gateway that plants and animals (vegetables and meat) pass through after we kill them. White is the color of the fangs of predatory animals we hope will not devour us. Scars are silvery white, and they mark the parts of our body that have survived not only physical assault but also the risk of infections, which could so often be more deadly than the wounds themselves. It is also the color of semen: white, and yet translucent. People have speculated for eons that the liquid male "seed" was somehow the essence of a conceived child, but the exact process of its "quickening," as well as the mother's contribution of an egg (and not just the loan of an incubating womb) was not understood by scientists until the late nineteenth century.[40]

White is the color of starlight. The Milky Way is also white, and has been considered a passageway through which souls enter and exit their lives on Earth. Also, in northern latitudes, white is the color of the ice and snows of winter—traditionally the deadliest season, because of food shortages, as well as epidemics among people who had to huddle together to keep warm. George R.R. Martin personifies this "hoary" principle in the figures of the White Walkers in his *Song of Ice and Fire* series. Further, greyish or whitish ashes may be all that's left after a body's full cremation. Today, many people still experience white as the color of death in the form of the "white light" they see in near-death experiences.

---

[40] See Dolnick. People have known there is relationship between a man and woman having sexual intercourse and pregnancies for a very long time. However, they were not aware that women produce eggs and that the "animalcules" swimming in semen that had been observed under microscopes were human reproductive cells, not bacteria or parasites such as the ones found elsewhere in the body. The closest guess for a long time was the "two-seed" theory of conception, which posited that female fluids and/or orgasm were necessary to create a baby. This is described in Bugge's article on fertility myths in the Middle Ages (208-210).

For all these reasons, white is often associated with personifications of Death, and also of pleas to be spared from it. In the Book of Revelations, Death rides an "ashen" or "pale" horse, and it is considered to be nearly the only thing one can count on as inevitable. Perhaps the association of death with necessary surrender is one of the reasons why white flags are flown by those who are desperate and close to death.[41] It is a plea for mercy when you can already see the misty breath of its mount: "Please, call this thing off! Just a little while longer!"

White is also a color of ghosts: for ages reaching even into our times, the stereotypical image of a ghost or spirit in popular culture appears white against a dark background. Until a few centuries ago, only the affluent could afford to be buried in wooden coffins; however, while the coffin has entered our visual repertoire of death imagery more recently, the archetypical winding-sheet had already been there for millennia. The fluttering often depicted in a ghost's shroud shows that the fabric is starting to unwind, hinting at what lies underneath. Sometimes it was just an immaterial spirit, but there were also popular legends of revenants in the early modern period featuring a reanimated corpse still trailing its winding-sheet. Because of this association with freshly-buried corpses, dressing in a sheet was a popular prank among friends and neighbors, and sometimes a disguise for burglars: superstitious victims would take fright and run away, leaving their household goods unguarded.

With this motif firmly established in the popular imagination, nineteenth-century spiritualist mediums and "spirit photographers" often used white sheets to depict spectral presences in their stagings. In the first half of the 20th century, before the development of more sophisticated special effects, the white sheet continued to be used in films so audiences could distinguish between living and ghostly characters. After visual media technology advanced, the sheets began to look campy, or cute and childish (as in Casper the Friendly Ghost) instead of frightening or "spiritual" in the necromantic sense.[42]

---

[41] The white flag has long symbolized a cry for help, or surrender with a plea for mercy. This has been true both in Europe and in China, where there is also an immediate association of white as a color of mourning. See Andrews.

[42] For more on the social history of ghosts, see Owen Davies.

While I have thus far focused on Indo-European traditions, the non-Indo-European pagan Hungarians also had an association between white horses and death, via the moon. They styled the moon as a white stallion (*mén*), and because of the moon's influence on the material world (early Hungarian tradition told that mountains were raised by the Earth's attraction to the Moon) as well as upon women, they held the moon in "great reverence." This chain of associations is preserved through the following words: *mén manó, manyó, menyecske, menny, monnó* (stallion, man, old woman, young woman, heaven, archaic one). They "knew that the Moon (*hold*) is a dead (*holt*) body and for this reason the White Horse was also used as a symbol of Death." In one Magyar legend, a young man sitting on a white horse lifts his girl up onto the saddle, telling her that the moon is shining beautifully. As everyone hearing the story knows, one approaches the saddle still alive, but a chill had to run through the young woman, because those who ride are dead, and the ghostly rider asks "are you afraid, my angel?"[43]

In Hinduism, white is the color of mourning, much as black has been in the West. However, the focus in dharmic religions is neither on the degeneration of the body nor on spirits that may linger and haunt the living: whiteness here represents the soul's escape from the material plane. In Chinese traditional culture, the color white was associated with death and mourning, as well as with autumn, metal, and the direction of West. Buddhists (Chinese and others) also tend to use white as a color for mourners' garments, flowers, and other funeral effects as a symbol of the deceased "escaping" from their past life and getting ready to be reborn.

Thus, it is not surprising that not only the dead themselves (in body and spirit), but also psychopomps or messengers that moved between the worlds, took on these mysterious deathly-white qualities. An intriguing example can be found in a tale of a white serpent collected by the Grimm Brothers. Those who eat the flesh of the magical reptile became able to understand the language of animals: a primordial condition of mystical connection, and the recovery of an ability that humans (in many worldwide

---

[43] See Tomory. The capitalization is in the original.

myths and traditional beliefs) lost at the end of a previous age in which humans were more connected to the wild forces of our world.[44]

Here is the beginning of this tale:

> A long time ago there lived a king who was famed for his wisdom through all the land. Nothing was hidden from him, and it seemed as if news of the most secret things was brought to him through the air. But he had a strange custom: every day after dinner, when the table was cleared, and no one else was present, a trusty servant had to bring him one more dish. It was covered, however, and even the servant did not know what was in it, neither did anyone know, for the king never took off the cover to eat of it until he was quite alone.
>
> This had gone on for a long time, when one day the servant, who took away the dish, was overcome with such curiosity that he could not help carrying the dish into his room. When he had carefully locked the door, he lifted up the cover, and saw a white snake lying on the dish. But when he saw it he could not deny himself the pleasure of tasting it, so he cut of a little bit and put it into his mouth. No sooner had it touched his tongue than he heard a strange whispering of little voices outside his window. He went and listened, and then noticed that it was the sparrows who were chattering together, and telling one another of all kinds of things which they had seen in the fields and woods. Eating the snake had given him power of understanding the language of animals...

It is this reclaimed capability to speak with the beasts of the air, water, and land (ravens, fish, and ants) that not only saves his life, but also gains him the hand of a very demanding princess and the fullness of life: "The youth, full of joy, set out homewards, and took the Golden Apple to the king's beautiful daughter, who had now no more excuses left to make. They cut the Apple of Life in two and ate it together; then, her heart became full of love for him, and they lived in undisturbed happiness to a great age."[45]

The poet Lisel Mueller sums up the feeling of the kind of communication people once had, and then lost, and then hesitatingly ask how they might reconnect. It is worth reading the poem in its entirety, but I'll summarize, saying that the poet tells us that "something happened," and people began

---

[44] Robin Artisson mentions this story in *An Carow Gwyn*, p. 99.
[45] A version of this tale in the public domain can be found at authorama.com.

to "trample and plunder" the earth. The animals fled, and their language became incomprehensible to us. But they became hungry and started returning to eat whatever scraps they could find, even becoming familiar with human food packaging. Their migration cycles were interrupted. And now hungry deer invade people's gardens, "as if they had been invited," ravishing the flowers and vegetables gardeners worked so hard to grow. Like all refugees, these deer arrive in defiance of the risks arrayed against them, because we're their last chance. "Shall we fit them with precious collars?" Mueller asks. For they have chosen the spaces close to us as their home.[46]

In one of the best-known poems from the twentieth century, e. e. cummings nicely brings the eldritch color symbolism together with the motif of hunted deer in the haunting verses of "All in green my love went riding," which I rediscovered while researching for this book. Readers will find an abrupt moment of transition from the gilded romance of a noble hunting expedition when the red deer are suddenly characterized as "paler than daunting death" (I added the emphasis). The narrator seems to follow the "lucky hunter's" ride as a ghostly observer who can take in both broad features of the landscape and small details, such as the dogs' smiles. The tension grows: suddenly, the rider's bugle is "cruel" and now her arrow is hungry for the kill. However, no deer die here: instead of the "hart" being felled, the poet's own heart is pierced by the hunter's apparent indifference.

> All in green went my love riding
> on a great horse of gold
> into the silver dawn.
>
> four lean hounds crouched low and smiling
> the merry deer ran before.
>
> Fleeter be they than dappled dreams
> the swift sweet deer
> the red rare deer.
>
> Four red roebuck at a white water
> the cruel bugle sang before.

---

[46] Lisel Mueller's "Animals Are Entering Our Lives" is cited by Terri Windling in her blog.

Horn at hip went my love riding
riding the echo down
into the silver dawn.

four lean hounds crouched low and smiling
the level meadows ran before.

Softer be they than slippered sleep
the lean lithe deer
the fleet flown deer.

Four fleet does at a gold valley
the famished arrow sang before.

Bow at belt went my love riding
riding the mountain down
into the silver dawn.

four lean hounds crouched low and smiling
the sheer peaks ran before.

Paler be they than daunting death
the sleek slim deer
the tall tense deer.

Four tall stags at a green mountain
the lucky hunter sang before.

All in green went my love riding
on a great horse of gold
into the silver dawn.

four lean hounds crouched low and smiling
my heart fell dead before.[47]

---

[47] Cummings, 15. Emphasis mine.

The White Deer in the Groves of Symbols

Ancient Tracks: Reindeer Lore and Nomadic Herders

Some of the stories of mystical stags or deer deities are very old, and may have originated in the Eurasian steppes and subarctic regions among reindeer herders. Reindeer previously had much wider habitat ranges than they do today, and they could be found in France and the British Isles during the Magdalenian epoch (17,000-12,000 BCE), a period also termed the "Age of the Reindeer" (*L'âge du renne*) by Édouard Lartet and Henry Christy. Unlike the cave lion and woolly rhinoceros, reindeer and wild horses survived the collapse of the mammoth steppe ecosystems, as well as the Pleistocene/Holocene transition in the British Isles and the lowlands of Northern Europe about 12,000 years ago. For around 3000 years, they coexisted with temperate fauna such as red deer and roe deer. They then gradually disappeared from northern central Europe and southern Scandinavia, as their habitats of light birch and pine forests were succeeded by thicker pine and deciduous forests.[48]

For humans, the Age of the Reindeer was also a kind of Paleolithic Renaissance, with extraordinary works of art appearing in Lascaux, Altamira, Santillana del Mar, Font de Gaume, Conquer Cave, the Cave of La Pasiega, Cueva de El Castillo, Pech Merle, La Marche, Creswell Crags, Nottinghamshire, Magura and Belogradchik (Bulgaria), and Astuvansalmi in the Saimaa area of Finland.[49] An image of a reindeer carved in Cathol cave in Wales around 12,500 BCE is considered to be the oldest known rock art in Britain.[50] However, reindeer persisted in Scotland much longer—probably until the 13th century[51]—which may explain this fairy lullaby:

> On milk of deer I was reared,
> On milk of deer I was nurtured,
> On milk of deer beneath the ridge of storms,
> On crest of hill and mountain.[52]

Early Central Asian and Siberian myths were brought to the Near East and Anatolia by Indo-Iranian nomads, where they met with other tribes and became absorbed into the older traditions of these regions. The Hungarians (Magyars), who are descended from nomadic tribes that came to the Carpathian basin from a homeland in the Ural mountains, or possibly from western Siberia or the Middle Volga region, are the most direct European heirs to these legacies.

In Zsuzsa Tomory's syncretic modern retelling of Hungarian history, she recounts how "our Csodaszarvas, Miracle Stag," emerges from the "dark twirling cloud which came about through the ancient 'Big Bang.'" Csodaszarvas carries the child Universe, who is also identified with the mythi-

---

[48] See Sommer et al.
[49] See Linda Iles, 127, in Wise.
[50] See BBC: "Gower Cave Reindeer Carving is Britain's Oldest Rock Art."
[51] See Hetherington.
[52] The original text from the *Carmina Gaedelica* reads:
Air bainne nam fiadh a thogadh mi,
Air bainne nam fiadh a shealbhaich,
Air bainne nam fiadh fo dhruim nan sian,
Air bharr nan sliabh 's nan garbhlach.
Alexander Carmichael's English translation is cited by Wise on p. 69.

cal Magyar ancestor Magor, the Sun, and the baby Jesus.[53] The holy baby sings this "ancient song of the universe," as such:

> ... The rising, shiny Sun is on my forehead,
> On my side the lovely, shining moon,
> On my right kidney are the stars of heaven ...

The stag's immense antlers cradle the newborn Sun, the Moon is on his chest, and Venus sits on his forehead—

> and thus does he walk the Magyar villages even today at Christmas time" (that is, just when the light begins to lengthen after the winter solstice). The stag's entire being is covered in star-dust. As he grows, the stars and galaxies multiply, too on his body. We can see even today his footprints as he walks on his road covered in star-dust.[54]

This is a tale told in linear time. An alternate interpretation of the solstice stag illustrates the annual cycle of light and dark period, rather than a creation story. In the version based in cyclical time, a great hunter pursues the magical beast and kills it around the winter solstice. The sun, held in the stag's antlers "of a thousand branches and knobs," escapes and becomes stronger, which brings back the spring. Its fawn then grows to maturity, and the cycle repeats in perpetuity.[55]

In the version of the tale with a linear progression of events, the Miracle Stag, "slowly emerges from the cumulus cloud" and "stops at the constella-

---

[53] Where did this baby come from? Before any Christian accretions, his mother was Tündér Ilona, the Hungarian fairy queen, who was called the mother of life. Her name, Ilona, seems to be derived from the Hungaro-Turkic root *él* or *éle*, meaning life, and *ana* or *anya*, meaning "mother." Her animal form is a swan, associated with the constellation of Cygnus, and she lays an egg from which Magor, the sun god, is hatched.

A very old origin for these stories is suggested by the effects of "precession." Over millennia, the apparent position of constellations shifts, caused by a 26,000-year cycle of the Earth's wobbling around its axis, much like a toy top wobbles as it spins. The view overhead in the Northern Hemisphere between ca. 16,500-13,000 BCE would have been different from the present: the Great Rift in the Milky Way would have been directly overhead and rotating around the Pole Star, which was Deneb for two thousand years, and some of the key stars in Cygnus would have been wheeling around it, in a phenomenon the Hungarians called the "turning of the fairies" (See Collins, pp. 101-2, in Wise). The name Ilona is also related to Helen/Helena/Elen, and the Cygnus constellation was later restyled as the Northern Cross or the Cross of Santa Helena. Recall here that the Greek myth of Helen of Troy also uses a swan motif, since Helen and her sister Clytemnestra are hatched from an egg resulting from a union between their mother and Zeus, who had disguised himself as a swan. This may even explain the anomaly I mentioned in a previous footnote of a female offspring resulting from rape by a god. Helen had been there for much longer than Zeus, but the patriarchal religions made her his child, conceived by trickery.

[54] See Tomory. She cites and retells much more celestial lore relating to stags, and the Hungarians' mythical forefathers and their wanderings (with a good deal of repetition), but this will have to suffice for the present volume. Andrew Collins, in his essay "Ellen and the Celestial Deer Path," describes how Csodaszarvas (the Miracle Stag) was associated in Hungarian star lore with the constellation of Ursa Major, located at the northern opening of the Milky Way's Great Rift. The stag's antlers are the flickering flames of a thousand candles burning upon the tips of his antlers. (See Collins in Wise's anthology *Finding Elen*, pp. 98-9.) Not surprisingly, the Great Rift has also been seen as a cosmic vulva, through which souls enter and/or leave the world.

[55] See Hmori. He also tells us Hun art all the way from Mongolia and the Dung Huan caves of western China depicts these magical events with the twin hunters, and the constellations we know as Orion (which he identifies with Nimrod) and Gemini (Nimrod's twin sons) and the wondrous antlered beast (Taurus or Ursa Major) help people recall the chase after the wondrous "horned doe" which led them to their new homeland.

tion Aquarius, a place which Magyar tradition calls Tóállás—a lake where he feeds on tender grasses to grow strong enough to continue his journey. His companions are two snakes: the blue snake represents the cold of space, the black snake is the darkness therein, but Magor even in his infancy is so strong that his radiance can render both harmless." His antlers then gradually took on the role of the World Tree, reaching up to the stars. Later versions of the myth would double the primal ancestor as twins called Magor and Hunor, who were understood to be human princes, and the stories then deal with migrations and nation-building instead of cosmic origin myths.[56]

Various medieval histories, including the *Gesta Hungarorum* (early 13th century), Mark of Kált's *Illuminated Chronicle* (*Képes Krónika* in Hungarian, 1358), the *Chronicle of the Hungarians* by János (John, Johannes) Thuróczy (1487), Mahmud Tercüman's Turkish chronicle *Tarih-i Üngürüs*,[57] and the chronicle *Hungária* by Miklós (Nicholas) Oláh pick up this thread. Each of them, with variations, recounts the tale of the two noble hunters pursuing a wonderful deer, and then kidnapping and "marrying" royal women. Their men usually "married" the common women who were attending the queens or princesses.

These sources agree that the Magyars' forebears originally came from Persia, that their king was named Nimrod or Menroth, and that his main wife was Enech/Enéh[58] (in Tercüman's work she is called Ankisa). The lady may have been not just an ordinary queen, though, as her name is very similar to the name of the Persian goddess Anahita. The royal couple's favorite sons were named Hunor (whose name probably derives from Onogor, the name of a people who lived nearby at the time) and Magor or Mag-

---

[56] See Tomory.

[57] Hmori has drawn quite a lot of his material from *Târîh-i Üngürûs* chronicle of Hungary published in the sixteenth century. The chronicle was compiled from older sources and translated, mostly from Latin, by Tercüman Mahmud (1510–1575), a translator and diplomat who worked for the Ottoman Empire. Mahmud had been born in Vienna, possibly to Jewish or Hungarian parents, and was originally named Sebold von Pribach. It is possible that he relocated to Istanbul after being taken prisoner following the defeat of the Hungarian forces at Mohács 1526. The *Târîh-i Üngürûs* was commissioned by Sultan Suleiman the Magnificent and produced with all the pomp and flair required for courtly historiography. Tercüman may have collaborated on the work with other Hungarian captives/state functionaries. His chronicle seems to draw primarily on the world history penned by the Roman historian Justin (Marcus Junianus Justinus Frontinus) and the *Chronica Hungarorum* (1488) written by Johannes de Thurocz (Thuróczy János in Hungarian), an aristocratic Hungarian historian. Suleiman wanted to celebrate his conquest of Hungary and use the chronicle for propaganda efforts (also see Papp, and Zoltan Simon's "Revised Chronology of the Hungarians.")

[58] Wait, wasn't Magor's mother called Ilona? *Enéh* can be interpreted as either cow/deer, or pine tree—or perhaps both, and it is also likely derived from *ana/anya*, meaning "mother," which would mean she is the selfsame mother of life (see Collins in Wise, 101).

yar. After reaching adulthood, these two brothers mustered a force of fifty-five mounted warriors and headed toward the borders of the kingdom on a scouting mission. There, they spied a wondrous deer. Some versions describe this deer as a hart, others as a hind, and some even as a hermaphroditic "horned doe," whose appearance is described as either pure white, or decorated with the sun, moon, and stars on her hide.

The numinous creature evaded the hunters by leaping into the Black Sea and swimming away. The hunters pursued it; when they made landfall, the deer was gone, but the men had found new and intriguing lands—either Crimea, or, according to Tercüman, the Northern Caucasus. In Tercüman's version, the princes asked their father's permission to go back and settle there, saying that cattle would have good grazing. With the king's blessing, they returned, spending five years in a temple they built in the marshes where the deer had vanished. In the sixth year, an exalted teacher came to them and taught them the ways of being a great king.[59]

They did not depart this place alone. Fred Hmori recounts how the princes and their men left their temple and looked around the nearby territories. They made camp in the evening, and woke to music emanating from a clearing in the forest. There, they found the wives and daughters (or just "maidens") unattended by their menfolk, singing and dancing in honor of the "horn" or "hind." The word *ino* or *iino* means both of those things in Hungarian,[60] and it could have indeed been a celebration of both, as the versions of the myth derived from Scythian sources describe the animal as a "horned hind."

Depending on which version of the tale is told, the women in the clearing were the daughters of the Bulars [Bulgarians], including the two daughters of "Belars" or "Bulars" (again, Bulgarians) or the Alan king Dula (*Gesta Hungarorum*). By contrast, the Persian version has one prince who marries the queen of the women. Her name is "horned doe" (*sar-istani*.)[61]

In the version with two princes, the brothers were so enamored of Dula's daughters that they resolved to marry them. Their companions then kid-

---

[59] From Mahmud Tercüman's *Târîh-i Üngürûs*, translated by Fred Hmori.
[60] See the commentary attached to the version of Simon Kezai's Gesta Hungarorum I provide in my references for the etymology, which is also echoed by Hmori, who comments: "the name of a hind is 'horned' in Hungarian.
[61] See Hmori.

napped all the rest of the women, taking them to an island in the lake. These ancestors had many descendants, eventually becoming the 108 clans of the Scythian nation. This number is hardly accidental: 108 has long been considered a holy number in Vedic as well as other ancient cultures. Some of the ratios early scientists could observe in the natural world include the average distance of the sun and the moon to the Earth, which is 108 times the diameter of each; the diameter of the sun is about 108 times the diameter of the earth; 108 is the angle found in each corner of a pentagon; and it is related to the Fibonacci sequence (which Indians knew about before Fibonacci). However, let us leave that aside for now: the important outcome is that the descendants of Hunor and one of the princesses became the nation of the Huns, while the descendants of Magor and the other princess became the nation of the Magyars.[62]

As indicated by etymologies which stem from different roots but still sound similar to the Hungarian name Ilona (mother of life), the complex of star and deer lore spread from Asia through the Caucasus and Anatolia on its way to Europe.[63] Andrew Collins suggests that people from the Maikop (Maykop) culture, who lived in the western Caucasus in the Bronze Age, were likely responsible for spreading a powerful interest in deer. This is evidenced by cast gold figurines bearing strong resemblance to artifacts found in Scythian sites and at the Chalcolithic site Alaca Höyük in Turkey. The Maikop buried their dead in Indo-European-style *kurgans* (burial mounds with stone chambers inside), and may have imparted this practice to the non-Indo-European Hattian natives of Anatolia, along with their language and their interest in deer. Another notable artifact is a seal that depicts an antlered deer standing in front of a tree whose branches extend

---

[62] Ibid.

[63] Via a reference to a greyish or brownish color, the proto-Indo-European root *h_1el- means deer or elk (and later, we get the word "elephant" from it). This gives rise to myriad related forms: the Old Armenian եղն (*eln*, "hind"); Armenian եղնիկ (*elnik*, "doe"); Proto-Balto-Slavic *elenias or *eleňь; Latvian *alnis* ("elk", "moose"); Lithuanian *élnias, élnis, álnis* ("deer"); Czech, Slovak, Polish, and Bosnian (as well as other Slavic languages) *jelen*; Old Prussian *alne*, Dutch *eland* (elk); Proto-Celtic *elanī or *elantī; *$h_1él-n$; Proto-Hellenic *élap^hos or *elnós; Ancient Greek ἔλαφος (*élaphos*, "red deer") or ἑλλός (*ellós*) or ὤλκη (*álkē*); Modern Greek ελάφι (*eláfi*); Proto-Germanic: *algiz, *elhaz; Latin: *alcēs*; Proto-Indo-Iranian *H*ŕ́ćyas; Proto-Indo-Aryan *H*ŕ́śyas, Vedic Sanskrit: ऋश्य (*ŕ́śya*); and thence the modern German *Hirsch* (a deer). See Wiktionary: h_1el (reconstruction).

above and below its main trunk (a "world tree"?)[64] This conforms with the etymology of Enéh, the name of Magor's mother, which refers to both deer and trees.

Deer Myths in Classical Antiquity

The Greek myth of the "golden" (or Ceryneian) hind perhaps reveals overlaps between the more ancient or exotic reindeer and the red or roe deer that lived in the Mediterranean region in the classical age. Artemis had seen five of these impossibly huge deer, with golden antlers and bronze hooves, grazing by a river in a location variously stated as Ceryneia or Thessaly; she was skilled enough to capture four of them, harnessing them to her chariot with golden bridles—but the fifth one got away. Capturing this animal was a challenge left to Heracles as his third labor. He pursued the hind for a year (perhaps recalling the solar cycles illustrated in the more archaic Hungarian tales), until he reached Hyperborea, a faraway mythical land in the North. There, he came upon her sleeping under a tree, and the myth variously relates that he caught her in a net, injured her, killed her, presented her to King Eurystheus (who was organizing his labors), or took her to Artemis, who told him to let the creature go. Most likely, this is a mythic account of reindeer, which are the only deer that can be harnessed, and which are very tall and have horned cows. However, Robert Graves had a more macabre alternate interpretation: "Historically, it may record the Achaean capture of a shrine where Artemis was worshipped at Elaphios (hind-like). Her four chariot stags represent the years of the Olympiad, at the close of each a victim dressed in deer skins was hunted to death."[65]

Once we enter a more literate era, an author who is known only as "Pseudo-Aristotle" (because their work was later attributed to the philosopher), related a legend about one of the warriors at the siege of Troy who was made famous in Homer's *Iliad*. Diomedes consecrated a white hart to

---

[64] See Collins in Wise, 114.
[65] See Wise, 80.

Artemis and placed a golden collar around its neck.[66] This work belongs to the ancient literary genre of "paradoxography," collections of stories that relate tales of abnormalities in humans and animals, monstrous births, ghost stories, mythical animals such as centaurs, and so on. Sometimes, the tone of these volumes is serious, and at other times it's rather tongue-in-cheek. The tale begins straightforwardly:

> Among the Peucetini they say that there is a temple of Artemis, in which is dedicated what is called the bronze necklet, bearing the legend "Diomedes to Artemis." The story goes that he hung it about the neck of a deer, and that it grew there, and in this way being found later by Agathocles, king of the Siceliots, they say that it was dedicated at the temple of Zeus.

However, it goes on to claim the deer was found 800 years later by Agathocles.[67]

Pliny the Elder's *Natural History* discusses deer in Chapter VIII, and mentions that sometimes white stags are found. He also references the pet hind kept by the renegade Roman general and statesman Quintus Sertorius (126-73 BCE). Plutarch's "Life of Sertorius" provides more detail: Sertorius had received the animal as a fawn from a commoner named Spanus, who found it when a doe that had just given birth was fleeing from hunters. When he came upon the fawn and noticed its unusual coloring, he captured it and made a gift of it to Sertorius. The fawn was very tame, and was trained by its master to come when it was called and to follow him, ignoring any crowds or bustle around it.

Eventually, Sertorious found further uses for his pet: he told the local people that the doe had been sent by the goddess Diana, and that it served as an oracle, delivering her messages. Sometimes, he claimed that military intelligence about imminent attacks had been imparted by the magical hind, or when he heard news of battles that had been won, he would bring

---

[66] You may recall the line in Lisel Mueller's poem that I shared in the last chapter, where the person who finds wild deer circling around her home asks: "Shall we fit them with precious collars?" This is a motif that seems to have originated in the Preclassical Age, was in use in Rome, then reverberated through the Renaissance when Classical imagery was revived—and poets still use it today.

[67] The editor of the volume of Pseudo-Aristotle that I refer to commented in endnote 'e' that a tale similar to the one about Diomedes' deer with the golden collar has also been told about Charles VI of France. "... in 1390, ... a twelve-year old boy already fond of the chase, is said to have come upon a deer bearing a collar inscribed *Hoc michi Caesar donavit*—most often ungrammatically quoted as *Hoc me Caesar donavit*—when Caesar had been dead for 1400 years. It can be remarked that if *michi* was the exact reading on the collar, it's a medieval spelling of the word, and the boy's uncle Louis d'Anjou, who organized the hunt, becomes a prime suspect; the aim of the imposture possibly being to raise the boy's self-esteem."

out the hind wearing victory garlands before the official announcements were made. When the animal appeared with these garlands, he told his men to sacrifice to the gods to ensure a good outcome. Both Plutarch and Pliny agree that he used her to take advantage of superstitious Spanish country people.[68]

However, Pliny himself ascribed magical virtues to deer, including incredible lifespans. He claimed that some had been captured one hundred years after they had been fitted with golden collars by Alexander the Great. They had grown so plump that the collars were entirely concealed by rolls of skin and fat. He also claimed that they were immune from fevers, and that eating their flesh every morning (provided that the animals had been killed with a single wound) would allow "princely women" to "arrive at an extreme old age, free from all fevers."[69]

The connection between Alexander the Great and the stag begins with the classical Greek myth of Artemis (who is later called Diana by the Romans) and the hunter Actaeon. When Artemis was bathing in a pool with her nymphs, Actaeon came upon her there and either merely observed her like a peeping tom (a sacrilege), or he tried to rape her. The vengeful goddess transformed him into a stag, and he was killed by his own dogs. This scene is depicted in the "Stag Hunt Mosaic (c. 300 BCE) installed in a wealthy home called the "House of the Abduction of Helen" or the "House of the Rape of Helen" in the Macedonian capital of Pella, where Alexander was born.

Alexander used depictions of the motif of dogs attacking a stag in explicit reference to the Persians he intended to conquer as vengeance for the sacking of Athens and destroying temples there—including the Parthenon, which was dedicated to the maiden goddess Athena.[70] The connection, or the sympathetic magic intended, was the "hunter being hunted" as retaliation for sacrilege against a goddess (Artemis in her bath, and the damage to Athena's temple), which ought to invoke divine help.

---

[68] Pliny the Elder, 95; Plutarch, 30-33.
[69] See Pliny the Elder, 94-5.
[70] See Ros.

Another connection between a conquering hero and the restoration of the honors due to a maiden goddess is found in the story of Brutus, the great-grandson of Aeneas of Troy and legendary founder of Britain. A soothsayer predicted that he would accomplish great things, but that he would also kill his parents. He killed his parents, as foretold, and was banished. At one point in their journeys, Brutus and his band of Trojan warriors landed on the shores of an island that had once been inhabited, but it was deserted when they arrived. There, they discovered a temple of Diana and performed rites in her honor. That night, Brutus fell asleep in front of her statue and he received a dream of the land where he would settle, an island to the west inhabited by giants. After he reached the island, he erected a temple for Diana overlooking the Thames.

Christians later rededicated the site of the old temple to St. Paul, a fanatic who made a special priority of suppressing worship of Diana after his religious conversion.[71] Between 1675 and 1710, a cathedral was erected, which was known for various relics associated with St. Helena (which offers echoes of the life-giving deer goddess known as Ilona, Elen, and variations thereof). Curiously, the lore of St. Paul's Cathedral has persistently reflected Dianic themes and distinctive customs connected to deer and hunting. For example, hunters would lay carcasses of deer they had killed on the cathedral stairs, and several deer-themed hunting festivals were documented. On Candlemas (February 2), on the Feast of the Conversion of St. Paul (January 25), and on the feast of the Commemoration of St. Paul (June 30), deer—either bucks or does, depending on the day—would be led to the cathedral's west door. Clergy wearing crowns of roses and robes embroidered with bucks or does to match the sacrificial victim were waiting, and the deer were killed. Huntsmen blew their horns, and the deer's head, fixed on a pole, was solemnly taken to the high altar.[72]

There has also been a strong theme of the suppression of Diana throughout the cathedral's existence, as though she continued haunting the site. John Clark offers a few examples, such as Richard Corbet, bishop of Norwich, appealing in his diocese for funds for the repair of St Paul's

---

[71] Wise, 35-36.
[72] ibid.

Cathedral in London in 1634. He pointed out that the cathedral had replaced a shrine of Diana and guided them in a visualization: "See a mystery in the change: St. Paul confuting twice the Idol: there, in person, where the cry was 'Great is Diana of the Ephesians!'" and then imagining that, here and now, "Paul installed while Diana is thrust out."

Much later, a contributor to the *Guide to Legendary London* prescribed a similar spiritual exercise for the Christian faithful (or xenophobes who fear brown-skinned immigrants) to carry out in the same place: "visualise a figure of the goddess Diana/Artemis, 'a tall brown-skinned lady dressed in skins and bearing antlers on her head. She is standing on the high altar and her powerful presence fills the cold, oppressive building...'" [73] However, eventually, sympathies for Diana came back to the fore, and some now visit St. Paul's expressly because of the old associations. Among twentieth-century occultists, there was even a theory that the wedding of Prince Charles and Lady Diana Spencer in 1981 took place at St Paul's rather than at Westminster Abbey because of "the Dianic influence still embodied in the site."[74]

Deer in Celtic Myths and Legends

Like the Greek stories, Celtic legends also use encounters with otherworldly creatures to illustrate that someone has transgressed boundaries, and that one of the key things that must be restored is the bodily self-determination of a divine female. *Pwyll Pendefig Dyfed* (Pwyll, Prince of Dyfed),[75] the first of the Four Branches of the Mabinogi, tells the story of the friendship between a human prince, Pwyll, and Arawn, the lord of Annwn. One night, Pwyll is seized with a desire to go hunting. He sets out early the next day with his hounds, and becomes separated from his com-

---

[73] Quoted from John Clark.
[74] See Clark.
[75] The name Pwyll derives from the proto-Brythonic *puɬll and means mind, wisdom, and intelligence. In Welsh, it has many additional meanings, including discretion, prudence, judgement, and sanity. See Etymology Geek.

panions. He hears another pack of hounds whose belling tolled[76] in an entirely different register, and then he sees them in the distance falling upon a stag and pulling it to the ground. Pwyll is surprised at their appearance: they are dazzlingly white and have equally brilliant red ears: these are the *Cŵn Annwn*, whose barking or howling generally foretoken the appearance of the Wild Hunt and the death of those who hear or see them. (In later lore, the *Cŵn Annwn* would be become "Hell hounds" owned by Satan, who replaced Arawn and other Celtic deities as the lord of the dead.)

Undaunted or unaware of what he had come across, Pwyll rudely drives them off and allows his own hounds to move in, which angers their master. As his dogs were feasting on the stag's flesh, Pwyll sees a huntsman approaching on a huge dapple-grey horse, wearing a hunting horn around his neck. The deerstalker who had been cheated of his prey speaks first:

> "Chieftain," he said "I know who you are, but greet you I will not."
> "Aye," said Pwyll "perhaps you are so important you don't have to?"
> "God knows" he replied "it's not the dignity of my rank that's restraining me."
> "What is it then, Chieftain?"
> "Between me and God, it's your rudeness and discourtesy."
> "Chieftain, what discourtesy have I committed in your eyes?"
> "I've never seen a greater discourtesy by a man than driving off a pack which has killed a stag, and [then] feeding your own dogs on it." That, said he, "was the discourtesy, and though I won't be revenging myself on you, between me and God, I will be claiming dishonour from you to the value of a hundred stags."

The arrogant prince recalculates:

> "Chieftain, if I've committed an offence, I will redeem your friendship."
> "In what form will you redeem it?"
> "As appropriate to your rank—I don't know who you are ... "
> "A crowned king am I in the land I am from."
> "Lord," said Pwyll "good day to you. Which land is it that you are from?"

---

[76] An irresistible double entendre. Hemingway's famous novel *For Whom the Bell Tolls* takes its title from a line in John Donne (1572-1631), who wrote it in his *Devotions Upon Emergent Occasions, Meditation XVII*. The bells Donne refers to are funeral bells. The word "bell" is also a verb; an archaic term related to "bellow." A rather non-specific term, in more archaic English it can refer to the barking and other sounds made by hunting dogs and/or the low roars of their prey. Pwyll's impressions as he approached the scene would have included noises from both the hounds and the hart. As for tolling, its present sense of "to sound with slow single strokes" (intransitive) dates to the mid-15th century. It is probably a special use of *tollen* "to draw, lure," early 13th century variant of Old English *-tyllan* in *betyllan* "to lure, decoy," and *fortyllan* "draw away, seduce," of obscure origin. The usage of "tolling" for church bells, whether for regular services, funerals, or other occasions, is a metaphor that describes their action of luring people to church. So truly, the belling of the Otherworldly hounds was tolling irresistibly for Pwyll.

"From Annwvyn. Arawn king of Annwfn am I."
"Lord, how might I obtain your friendship?"

The kingdom of Annwn (alternately spelled Annwvyn in this text, and Annwfn elsewhere) is the Welsh name for the Otherworld, equivalent to the Irish Tir Na n-Og, the "Land of Youth." To set things right, Pwyll trades places with Arawn for a year and a day, taking on the fearsome king's appearance and duties. He feasts splendidly on the best food and drink, served in jeweled vessels. He is also allowed to lie beside the most beautiful woman he has ever seen each night, and then at the year's end he must fight Hafgan, a rival from a neighboring kingdom, and strike him down with a single blow. Pwyll fulfills all these conditions, and after Hafgan dies, Pwyll and Arawn meet again, are restored to their proper appearances, and go their separate ways. Because Pwyll had not meddled with Arawn's wife during the nights of the past year,

> ... thenceforth a strong friendship began between them, each giving the other horses, greyhounds, hawks and any other kind of treasure he thought might be pleasing to the mind of his fellow. And because of his sojourn that year in Annwfn, and his kingship [which had been] so prosperous there, and the forging of two kingdoms into one through his resilience and his fighting-power: the name "Pwyll Pendevic Dyfed" fell out of use and he became known as "Pwyll Pen Annwvyn" (Pwyll, Head of Annwn) from then on.[77]

The simplest interpretation of this story, which naturally also affords many other layers of reading, is that humans—and especially their leaders—must not rob their neighbors, or take that which does not belong to them. And part of the honor Pwyll showed in his dealings with Arawn was refraining from interfering with his otherworldly queen. However, at the end of the section above, we see that there is a lively exchange of animals and "treasure" between the kingdoms of the living (Pwyll's world) and the world of the fae or the dead (Annwn), which is a way of figuring a reciprocal exchange in the form of sacrifices offered, and fertility and abundance brought forth.

---

[77] See the medievalist Will Parker's translation of the *Four Branches of the Mabinogi* from the Middle Welsh (2005) for the complete tale at www.mabinogi.net, or his book *The Four Branches of the Mabinogi: Celtic Myth and Medieval Reality* (2007) for an in-depth examination of the symbolic and cultural contexts of the work.

Peredur is the hero of a middle Welsh romance titled *Peredur son of Efrawg* (or Evrawc). His name, his character, and his story have much in common with Perceval (Percival, Parzival, Parival, etc.), whose adventures were most famously portrayed in Chrétien de Troyes' unfinished *Perceval, the Story of the Grail* from the early 12th century. While Perceval has a Holy Grail motif and a Fisher King who is named as such, Peredur lacks the former and has a character somewhat reminiscent of the latter.

The relevant episode for this study is when the young hero enters the fabled Castle of Wonders. This castle is liminally situated in the middle of a lake, and people who live nearby and know of it do not know what kinds of wonders lie within. Peredur also has no idea of what he's about to encounter: his perceptions, judgement, and moral sense are all thrown into confusion.

When he arrives, the castle is open, as is the door to its great hall. Inside, he observes a magical chessboard[78] with pieces moving of their own accord. When the side he favored lost, he was "wroth" and threw the entire chessboard into the lake. A "black maiden"[79] comes in and chastises him for throwing away the Empress' property, which "she would not have lost for all her empire." She tells him that to regain favor there, he must fight and slay a black man, who "lays waste the dominions of the Empress." Peredur prevails in combat with this man: when the wretch begs for mercy, Peredur says he will grant it, if he restores the game board to its place. The knight returns to the castle, but the black maiden is not impressed and tells him he has failed in his mission: the chessboard is still not where it's supposed to be, so Peredur goes back to kill the man. He succeeds, but the black maiden is still not happy: Peredur must now kill another monster in the forest.

> "What monster is there?"
> "It is a stag that is as swift as the swiftest bird; and he has one horn in his forehead, as long as the shaft of a spear, and as sharp as whatever is sharpest. And he destroys the branches of the best trees in the forest,

---

[78] Charlotte Guest translates *gwyddbwyll* as chess, which is the word used in modern Welsh for the familiar game, but the original *gwyddbwyll* was a much older game that was associated with the gods, with royalty, and with divination. Clearly, throwing this kind of object into the lake is even ruder and more ill-fated than just destroying a regular game board.

[79] Note that "black" characters in these stories do not correspond to racial classification schemes; rather, this color identifies them as tutelary figures. (In Irish tales, however, a "black" character may simply have black hair or clothing.)

and he kills every animal that he meets with therein; and those that he doth not slay perish of hunger. And what is worse than that, he comes every night, and drinks up the fish pond, and leaves the fishes exposed, so that for the most part they die before the water returns again."

"Maiden," said Peredur, "wilt thou come and show me this animal?"

"Not so," said the maiden, "for he has not permitted any mortal to enter the forest for above a twelvemonth. Behold, here is a little dog belonging to the Empress, which will rouse the stag, and will chase him towards thee, and the stag will attack thee."

Then the little dog went as a guide to Peredur, and roused the stag, and brought him towards the place where Peredur was. And the stag attacked Peredur, and he let him pass by him, and as he did so, he smote off his head with his sword. And while he was looking at the head of the stag, he saw a lady on horseback coming towards him. And she took the little dog in the lappet of her cap, and the head and the body of the stag lay before her. And around the stag's neck was a golden collar.

"Ha! chieftain," said she, "uncourteously hast thou acted in slaying the fairest jewel that was in my dominions."

Oops! *But she did ask him to do this.*

The White Deer From Romance to Renaissance

Celtic themes of this type are taken up in early French romance literature, such as in the collection of ballads called the *Lais of Marie de France*. These songs make frequent reference to characters participating in Mass or Christian feasts, but the plots and characters appear to be taken from older sources, and the Christian overlays seem thin. References to Pagan figures and literature crop up, such as "Dame Venus" casting a copy of Ovid's *Remedia Amoris* [80] into flames while threatening to shun those who use its advice.

---

[80] Ovid's *Remedia Amoris* ("The Cure for Love") was a work that advised readers how *not* to fall in love and get hurt, or how to fall *out of* love if they are already ensnared. Essentially, it was a guide for ancient Roman pick-up artists. Readers could attempt to prevent or fix broken hearts by focusing on their beloved's defects, having two lovers instead of one, playing it cool, trying to work up a stage of disgust by thinking about genitalia, and avoiding alcohol and romantic poetry—but for goodness' sake, he advised, don't resort to witchcraft! Because the last thing Dame Venus is going to stand for is people learning magical hacks to undo her handiwork. Of course, the entire enterprise of preventing or curing love is doomed to failure, because explicit warnings of this type tend to draw attention to the thing they are ostensibly warning about. I assume this was actually the intention, not only in Ovid's work but also in Marie's lay, in a spirit of: "It sure would be a great big shame if anyone were to read Ovid and then cast all caution into the flames and submit to whatever Venus had in store for them." Perhaps the author was mindful of censorship, but it seems more likely she was displaying a droll sense of humor.

In the Lay of Guigemar, the "Knight of Little Brittany" goes on a hunting expedition and encounters a hermaphroditic deer (again, this may be the "horned doe" derived from travelers' stories of reindeer) that had just given birth. There are several mentions in the short text of his haste, and of his "overpassing" his quarry. When he finally looks around himself, he sees the strange animal, but his dogs, oddly, do not want to attack it. Passionate hunter that he is, he takes his bow and arrow from a servant and shoots. The arrow hits the deer above the hoof (an Achilles' heel?)[81] and then rebounds upon his own "thigh" (manly bits); then, in its death throes, the deer speaks with a human voice and curses his life and his romantic relationships.

> The night being come, Guigemar summoned his prickers and his squires, and early in the morning rode within the forest. Great pleasure had Guigemar in the woodland, and much he delighted in the chase. A tall stag was presently started, and the hounds being uncoupled, all hastened in pursuit—the huntsmen before, and the good knight following after, winding upon his horn. Guigemar rode at a great pace after the quarry, a varlet riding beside, bearing his bow, his arrows and his spear. He followed so hotly that he over-passed the chase. Gazing about him he marked, within a thicket, a doe hiding with her fawn. Very white and wonderful was this beast, for she was without spot, and bore antlers upon her head. The hounds bayed about her, but might not pull her down. Guigemar bent his bow, and loosed a shaft at the quarry. He wounded the deer a little above the hoof, so that presently she fell upon her side. But the arrow glanced away, and returning upon itself, struck Guigemar in the thigh, so grievously that straightway he fell from his horse upon the ground. Guigemar lay upon the grass, beside the deer which he had wounded to his hurt. He heard her sighs and groans, and perceived the bitterness of her pity. Then with mortal speech the doe spake to the wounded man in such fashion as this:
>
> "Alas, my sorrow, for now am I slain. But thou, Vassal, who hast done me this great wrong, do not think to hide from the vengeance of thy destiny. Never may surgeon and his medicine heal your hurt. Neither herb nor root nor potion can ever cure the wound within your flesh: for that there is no healing. The only balm to close that sore must be brought by a woman, who for her love will suffer such pain and sorrow

---

[81] See Godfrey on why the heel was considered to be extraordinarily vulnerable, and foot wounds are often fatal in mythology—not just for Achilles, but for many other figures in mythology, such as Paris, Pholus, Diarmuid, and Brân the Blessed.

as no woman in the world has endured before. And to the dolorous lady, dolorous knight. For your part you shall do and suffer so great things for her, that not a lover beneath the sun, or lovers who are dead, or lovers who yet shall have their day, but shall marvel at the tale. Now, go from hence, and let me die in peace."

Guigemar was wounded twice over—by the arrow, and by the words he was dismayed to hear. He considered within himself to what land he must go to find this healing for his hurt, for he was yet too young to die. He saw clearly, and told it to his heart, that there was no lady in his life to whom he could run for pity, and be made whole of his wound.[82]

Guigemar travels to a distant land where he meets a woman who suffers as much for his love as he suffers for hers. At one point, after escaping from her loveless marriage, she is taken prisoner by a certain Lord Mériaduc who intends to rape her. However, Guigemar has tied a knot in her girdle that only he can untie, so the villain is unable to carry through with his foul intention. After much bloodshed, Guigemar prevails.

In 1485, William Caxton published the best-known version of the legends of King Arthur, Queen Guinevere,[83] and the Knights of the Round Table. Thomas Malory's *Le Mort d'Arthur* was (probably) compiled by an aristocrat who lived a rather adventurous life himself, and he claims to have written the book while imprisoned. In any case, in the version of the white hart story he presents, the wizard Merlin seemed to have foreknowledge that a "strange and marvellous adventure" was just about to unfold. He told everyone to sit still, and just then:

there came running in a white hart into the hall, and a white brachet[84] next him, and thirty couple of black running hounds came after with a great cry, and the hart went about the Table Round as he went by other boards. The white brachet bit him by the buttock and pulled out a piece,

---

[82] The Lay of Guigemar, from the *Lays of Marie de France*, comes from a collection of courtly tales most likely composed in the 1170s by a French poet who entertained at the court of Henry II in England. She is widely believed to be an illegitimate daughter of Geoffrey IV of Anjou, the founder of the Plantagenet dynasty. As befits a royal "bastard" daughter, she eventually became an abbess, a function she served in at Shaftesbury. Breton *lais* (or lays) are a form of ballad that is composed in rhyming octosyllabic couplets, and they were composed for minstrels to sing. The texts of individual lays are short: around 600-1000 lines, and they feature romantic and chivalric content, often with a Celtic otherworldly flavor. The word "lay" (or *lai*) is not what modern readers might snicker about, but is probably derived from Irish or German words for song or melody.

[83] The name of Arthur's queen takes various spellings, from Guinevere, which is probably the most familiar, to Guenievere, Gwynnever, Gwenhwyfar, Guanhumara, and others, depending on the region and language. As with other names that take different spellings, such as Annwn/Annwfn/Annwvyn, I use the spelling provided by the source materials I'm discussing and do not unify it within my text.

[84] A brachet is a female hound that hunts by scent. A palfrey is a smooth-gaited saddle horse, considered suitable for female riders (as opposed to plow horses, war horses, etc.) It is likely that the palfrey's white color is a significant detail.

> wherethrough the hart leapt a great leap and overthrew a knight that sat at the board side; and therewith the knight arose and took up the brachet, and so went forth out of the hall, and took his horse and rode his way with the brachet. Right so anon came in a lady on a white palfrey, and cried aloud to King Arthur, Sir, suffer me not to have this despite, for the brachet was mine that the knight led away.

Sir Gawaine and his brother Gaheris set off to hunt the hart. Along the way, they found two brothers who were fighting over the hart and brachet, which had just passed by, and they sent the pair to Arthur. They crossed a river, and Gawaine killed a knight who was defending the land on the other side. Further along the trail, they set six greyhounds after the hart, and the dogs pursued it into a castle. Two of the dogs were killed by a knight who emerged from within it, and the rest were chased off. Gawaine was furious about the killing of his greyhounds, and the knight was furious over the rude invasion of his home. The two men engaged in bloody combat, and Gawaine prevailed.

> Sir Gawaine smote the knight so hard that he fell to the earth, and then he cried mercy, and yielded him, and besought him as he was a knight and gentleman, to save his life. Thou shalt die, said Sir Gawaine, for slaying of my hounds. I will make amends, said the knight, unto my power. Sir Gawaine would no mercy have, but unlaced his helm to have stricken off his head. Right so came his lady out of a chamber and fell over him, and so he smote off her head by misadventure. Alas, said Gaheris, that is foully and shamefully done, that shame shall never from you; also ye should give mercy unto them that ask mercy, for a knight without mercy is without worship. Sir Gawaine was so stonied of the death of this fair lady that he wist not what he did, and said unto the knight, Arise, I will give thee mercy. Nay, nay, said the knight, I take no force of mercy now, for thou hast slain my love and my lady that I loved best of all earthly things. Me sore repenteth it, said Sir Gawaine, for I thought to strike unto thee; but now thou shalt go unto King Arthur and tell him of thine adventures, and how thou art overcome by the knight that went in the quest of the white hart.

In the aftermath, four knights attacked Gawain, and then four ladies of the castle begged for mercy, which resulted in him being taken prisoner instead of killed. After they discover whom they had the honor of hosting, they sent him back to his uncle, King Arthur. He bore the hart's head as a prize, and he was also forced to wear the lady's head around his neck as a sign of his shame. Her body was sprawled in front of him on his horse's neck: his captors made themselves clear that that this was the way that he must arrive home, so everyone can see the infamous spectacle of a knight who has slain a noble lady.

> Thus was Gawaine sworn upon the Four Evangelists that he should never be against lady nor gentlewoman, but if he fought for a lady and his adversary fought for another. And thus endeth the adventure of Sir Gawaine that he did at the marriage of King Arthur. Amen. [85]

Even in the early Renaissance period, the white stag was still associated with kingship, liminality, taboos, and otherworldly visions on the European continent.

> A white doe appeared before me
> On the greensward, with horns of gold,
> Between two river banks, in the shade of a laurel tree
> As the sun rose over the springtime.
> She looked so sweetly proud,
> that I left all my toil to follow her:
> As the miser whose delight in seeking treasure
> Assuages all his pains.
> Around her fair neck was writ in diamond and topaz
> "Touch me not, for Caesar wills my freedom"
> The sun was already nearing the noonday peak,
> And my eyes were weary from gazing, but not sated
> When I fell into the water, and she vanished. [86]

And, as Petrarch's poem demonstrates, the classical Greek and Roman motif of the white deer enjoying the ruler's personal protection, symbolized by the collar, still persists. Here I want to point out a fundamental difference between the Celtic and Celtic-influenced myths, and the imperial myths of antiquity. In the former, the wild animal appears as a warning that someone has transgressed boundaries of morality, or even the boundaries between the human world and a world of fateful powers. In the latter, the human ruler is so powerful that the relationship is inverted: the magi-

---

[85] Malory, *Le Mort d'Arthur*, Book III, Chapters V-VIII.
[86] Francesco Petrarch (1335-1374), Canzoniere, CXC, quoted in Eco, 109.

cal deer is a pet, living under his power and his protection. The exalted lady associated with the deer in the early Greek and Roman myths was Artemis/Diana, and she seemed to be entirely absent in these late echoes, except for her persistent presence at St. Paul's Cathedral. As we shall see, both types of stories persist from the Middle Ages through at least the Renaissance, in parallel to the emergence of newer or rewritten stag legends that serve Christian agendas.

Deer and Unicorns in Christian Folklore and Hagiography

In the course of conquering Paganism, Christianity took over its supernatural deer lore. One of the earliest legends illustrating this process is of St. Osyth or Osgyth, who lived in the 7th century. She had wanted to become an abbess from an early age, but her family planned for her to make a strategic marriage. The young woman was wedded to Sighere, the king of Essex, and bore him a son. When her husband left her alone while he hunted a white stag, Osyth convinced some local bishops to let her take a nun's vows. Later, she established the convent she had always dreamed of at Chich in Essex, and served as its first abbess. She was eventually executed (martyred), but rose after the decapitation was carried out, holding her head in her hands and carrying it all the way to the door of a nearby convent, where she finally expired.

In the legend of St. Winifred there is no white deer, but she was a maiden who fled from a local chieftain called Caradoc who had attempted to rape her. When Caradoc caught up with her, he beheaded her at the door of St. Beuno's church. A healing spring of water burst forth at the place where her head hit the earth (and this upwelling of water achieved renown as a healing spring: the "Lourdes of Wales"). Winifred's uncle St. Beuno then put her head back on her neck and she was restored to life—and wicked Caradoc was swallowed up by the land.

By placing these two legends side by side, we see women who sought freedom for self-realization in a calling (Osgyth) and bodily self-determination (Winifred, who is officially the patron saint of the victims of unwanted advances). The deer facilitated the first project, but as we will see below, it is a motif that was beginning to destabilize and wane in this period. Thus, it wasn't automatic to see deer connected with the motif of women's bodily autonomy the way that the rape and the killing of a deer are associated in the story of Gawain and Ragnelle. However, there are still some interesting and archaic themes that deserve further discussion.

Cephalophore (head-carrying) saints were fairly widespread in Christendom (there are at least 120 known examples, with particular prevalence in France), but the motif is much older. Some modern scholars believe the links between the Christian cephalophores and older Celtic legends, such as the Irish *dullahan* (headless fairy riders) and the Bronze-Age cult of severed heads and skulls in human sacrifices are tenuous.[87] I'm more inclined to believe that the connections exist on the basis of the great prevalence of these tales across so many ages, places, and traditions. Oracular, truth-telling, and singing heads were known in the Greek and Roman worlds (such as Orpheus' head, which had been torn off his body by maenads but continued to sing), and in Norse legends (the oracular severed head of Mímir). The head of Brân the Blessed, who was a giant and a king in Welsh mythology, was cut off at his request after he received a fatal wound in his foot. In accordance with his further instructions, it was then taken to the White Hill of London, which may be the site where the Tower of London now stands. We also find sentient severed heads or skulls in Russian fairy tales, such as the skulls with shining eyes on Baba Yaga's fence.

With the gradual ascendance of Christianity, which proceeded with varying degrees of "enthusiasm" in different lands, the legends of white deer sometimes betrayed a certain ambivalence. There are some cases

---

[87] See Sarah Laskow for a quick discussion of cephalophore saints and of scholars who believe cephalophores are not part of a continuous trajectory of development of Pagan motifs. But if you are intrigued by the subject, also read John Grigsby's *Warriors of the Wasteland* for much deeper analysis of sacrificial motifs and oracular heads in Bronze Age culture. He notes on p. xv that there was even a legend in Dover that the head of King Arthur's protégé, Sir Gawain, had once been kept at Dover Castle, and on p. 20 that most of the magical talking heads found in Celtic romances were not taken from warriors killed in battle, but from kings or chieftains who were slain in unusual and highly symbolic ways. These were deaths that (like those of the Christian martyred saints) set them aside from other mortals, and, because they were specially blessed, the heads continued to facilitate healing.

Later echoes of the motif are found in early modern works that cast medieval men of science, such as Roger Bacon, as wizards. The "brazen heads" they commanded were either powered by mechanical devices (i.e., they were automata) or by magic, and they would provide correct answers to questions. The idea may have been inspired by alchemical symbolism, or perhaps by the bronze heads that were left within Hadrian's Wall during the Roman period (as an ersatz sacrifice?) Eventually, the oracular function of the heads fades away and folklorists record stories of old houses inhabited by "screaming skulls" that haunt the premises—and people's moral consciences. For example, it is told that an African slave owned by Azariah Pinney in Bettiscombe had died with a determination that he should be buried in his homeland of Trinidad. Pinney buried the man in the local graveyard, but he made so much noise and haunted the manor so persistently that they eventually dug up his skeleton and brought it back to the spirit. While this wasn't exactly what the man had wanted, it was enough to quiet his restless spirit. See Ingram, and Anna Green.

where the deer is clearly co-opted as a Christian symbol, but in others it may be understood as something superstitious or atavistic, but nevertheless effective. In one Welsh legend about using a white deer as a foundation sacrifice, one could say that either it was proof that the old ways were still the best ways, or it was an act of sacrilege against the holy forces connected with the animal (and I believe it was more likely to be the latter.) [88] In the northeastern Welsh town of Llangar, there is a church now known as the Church of All Saints Parish, but it was originally called the Church of the White Stag. The builders who wanted to erect the structure found the site to be cursed:

> The workmen set to work with the zeal of the righteous and well paid, and after a full day of back breaking work in the building of this house of God, they retired to their homes, much pleased with their efforts. However, come the morning, the three were horrified to find their work of the previous day ransacked. Footings and scaffolding lay shattered about the site, wood and masonry cast about as if with a giant's frenzied strength. All was ransacked and broken, a full day's effort reduced to splinters. Indeed, the signs of frenzy were deeply unnerving, and it was with real fear that the workmen looked upon the ruin.
> "Who has done this?" asked one of the workmen, fearful and trembling. "Who would do this?"
> "This is the work of y Gwr Drwg," [the 'bad man'] muttered the second. "Who else would find our worthy work so offensive?"[89]

The nocturnal rampages continued, so they consulted with a cunning man named y Dyn Gysbys, who told them that they were working in the wrong location. They needed to build their church at a place where they found a white stag. When they saw him, they should lay their foundations

---

[88] I don't think deer sacrifices were likely to be a typical practice, because—for obvious reasons—domestic animals or animal products were more suitable to claim space for domesticity. Horses, goats, cattle, poultry, or even eggs might be used. Exceptionally, sometimes human beings were killed either actually or in effigy. See Claude Lecouteaux's *The Tradition of Household Spirits* (2000). Moreover, Miranda Green marshals a good deal of evidence from faunal analysis that indicates that even during the Iron Age, sacrifices of wild animals were very rare.
Also see Green's passage on the sacrifices described in the Iguvine Tablets (also known as Tables of Iguvium—her usage—or Eugubian or Eugubine Tablets) from Umbria, a set of bronze tablets inscribed sometime around the 3rd century BCE in the native Umbrian alphabet. These writings by a collective of priests of Jupiter are the only near-complete documents that describe the actual auguries, sacrifices, and prayers important functionaries performed. Like the foundation sacrifices made at building thresholds, it is an act of offering to appease the spirits displaced by the human intrusion or displeased for various reasons. Here, again, only domestic animals are used: oxen, pregnant sows and suckling pigs, and ewe-lambs. Green points out that, by comparison with what is related in these tablets, modern scholars' knowledge of Celtic rites is scant, though the rock art at Camonica Valley depicts sacrifices with a temple, animal, and altars, and at the Gaulish sanctuary of Gournay, oxen were sacrificed to guard the shrine. The Celts, altogether, performed far more sacrifices of domestic animals than wild ones (Green, 94, 96).

[89] See *Myths, Oddities & Legends of Northeast Wales*; Artisson, 141-2; and Evans "Legend of the Church of the White Stag."

on that site, and then kill him and mix his blood with the mortar, and this is what they did. The place where they killed it has been known ever since as Moel Lladdfa, the Hill of Slaughter, and the church remains undisturbed. So, it seems that appropriating or subduing the power of the creature that represented or embodied an older faith enabled these builders to further the aims of the new one.

Other deer that assisted in church-building—more willingly than the one in the above story—came to the aid of St. Wihtburh (Withburga, Venerable Withburgh). Wihtburh, who may or may not have been the daughter of King Anna of East Anglia and the youngest sister of St. Aethelthryth of Ely, was having a monastery built at Dereham (a place-name that translates to "deer enclosure") in Norfolk. Somehow, deer arrived on the site and fed her workmen their milk, a miracle that is still commemorated in church iconography.[90]

The story of Domneva's deer from Kent also represents a transitional stage in the stories: wicked Pagans with Pagan names (Thunor being equivalent to Thor) yield their land to representatives of the Church, and then they are dishonorably buried in the earth. In the seventh century CE, the twin brothers of Kentish princess Domneva[91] were murdered on orders from their kinsman Ecgbehrt (Egbert). Allegedly, Ecgbehrt had been influenced to do this by his Pagan reeve, Thunor, in order to prevent them from claiming the Kent throne.

Thunor had them buried under the king's throne, but a beam of light as bright as the sun rose up in the middle of the night through the roof of the hall. This revealed the grave and the crime, and Domneva was offered *weregild* (blood money) for their deaths. However, instead of the financial compensation due to her, she insisted on receiving a land grant because she wanted to found an abbey. She asked her uncle Ecgbehrt to grant her as much land as her pet hind could run across. The nimble creature traversed the Isle of Thanet from Westgate to Minster, but during its course, Ecgbehrt's reeve Thunor, the culprit behind the assassination of her broth-

---

[90] See A Clerk of Oxford, "St. Wihtburh and the Miracle on Holkham Beach." Let us also recall that at this time there were still reindeer living in Scotland, and the "fairy lullaby" that describes children being raised on the milk of (rein)deer reflected something still possible on the island of Great Britain.

[91] Domne, which is a local version of the Latin *domina*—lady—is probably the title the princess used as an abbess; her name is also rendered as Eafe or Éue, and her title as Æbbe or Ebba for abbess.

ers, objected to how much land was being marked out for Domneva and tried to stop it.

At this point, one version tells that the earth opened up and swallowed him (which is the same thing that befell St. Winifred's would-be rapist) at a place that was then renamed *þunores hlæwe* ("Thunor's mound," perhaps this was once a tumulus somehow associated with the god Thor or Thor's devotees?) Other versions tell that the wicked reeve Thunor was simply thrown into a pit as punishment for his crimes. Either way, he didn't cause any more trouble. The deer's run, the "Cursus Cerve," was recognized as a valid boundary. Domneva's daughter, St. Mildred, became the next Abbess of Minster Abbey, and the Cursus Cerve was later called St. Mildred's Lynch (linch = Old English *hlinc*, "ridge, rising ground").[92]

Christianity eventually accommodated the white deer not only to its claims to land that was wanted for religious facilities, but also to its symbolic repertoire, transforming the animal into a guide that leads royalty toward religious experiences and also into a symbol of Christ. This process did not take place at the same pace everywhere across Europe, and—as we will see below in the story of St. Hubertus—there are also cases where Christian authors help themselves out by back-dating events.

Hagiographical accounts place the life of St. Eustace (born Placidus) in the second century CE. There are churches named for him in Rome and in Paris which claim to own his relics. The British Museum also owns a reliquary shaped like Eustace's head that it acquired from the cathedral treasury of Basel, Switzerland. The cult of this saint has been traced back to the 8th century CE, but the fame of St. Eustace was promulgated most effectively by Jacobus de Voraigne's *Legenda Aurea* (The Golden Legend), a collection of hagiographies he compiled in the mid-13th century. The chapter on Eustace tells of a master of chivalry who served Emperor Trajan and was named Placidus before his baptism. He was "right busy in the works of mercy, but he was a worshipper of idols," and his wife was of the same sort.

One day when he was hunting near Tivoli, Placidus came upon a herd of harts. One of them was "more fair and greater than the others," and it ran into the thickest part of the forest. He gave chase, desiring to kill the hart,

---

[92] I am grateful to John Grigsby for drawing my attention to this legend. The version I relate above is retold on the basis of Sara Trillo's and the author known as "A Clerk of Oxford's" versions of the legend compiled using Old English texts.

but then he spied a cross shining "more clear than the sun, and the image of Christ, which by the mouth of the hart ... spake to him, saying: "Placidus, wherefore followest me hither? I am appeared to thee in this beast for the grace of thee. I am Jesu Christ, whom thou honourest ignorantly, thy alms be ascended up tofore me, and therefore I come hither so that by this hart that thou huntest I may hunt thee ..." Needless to say, Placidus was instantly converted. He "fell down again to the earth, and said: I believe, Lord, that thou art he that made all things, and convertest them that err. And our Lord said to him: If thou believest, go to the bishop of the city and do thee be baptized."[93] The emblems of St. Eustace include a cross, the stag, and an oven.

It is noteworthy that neither the texts that describe Eustace's encounter with the stag nor his iconography remain consistent about the stag's color. It is a detail that sometimes emerges and sometimes disappears, because it seems to be losing relevance over time. However, the stag itself is a powerful association, and, because of it, he is considered one of the patrons of hunters.

Eustace's fame was eventually overshadowed by another saint. St. Hubert (or sometimes Hubertus), the "Apostle of the Ardennes," was born in the year 656 CE into an aristocratic family in Aquitaine. He is the patron saint of hunters, opticians, metalworkers, and mathematicians. Accounts written by his contemporaries only provide a few biographical details, such as his marriage to a noblewoman named Floribanne, appointment as the first bishop of Liège in the year 708, and death in 727.

Later hagiographies provide considerably more details and flourishes to his life story. For example, they tell readers that because he was grieving the death of his wife, who died giving birth to their son Floribert, he tried to distract himself by hunting. He set out on Good Friday, a day when people were expected to be in church commemorating Jesus's crucifixion and not engaging in sporting pastimes. In the deep forest, he chased a magnificent stag, and when the animal turned toward him, Hubert saw a crucifix hovering between its antlers. A voice spoke to him: "Hubert, unless thou turnest to the Lord and leadest a holy life, thou shalt quickly go down into

---

[93] See De Voraigne, *The Golden Legend*, "St. Eustace."

Hell." Hubert dismounted and prostrated himself, and after asking "Lord, what wouldst Thou have me do?" he was told "Go and seek Bishop Lambert, and he will instruct you."[94] He gave up his wealth and titles and sought out Lambert. Then, after he had studied with him, Hubert became a hermit, then a priest, and finally a bishop.

This series of events was clearly borrowed from the legend of Placidus/Eustace, and was only attributed to St. Hubert in the 15th century—some seven hundred years after his death. As with his Roman progenitor, the color of the stag is not stabilized in Hubert's iconography: only the cross is of critical importance. Even now, the stag's head with a cross between the antlers that is used as a logo by Jägermeister (Hunt Master) liqueur, and which was explicitly drawn to honor St. Hubert, is piebald (particolored) rather than purely white.[95] While two-toned deer do exist, they are rare, and this choice seems to depict uncertainty in selecting an authoritative version of the legend.

However, Hubert's legacy extends well beyond out-of-the way forest chapels and the logo of a bitter digestif. In some versions of the story, the stag did not only lead Hubert to Christ, it also instructed him to consider the dignity of animals and to engage in ethical hunting practices. These included only shooting when it is possible to make a quick, clean kill, and targeting old, sick, or injured animals instead of those that are in their prime. Additionally, females with young should be spared, so that the offspring can be properly nurtured to adulthood. These precepts were codified and institutionalized in 1695 for aristocratic hunters in the Habsburg Empire, when Count Franz Anton von Sporck founded the Venerable Order of St. Hubertus, a hunting society and knightly order. The Order still exists today as the International Order of St. Hubertus, and its motto remains *"Deum Diligite Animalia Diligentes"* (Honoring God by Honoring his

---

[94] Cited from Herbermann.

[95] Despite persistent rumors, Jägermeister is vegan and does not contain any stag blood. And the German verse printed in an old Gothic font that runs along the edges of the label comes from the forester and poet Oskar von Riesenthal's poem "Waidmannsheil" (Hunter's Salute), which honors the teachings attributed to Hubert. An approximate translation would be: "This is the hunter's shield of honor; he protects and looks after his game. He hunts sportsmanlike, protecting and looking after his game; honoring the Creator in the creatures, as is fitting." See Mike Newman.

Creatures).[96] Chapels to Hubert still stand in many wooded areas, and his legend is revered even by non-religious hunters, especially in the Central European countries with highly organized hunting clubs such as Germany, Austria, and the Czech Republic, as well as the masters of the French *chasse à courre*.

Elements from the legends of Eustace and Hubert, as well as the stories about the founders of nunneries, are also echoed in a tale about David I, King of Scotland. David was exceptionally fond of hunting stags in the forests around Drumshugh, and, like Hubert, he wasn't particular about observing religious holidays. Thus, in 1128, David planned a hunting expedition on the Feast Day of the Holy Rood (Holy Cross). His priest had warned him that he should not take the day lightly by pursuing his sport, but he paid no heed and set off with his huntsmen. David was separated from his companions, and he met a large white deer and gave chase. When his horse threw him off, David cried out to God to save him. The stag lowered his antlers and charged. The king grasped the fierce beast's antlers in order to wrestle with it, but just as he did so, the antlers twisted and miraculously transformed into a cross. The animal then vanished either in a puff of smoke or by fleeing into the deeper parts of the forest, depending on the version of the tale.

That night, David received instructions in a dream to build the Holyrood Abbey for the Augustinian Canons, at the site where he had defeated the stag. From this time on, the white deer was translated into a Christian symbol of purity, redemption, and *good* fortune[97] (rather than a fey warning or omen) in Scotland. It is also notable that all three of these stories lack significant female characters—the element of a woman who must be honored, defended, or avenged is simply missing.

A few centuries later, the white stag would be adopted by an English ruler: King Richard II (1367-1400). The white hart was Richard's heraldic

---

[96] The IOSH asks all members to voluntarily subscribe to these principles and use them to guide their behavior:
- To promote sportsmanlike conduct in hunting and fishing
- To foster good fellowship among sportsmen from all over the world
- To teach and preserve sound traditional hunting and fishing customs
- To encourage wildlife conservation and to help protect endangered species from extinction
- To promote the concept of hunting and fishing as an intangible cultural heritage of humanity
- To endeavor to ensure that the economic benefits derived from sports hunting and fishing support the regions where these activities are carried out
- To strive to enhance respect for responsible hunters and fishermen

[97] See Muir and MacIntyre, and also Dunk.

badge or "emblem," a personal symbol not necessarily identical with the more official royal coat of arms. Richard used this emblem, for instance, when he had his portrait painted wearing a gold and enameled jewel displaying the device of the white stag. The reason behind his choice is unclear, but it is possible that his choice reflects a pun on his name: Rich-hart.[98]

Scotland adopted the unicorn as a national symbol, perhaps because it was considered to be the enemy of the lion: the symbol of England. Or, perhaps because there was slippage between unicorns and deer or stags, especially since in some of the legends the magical beast only had one horn. An example was already mentioned: the "stag" the black maiden sends Peredur to slay, which was "as swift as the swiftest bird; and he has one horn in his forehead, as long as the shaft of a spear, and as sharp as whatever is sharpest."[99]

Unicorns were variously described or illustrated as horselike, goatlike, asslike, or sometimes also deerlike. According to Robert Graves, the hircocervus, a goat-stag, was a symbol of resurrection and immortality in the Dionysian Mysteries. He adds that when the Hyperborean druids visited Thessaly, they recognized this goat-stag, which was associated with apples, as the same as their own immortal hart or hind also associated with apples. This creature is responsible for later unicorns sometimes displaying a beard.[100] Both Plato and Aristotle discuss the hircocervus, though in the latter's work it is clear that he considered it to be fictional. Strabo and Pliny the Younger referred to unicorns, and the Biblical creature called the *re'em* (Hebrew: רְאֵם) has sometimes been translated as "unicorn," and at other times interpreted as a more mundane animal such as an oryx or wild ox, or perhaps the extinct aurochs.

Just like natural beasts, unicorns were also imbued with symbolic and didactic meanings that were intended to reinforce Christian doctrines. In

---

[98] Fox-Davies, 470.

[99] Charlotte Elizabeth Guest (trans.), "Peredur, son of Evrawc" in her *Mabinogion*.

[100] Graves, 411. On p. 412, he cites a rare Hermetic tract, the *Book of Landspring*, which has an illustration of a deer and a unicorn standing together in a forest. The accompanying text reads:
"The sages say truly that two animals are in this forest: one glorious, beautiful and swift, a great and strong deer; the other an unicorn ... If we apply the parable of our art, we shall call the forest the body ... The Unicorn will be the spirit at all times. The deer desires no other name but that of the soul ... He that knows how to tame and master them by art, to couple them together, and to lead them in and out of the forest, may be justly be called a Master."

bestiaries (encyclopedias of mythical and living animals), the unicorn often figures as an allegory for Christ's death, for it, too, is captured and killed for the sake of mankind. As Chrystal Perez recounts for the Getty Museum blog,[101] one such bestiary held in the Bodleian Library narrates the unicorn's story and follows it with the much older Psalm 92:10: "My horn shalt thou exalt like the horn of a unicorn."

Besides representing the crucifixion, unicorns also had an affinity with maidens: this seems to hark back to the white deer's association with women's bodily autonomy. In the *Physiologus*,[102] a didactic natural history compiled in the early CE centuries, the entry on the unicorn has the beast encountering a maiden, who represents the Virgin Mary. Entranced by her, he lays his head on her lap and falls asleep. This allegory would go on to shape ideas about unicorns for many centuries afterward.

Sometimes the association between women and unicorns was chaste. For example, Leonardo da Vinci made a pen and ink sketch of a maiden holding a leashed unicorn and wrote in a notebook where he kept descriptions of mythical animals:

> The unicorn ... because of its intemperance, not knowing how to control itself before the delight it feels towards maidens, forgets its ferocity and wildness, and casting aside all fear it will go up to the seated maiden and sleep in her lap, and thus the hunter takes it.[103]

However, the obvious eroticism and phallic symbolism came to the fore in other works. Already in the early 600s CE, Isidore of Seville specifies that a maiden must bare her breast to lure unicorns. More than seven hundred years later, Richard de Fournival published his more lyrical, lovestruck, and sensual *Bestaire d'Amour*, which claims that the unicorn is drawn to maidens by their "sweet odor alone."[104] Rabelais gets more explicit with his commentary on the horn: "Commonly it dangles like a turkey-cock's comb, but when a unicorn has a mind to fight or put it to any other

---

[101] See Perez.

[102] The *Physiologus* also includes Christian allegories of lion cubs who are born dead and come back to life when the old lion breathes on them; the pelican that sheds its blood to sprinkle on its dead chicks (again, to bring them back to life), and the phoenix, which rises on the third day from its own ashes.

[103] See the Universal Leonardo pages maintained by University of the Arts, London, which aim to present a comprehensive overview of the Renaissance man's oeuvre.

[104] See Dressler and Maynard.

use, what does he do but make it stand, and then it is as straight as an arrow." And Aubrey Beardsley's *Venus and Tannhäuser* (1907) contains a chapter about the goddess Venus's pet unicorn Adolphe, who has "no mate except the queen herself." Adolphe "is insanely jealous of her," but Venus does indeed appreciate him and gets her days "off" to a lusty start by masturbating him and drinking his semen as an apéritif before breakfast.[105]

In the mid-sixteenth century, the Italian humanist and mythographer Natale Comes (aka Natalis Contis) published an untitled hunting poem, which combines motifs of raw natural power, magical virtue, and sensuality in a beast that is, alas, also rather foolish:

> Far on the edge of the world and beyond the banks of the Ganges,
> Savage and lone, is a place in the realm of the King of the Hindus.
> Where there is born a beast as large as a stag in stature,
> Dark on the back, solid-hoofed, very fierce, and shaped like a bullock.
> Mighty and black is the horn that springs from the animal's forehead,
> Terrible unto his foe, a defence and a weapon of onslaught.
> Often the poisoners steal to the banks of that swift-flowing river,
> Fouling the waves with disease by their secret insidious poisons;
> After them comes this beast and dips his horn in the water,
> Cleansing the venom away and leaving the stream to flow purely
> So that the forest-dwellers may drink once more by the margin.
> Also men say that the beast delights in the embrace of a virgin,
> Falling asleep in her arms and taking sweet rest on her bosom.
> Ah! but, awaking, he finds he is bound by ropes and by shackles.
> Strange is the tale, indeed, yet so, they say, he is taken,
> Whether it be that the seeds of love have been sown by great Nature
> Deep in his blood or for some more hidden mysterious reason.[106]

The explicit references to the magical virtues of the alicorn (the unicorn's horn, or the magical substance it was made from) highlight the fact that these horns (or whatever animal parts or substances were sold under the name by charlatans) were a valuable commodity. Thus, stories speak of maidens used as a lure by hunters who intend to kill unicorns for fame or gain. Illustrations in bestiaries show well-armed men piercing their hap-

---

[105] See the article by the erudite collective who call themselves "Filthy Staff" titled "Unicorns as Phallic Symbols."
[106] Ibid.

less prey with swords and lances; the unicorns' wounds run red with blood, a symbol of Christ's sacrifice. The complicit virgin stands next to the dying animal or holds it in her lap, often looking remorseful for the role she has played.[107]

In none of these cases (chaste, lewd, or commercial) does the maiden or Virgin appear as an independent subject—she is merely symbolic of abstract virtues, she is desired, or she is the "cool girl" who goes along with what the guys want, even though she knows she shouldn't. Her honor is neither threatened nor defended, she presents no challenge that calls the knights to become better men, and there doesn't seem to be an ethical dilemma in the hunting of what had to be considered an endangered species.

Unicorns' long heyday in the late Middle Ages and Renaissance period ended when they were canceled by the Church. Despite their Biblical credentials, they were included in a crackdown on unauthorized religious imagery proclaimed at the last session of the Council of Trent. Johannes Molanus's *Treatise on Sacred Images* then interpreted the Council's decrees in much more detail, and specifically proscribed many previously popular motifs. With no more unicorns, we find some Pagan myths of deer revived at the end of the sixteenth century, such as when Shakespeare styles the slain Julius Caesar as a deer:

> Pardon me, Julius! Here wast thou bay'd, brave hart;
> Here didst thou fall; and here thy hunters stand,
> Sign'd in thy spoil, and crimson'd in thy Lethe.
> O world! thou wast the forest to this hart,
> And this indeed, O world, the heart of thee.
> How like a deer, strooken by many princes,
> Dost thou here lie![108]

White deer were put in a new role in the Restoration era by the poet, playwright, literary critic, and translator John Dryden. He was so famous in his era that he was known as "Glorious John" and the Restoration period

---

[107] See Perez.

[108] These are lines 205-211 in Act III, Scene 1 of William Shakespeare's play *Julius Caesar* (p. 1119). "Bayed" refers to dogs cornering a hunted animal and barking at it. "Signed in thy spoil" refers to Caesar's blood marking the murderers' hands: "spoils" are prizes taken by acts of violence, either by hunters or by those engaging in raiding and pillaging. Lethe is one of the rivers flowing in Hades' underworld. *Lethe* (λήθη) means "forgetfulness," "oblivion" or "concealment" and it is an antonym of the word for truth: *Aleithia* (ἀλήθεια): those who sip from the river Lethe forget their previous lives.

in English history is often referred to as the "Age of Dryden." Sometime around 1686, Dryden converted to Catholicism, and in 1687 he published "The Hind and the Panther," an allegorical bestiary written in heroic couplets that illustrated moral and ecclesiastical ideas using animals as symbol bearers. In the third part of this work he describes the Catholic Church as a "milk white hind ... unspotted and innocent within." The hind "knows no sin" and fears no danger, despite being hunted with horns and hound. We know that she is no ordinary animal because he tells us she is "doom'd to death though not fated to die."[109]

Dryden characterized the rival Church of England as a black, spotted panther to represent its impurity, and some of the other qualities he attributes to this beast include coldness, scorn, malice, surliness, and insincerity; meanwhile, other sects were also given animal emblems, such as a bear, a wolf, and a hare, and these were also understood in entirely negative terms. Many critics found Dryden's thematization absurd, and they questioned his personal motives for conversion since he did it more or less simultaneously with the coronation of the Catholic king James II. Satirists and pamphleteers lampooned him personally, along with his tropes of animals arguing about theology; however, other critics praised the work for its erudition and formal merits.

In any case, what is noteworthy for us to mark is the way the white deer has again shifted its function: it is no longer an omen or foretoken of what shall be, or a warning that appears when someone exceeds the bounds of good behavior; it is not a helper with church construction projects; it isn't leading an individual to their conversion; nor does it represent innate and personal qualities of sovereignty (as we saw with Shakespeare's "brave hart," Julius Caesar); it also isn't Christ himself—even though he often has been portrayed as a little white lamb. Instead, Dryden's white hind represents the Catholic Church as an *institution* which possesses the powers of immortality and transcendence beyond time itself. He writes: "Let those remember that she cannot dye / Till rolling time is lost in round eternity."

As I will discuss in the "Loathly Ladies" chapter, the idea that Christian linear time, which would terminate on Judgment Day and yield to a divine-

---

[109] For analysis of Dryden's use of symbols and the context in which he was writing this work, see Mambrol. To read the poem in its entirety, see Dryden. I owe a debt of gratitude to Daniel Lamken for drawing this work to my attention.

saturated eternity, will overcome Pagan cyclical time was a fundamental Church doctrine and was used to accommodate and subordinate survivals of older myths. In this light, the hind's white color naturally no longer stands for any of the physiological changes associated with death (nor does it represent death or the dead in any way) but instead represents a final and complete vanquishing of death. Thus, rather than functioning as a fey warning or a symbol of imbalance between humans and otherworldly powers—which he believed were all doomed—Dryden's deer flaunts the Roman Catholic Church's predestined victory over time, the world, human mortality (and, of course, rival sects).

The White Doe: An Early Modern Fairy Tale

In the late seventeenth century, Marie-Catherine Le Jumel de Barneville, Baroness d'Aulnoy, composed a literary fairy tale called "The White Doe," as one of the many fantastical stories of magical transformations she wrote about in her prolific oeuvre. During her lifetime, she was famed for her wit, beauty, high spirits, and adventures that could have been side quests in Dumas' *Three Musketeers*. Sadly, her reputation faded when children's literature experts declared her work frivolous.[110]

The tale begins like this:

> Once upon a time there lived a king and queen who loved each other dearly, and would have been perfectly happy if they had only had a little son or daughter to play with ...

The queen's wish was fulfilled by a fairy that appeared to her in the shape of a large crab. When her daughter was born, she was named Desiree because her parents had so desired her. The queen honored her debt of gratitude to all the fairy godmothers who blessed them. However, she neglected to invite the crab-fairy, the one she was most obliged to, to come and bring gifts for the tiny princess. Scorned and furious, the crab-fairy appeared at the festivities intending to kill Desiree. The other fairies persuaded her to

---

[110] See Marina Warner's *Wonder Tales* for a spirited rehabilitation of the aristocratic authors of salon *contes de feés*—fairy tales—a term d'Aulnoy coined.

refrain from deadly vengeance, but she was still determined to punish the child for her mother's ill manners: she declared that if a single ray of sunlight touched the girl before her fifteenth birthday, she would have much to regret, and her life would be in peril.

The king and queen arranged for Desiree to live in a palace that allowed no light in. Since she couldn't socialize like other girls, when she approached the age of marriageability, the queen arranged for her portrait to be painted so eligible princes could see her. One of them became so obsessed with the picture of the homebound princess that he told his parents he wanted to cancel his engagement to another girl, and to arrange to marry Desiree instead.

When the prince received the news that Desiree agreed to become his bride he was overjoyed, but he was also crushed to hear about the curse, which meant she couldn't marry him until after her fifteenth birthday. He became ill because he had "never been taught to deny himself anything or to control his feelings." "If I have to wait three months before I can marry the princess I shall die!" was all that the spoiled prince would say—and his parents obliged his wish to hasten the wedding plans.

It was decided that Desiree would go to him in a carriage that allowed no light in, only traveling by night. At the prince's palace, she would dwell in an underground chamber where no sunlight could reach her. She was accompanied on her journey by her maid of honor, Eglantine, and her lady-in-waiting, Cerisette—who had fallen in love with the prince's magic portrait—and Cerisette's mother.

Trouble ensued when the fairy godmother of the prince's scorned fiancée put treacherous thoughts into the minds of Cerisette and her mother. At night, when the carriage was opened to air it out, they cut a large hole in the side. No one noticed until the next day when the sun was up, and the sun's light caused Desiree to be transformed into a white doe. She sprang out of the carriage and fled into the forest.

The maid Eglantine pursued her, and Cerisette and her mother rejoiced. They patched up the hole in the carriage, and Cerisette put on the princess's clothes and her diamond crown. When they arrived at the prince's castle, their ruse was discovered because Cerisette not only looked nothing like Desiree's portrait, but she was actually quite ugly, and the princess's dress was too small on her. Cerisette and her mother were sent to prison. The despondent prince decided that as soon as he recovered enough of his strength he would escape from the castle and live out the rest of his life in solitude with his favorite attendant. He left a note for his father explaining what he had done.

Guided by a helpful fairy, Eglantine eventually found Desiree the doe, and the fairy sent the two of them to a small hut where they could take shelter. There, an old woman offered the girl and the doe lodging. After the sun set, Desiree was restored to her human shape—because the curse of the animal form was only in effect during daylight hours. The next day, the prince and his attendant were also wandering through the wood. They, too, found the old woman's cottage and arranged for lodging there. Eglantine and the doe managed to return to the hut while the two men were out, and the two parties had no idea of each other's presence.

At first light, the prince arose and went out. He saw the white doe grazing in the middle of a wide open space. She fled when she sighted him, but not fast enough to escape several arrows that he had let fly without thinking. Desiree was kept safe thanks to an intervention by her fairy godmother. Desiree reached the old woman's hut well ahead of the prince, and her maid let her in. At darkfall, when she was once more capable of human speech, she related her frightful encounter. Eglantine counseled Desiree to remain in the hut the next morning, but once the change came upon her, she couldn't resist her longing to return to the forest, so she sprang out the door.

The prince also went back to the forest that day, seeking her. Eventually, he became tired and fell asleep. Just as he drifted away, the white doe emerged from a thicket. She was terrified to see her mortal foe lying there, but also somehow thrilled by him. She kissed him on his forehead, which awakened him. He recognized the doe he had pursued the previous day, and her animal instincts aroused her to terror and flight. The prince gave chase, but this time without a desire to harm or kill his beautiful quarry. He called out to her, but she fled as long as she could, and when the prince reached her she was stretched out on the grass, waiting for the death blow.

However, instead of striking her, the prince knelt at her side and told her that she had nothing to fear. They remained there peacefully until the sun was near to setting, and Desiree was anxious that the prince not see her human shape. She feigned thirst by lolling her tongue out, and the prince set off to fetch her some more water. She fled back to the hut, and, once back in her own form, confessed to Eglantine that her pursuer was the prince himself—and that he was even more handsome than his talking portrait.

The prince arrived at the hut, aggravated that the doe whom he had treated so kindly had fled from him. He vowed that he would hunt her until he finally caught her. The next morning, she again left the hut and fled to a thicket where she thought he could not find her—but her whiteness betrayed her. Desperate to capture her, the prince loosed an arrow at her leg, which caused her to fall to the ground. Using water and healing herbs, he tried to soothe the pain of her wound.

Eglantine had also been searching for the doe, and when she found the two of them, she proved to the prince that the injured animal "belonged" to her by asking Desiree to touch her heart with a hoof. When the doe did this, the prince had to acknowledge Eglantine's right to the animal, and the maid carried her back to the hut.

That evening, the prince's friend cut a small hole in the wall so they could observe their neighbors in the next room. And—just as they had guessed—they saw the beautiful princess whose face they knew from her portrait, with Eglantine tending her wound. Desiree was lamenting how cruelly she had suffered from being unable to speak to the man she loved.

The prince knocked at the door and Eglantine opened it, expecting the old woman bringing their supper. He flung himself at Desiree's feet and poured his heart out to her. The two conversed until dawn, and they realized when the sun was high in the heavens that her enchantment must be broken, because she no longer had the doe's form.

The mistress of the hut, who was Desiree's fairy godmother in disguise, made the couple "such a wedding feast as had never been seen since the world began. And everybody was delighted, except Cerisette and her mother, who were put in a boat and carried to a small island, where they had to work hard for their living."[111]

White Stags in the Modern Age

White stags have retained a symbolic resonance even in more recent times. Several generations of children have grown up reading C. S. Lewis's *Narnia* tales, in which white deer appear twice. The White Witch's sleigh was drawn by white reindeer, but they did not participate in the plot of the story; along with their mistress, they generally signified an inhuman physical and moral coldness, and this reflects the theme of whiteness as death. However, there is another white stag: Mr. Tumnus (the faun) tells the Pevensie children that the animal can grant them wishes if they catch it. The chase leads them to the Lantern Waste, the liminal zone where they had first entered Narnia, and they become unsure how to proceed. They end up stumbling back through Digory Kirk's wardrobe into their house and their childhood, thus ending the Golden Age of Narnia and initiating its Dark Age.

In this modern incarnation, the white stag is reduced to a mere vision of "luck." There are no ethical precepts attached to it relating either to how the land or women should be treated, though it is perhaps telling that the children's greed leads them back through a wasteland into the mundane world. However, there, they can share their stories with their friends and they are assured that they will have more marvelous adventures in the future. Lewis at first claimed not to have had explicit intentions of inculcating Christianity in young readers of the *Narnia* series, but in private correspondence admitted the parallels and wrote that his works systematically laid out the Christian story. In one of his last letters, Lewis wrote:

> Since Narnia is a world of Talking Beasts, I thought He [Christ] would become a Talking Beast there, as He became a man here. I pictured Him becoming a lion there because (a) the lion is supposed to be the king of beasts; (b) Christ is called "The Lion of Judah" in the Bible; (c) I'd

---

[111] This tale, which I have greatly abridged in this retelling, was anthologized by Andrew Lang in *The Orange Fairy Book*. The connection between an insult to a crab and the plight of deer is coincidental, but evocative—as you will see in the chapter on "All Devouring Appetites." I also want to point out that it seems to owe a large debt to Marie de France's *Lay of Guigemar*.

been having strange dreams about lions when I began writing the work. The whole series works out like this.

> *The Magician's Nephew* tells the Creation and how evil entered Narnia.
> *The Lion, the Witch and the Wardrobe* the Crucifixion and Resurrection.
> *Prince Caspian* restoration of the true religion after corruption.
> *The Horse and His Boy* the calling and conversion of a heathen.
> *The Voyage of the "Dawn Treader"* the spiritual life.
> *The Silver Chair* the continuing war with the powers of darkness.
> *The Last Battle* the coming of the Antichrist (the Ape), the end of the world and the Last Judgement.[112]

The white stag was appropriated into Lewis's work for didactic purposes, ultimately only helping the children be recognized for their personal achievements.

Robert Stephenson Smyth Baden-Powell, the British military officer who founded the Scouting movement, also used the stag as a symbol. He highlighted its characteristics that children might emulate: it should inspire them to self-improvement and community-improvement. Drawing on the old Hungarian myths of Csodaszarvas, when he addressed the 1933 Fourth World Jamboree in Hungary, he told the gathered crowd:

> The Hungarian hunters of old pursued the miraculous Stag, not because they expected to kill it, but because it led them on in the joy of the chase to new trails and fresh adventures, and so to capture happiness. You may look on that White Stag as the pure spirit of Scouting, springing forward and upward, ever leading you onward and upward to leap over difficulties, to face new adventures in your active pursuit of the higher aims of Scouting—aims which bring you happiness. These aims are to do your duty wholeheartedly to God, to your country, and to your fellow man by carrying out the Scout Law. In that way you will, each one of you, help to bring about God's kingdom upon earth—the reign of peace and goodwill. Therefore, before leaving you, I ask you Scouts this question—Will you do your best to make friendship with others and peace in the world?

Certainly, this was an exhortation to fulfill a godly purpose, but it was to be peace and goodwill, and not a Final Judgement.[113] It's also possible to say

---

[112] See Paul Ford's *Companion to Narnia*.
[113] See whitestag.org/history/farewell.html.

that Baden-Powell seems to draw upon the principles of sportsmanlike hunting espoused by the St. Hubert groups and extends them to all of humanity.

Ezra Pound also used the white stag as a secular symbol of personal glory:

> I ha' seen them mid the clouds on the heather.
> Lo! they pause not for love nor for sorrow,
> Yet their eyes are as the eyes of a maid to her lover,
> When the white hart breaks his cover
> And the white wind breaks the morn.
>
> "'Tis the white stag, Fame, we're a-hunting,
> Bid the world's hounds come to horn!"

In this poem, Pound was referring to the incident in Sir Thomas Malory's *Le Morte d'Arthur*, when a pursued white hart bursts in on Arthur and Guinevere's wedding feast. He published it in *Personae* (1909), a collection that he felt was a major breakthrough, and which won him the praise of W. B. Yeats.

At the end of the 20th century, we find literary stags symbolizing family or clans. In Harry Potter's family, the deer was a Patronus (spirit protector) that Harry, both of his parents, and the tormented Professor Snape (who loved Harry's mother) all had in common. As an animagus, Harry's father was also able to change his physical form into a stag. It takes fairly advanced magic in this world to summon a Patronus, but once mastered it is a powerful form of protection against Dementors, a kind of demon that feeds on positive emotions and leaves its victims drained and despairing. The deer can be described as a symbol of self-sacrificing love that wards off the effects of cruelty and indifference.

There are other examples of white stags found in films (Snow White and the Huntsman), video games (The Elder Scrolls V: Skyrim; Quest for Glory; Warcraft), web comics, anime, and other media. My aim here is not to provide an exhaustive survey of every deer that has appeared on printed pages or on big or little screens. Rather, it is to highlight some of the main themes that have persisted since ancient times, despite the efforts by medieval and twentieth-century Christians (i.e., Lewis) to empty them of their earlier edifying potential.

The last and most recent example I will mention of a white hart in literature is in *Game of Thrones*, the first volume in George R. R. Martin's *Song of Fire and Ice* series. These books feature complex plot lines with the Baratheon family, who are symbolized by a stag, and the Stark family, whose symbol is the direwolf, and symbolic and real violence against actual animals and the people who use them as their emblems.[114] For example, teenaged Sansa Stark dreamed that her fiancé Joffrey Baratheon would kill a hart with a golden arrow. His father, King Robert Baratheon, went out seeking the hart, but did not have a chance to take it: portentously, it has already been killed and eaten almost entirely by wolves. Disappointed, Robert set off again to chase a huge boar that had been sighted even deeper in the forest. Like many a dissolute monarch in Celtic legends, Robert is grievously wounded. He was ripped open "from groin to nipple" by the beast's tusks, because he "missed his thrusts."[115]

These last three words uttered by the dying king are a very economical rendering of the entire Fisher King complex: the echo of the old injuries to the "thigh" and the idea of sexual transgressions from the old legends rings clear. Although Robert was never impotent or infertile (and had numerous bastard children), he lacked a legitimate heir. After he dies of his wounds, he is succeeded by Joffrey, the son of his wife from an incestuous liaison. However, because Joffrey is neither well liked nor much recognized, a civil war breaks out that metastasizes into the War of Five Kings, a multi-theater conflagration that rages across lands near and far. It wouldn't be too farfetched to compare Robert Baratheon's hunting accident with a legend of what befell the historical figure of Archduke Franz Ferdinand, whose death became the spark that ignited the First World War.

---

[114] There are a few more minor details before and after Robert Baratheon's death that involve direwolves and deer, both real and symbolic. Earlier in the story, the pet direwolf owned by Sansa's sister Arya attacks Joffrey while he is hunting, and Sansa's direwolf Lady is killed in her place at the urging of several of the Baratheons, and her father Ned carries it out. But after his father dies, Joffrey also orders the execution of Ned himself on the pretext that he had conspired to murder Robert, and Sansa is kept hostage. In the second book, *A Clash of Kings*, Joffrey commands a war ship called the *White Hart*, which had a perfidious master who Joffrey executes to make an example. During the Battle of the Blackwater, in which his uncle Stannis attempts to make a claim on the throne because of Joffrey's illegitimate parentage, the *White Hart* is boarded by the crew of one of Stannis's ships and ultimately sinks in a huge blaze started by wildfire.

[115] George R. R. Martin, *A Game of Thrones*, 503.

All-Devouring Appetites

As quaint as the old legends and literary tropes are, the death of a white deer also presaged millions of deaths on battlefields around the world, as well as the other miseries wrought by human beings in chain reactions to the wars of the twentieth century. All of this was set into motion in 1914, when the Serbian anarchist Gavrilo Princip raised his Browning model 1910 semiautomatic pistol in a jostling crowd. With two shots he took without aiming and with his head turned aside—shots that seemed to defy any kind of odds—he killed both Archduke Franz Ferdinand and his wife Sophie, the Duchess of Hohenberg.

Oddly, this happened because Franz Ferdinand wasn't where he was supposed to be at the time: he changed his plans after an earlier assassination plot failed that day. He had survived a bomb that bounced off his car and exploded underneath another vehicle in his motorcade, injuring several of his men. The archduke made a spontaneous decision to visit these injured companions in the hospital; however, his chauffeur was unfamiliar with the route, and had to stop the car to recalculate. Fatefully, he stopped six feet away from the only person in the crowd of thousands who had murderous intentions and the means of accomplishing them.

Gavrilo Princip didn't have space in the close-packed throng to pull out and prime the bomb he had brought for use earlier in the day, so he simply stepped up to the footboard of the car and drew his pistol. He would later confess to prosecutors: "Where I aimed I do not know ... I even turned my head as I shot."[116]

His extraordinarily providential shots fatally wounded the Archduke by severing his jugular vein, and hit his wife, Sophie, in the stomach. She had been sitting next to her husband in the car, and by some accounts threw herself in front of his body, sacrificing herself in an attempt to save him.[117] Sophie was dead on arrival at Governor Oskar Potiorek's residence, where the Imperial couple were taken for medical care and last rites. Franz Ferdinand died ten minutes later.

Princip wanted to shoot himself in the head immediately after assassinating the pair, but he was seized by the crowd and taken into custody. Because he was 27 days away from his twentieth birthday, Austrian law wouldn't allow for him to be hanged. Instead, he was sentenced to twenty years' imprisonment, chained to a wall in the prison in Terezín (a military fortress and garrison 70 km to the northwest of Prague, which would later become a Nazi-run concentration camp). There, he died of disease and mistreatment, and he was buried in an unmarked grave.

Even more surprising than Princip's improbably lucky shots was the fact that Franz Ferdinand expected something like this to happen. He even believed he deserved it. As historian Mike Dash recounts, "if he could return from beyond the veil and share his reflections with us about the event, Franz Ferdinand himself would have said that he couldn't have been less surprised. He had spoken of premonitions of an early end, and according to one of his relatives, he had told some friends the month before Princip shot him "I know I shall soon be murdered." Another source described him as "extremely depressed and full of forebodings" a few days before his fateful motorcade.[118]

---

[116] Quoted in Mike Dash's article for *Smithsonian*.

[117] See the report from *The Times of London* 28 June 1914 titled "Heroism of the Duchess" reprinted in *Irish Times* 2014 (Hennessy).

[118] See Dash.

An oral tradition among hunters in Austria at that time tells that the archduke had shot a rare white stag in 1913. It was commonly believed that this would cause the hunter or a member of his family to die within a year.[119] It's certainly not the case that the man had delicate sensibilities about slaughtering his animal brethren: according to his own "meticulously kept" hunting records, he had gunned down a total of 274,899 animals, some of which had been sprayed with ammunition from machine guns.[120] Five thousand of the dead animals were deer, and his personal record for the most kills logged in one day was 2,140.[121]

The archduke had no respect for the customs or laws of the places he visited; for example, when he was at Yellowstone, where guns are not allowed, he and his companions used sticks and rocks to kill six squirrels, a skunk, and a deer so they would have trophies from their trip. His last kill was an ordinary cat that he shot while sitting in a parked car at his estate at Chlumec a week before the fateful assassination. He kept trophies of domestic and exotic beasts on the walls of "every wall of every room" of his palaces and hunting lodges, and he wished to one day open a museum to show them off to even more admirers. Not everyone was impressed: his uncle, Franz Josef, Emperor of the Austrian Empire, considered his nephew's hobby "mass murder."[122]

Just as Gavrilo Princip had shot blindly and killed Franz Ferdinand and Sophie, so the Archduke had probably shot the white stag without having any idea of how he did it. Because of the labor-intensive aristocratic style of hunting he used, in which teams of beaters flushed large number of game out of thickets while loaders kept his guns ready to spray anything that moved with bullets, it was probably inevitable he would eventually kill a white deer. However, despite this blind savagery, he believed a white deer was not only owed special protection, but actually had the power to curse him, his family, and others as well. And so it transpired.

---

[119] Ibid. These beliefs are not only limited to Austria or to the early 20th century. Many contemporary hunters, too, also believe that killing a white deer will bring misfortune on themselves and their families. Several have shared their stories with a reporter from the National Deer Alliance (see National Deer Alliance).

[120] See Curzon.

[121] See Ratner.

[122] Ibid.

Franz Ferdinand was an exceedingly greedy and callous taker of life.[123] We might see photographs of one of his old castles with hundreds of animal trophies on the walls and scoff in disgust, wondering if his aristocratic title somehow made him so inhumane. However, when we take a look at what humbler folk were doing in the eighteenth century, it seems that the archduke was anomalous more in his opportunities than in his mindset. Consider some of the more plebeian hunting practices that were prevalent in the American territories in the nineteenth century. One notorious example was use of the punt gun, an extremely large hunting shotgun that could fire over a pound of shot, slaying fifty to one hundred birds with one round. Many states in the US outlawed their use by the 1860s, and the Lacey Act (1900) and Migratory Bird Treaty Act (1918) effectively made these firearms extinct. However, unfortunately, so were the passenger pigeons.

The situation was similar with the American bison, whose numbers were reduced from tens of millions to only 325, after massacres driven both by commercial interests and a determination to deprive Native Americans of their livelihood.[124] By killing the bison, it was hoped Native Americans would then either die or give up all forms of resistance to the colonizing forces. As one US Army Colonel told a wealthy hunter who had pangs of conscience after shooting 30 of the animals on a trip organized by Buffalo Bill Cody: "Kill every buffalo you can! Every buffalo dead is an Indian gone." Colonel Dodge wrote, "where there were myriads of buffalo the year before, there were now myriads of carcasses. The air was foul with a sickening stench, and the vast plain, which only a short twelve months before teemed with animal life, was a dead, solitary desert." Settlers and Natives

---

[123] However, the Austrian Archduke was an amateur in comparison with Frederick Oliver Robinson, 2nd Marquess of Ripon (usually just called "Lord Ripon"), who managed to slaughter 556,813 animals between 1867 and 1923. Ripon was not only the most bloodthirsty hunter ever to wage war on the animal kingdom, but he was also noted for being extremely uncouth: sons of old gamekeepers would tell that if his lordship "saw his beaters getting out of line, [he] was not above putting a few pellets into their legs" or shooting a grazing sheep just to spite his men by making them carry it home. Between February and August when game was not in season, he would shoot insects. As an example of his boorishness: "there was the day when the vicar shot more bumblebees than he did. In furious silence Ripon jumped into the dogcart and drove off, leaving the aged cleric several miles to walk home" (see Sports Illustrated staff). Both of these indiscriminate butchers could have taken a few lessons from the Venerable Order of St. Hubertus.

[124] Some of the philosophical foundations for these policies go back to John Locke's *Second Treatise of Government* (1690), which presented the argument that it is necessary to "mix one's labor" with the land in order to make a legitimate claim to it. Locke's followers didn't believe that "lazy natives" were "improving" land that they hunted and gathered on. As David Graeber and David Wengrew write, with reference to James Tully, an expert on indigenous rights, "land used for hunting and gathering was considered vacant, and 'if the Aboriginal people attempt to subject the Europeans to their laws and customs or to defend the territories that they have mistakenly believed to be their properties for thousands of years, then it is they who violate natural law and may be punished or 'destroyed' like savage beasts." (Graeber and Wengrew, 149).

alike scavenged the bones and sold them for fertilizer. A railroad inspector ruefully commented on the fact that this provided the latter with a livelihood, but "it is a mercy that they can't eat bones. We were never able to control the savages until their supply of meat was cut off."[125]

Monstrous, barbaric atrocities! We think we would never engage in such outrages against wildlife, or against humans who have tried to steward their lands and maintain the animal populations—or would we? Well, maybe not as individuals, but collectively we certainly do, with our "civilized" consumption patterns everywhere around the world. "How did you go bankrupt?" Bill asks Mike in Ernest Hemingway's *The Sun Also Rises*. "Two ways. Gradually, then suddenly."[126] The same is true of our loss of ecological diversity. A report released by the Intergovernmental Science-Policy Platform on Biodiversity and Ecosystem Services (IPBES) in May 2019 revealed that around 1 million species (about one quarter of them) are at risk of extinction in the near future. At present, we are exterminating about 150–200 species *per day*, which scales up to 13–18% of all species each decade at the present rate.[127]

In hunting and gathering societies, the human population density has to be kept in balance with available food: where there are harsh winters or long dry seasons with little to no edible vegetation or other foods to forage, people must hunt scarce animals for meat. The seasonal "bottleneck" means that, even if there were seasons of abundance, the amount of food available during the lean season puts constraints on the size of the human population.[128] But when the population has no compunctions about "clearing" forests, any land can become grazing land. Deforestation took many centuries in most of Europe and Asia, but it only took settlers in North America about a century to reduce the old growth forests by 80%.[129] The

---

[125] See Phippen.

[126] Cited by Gordon White, p. 21.

[127] See Will Marshall's article for Medium.com, which summarizes the findings from IPBES, the WWF, and other sources.

[128] See Zhu et al. There is also an intriguing parallel to the idea of the balances of species populations in Buddhism that was mentioned by Pierre Madl. The author claims that when excessive populations of certain species occur it's an indication that many human beings who recently died have sunk to a lower level of incarnation because of their undesirable behavior. This is then the mechanism driving sudden overpopulations of grasshoppers, starfish, rabbit, cockroaches, etc. It's not exactly a concept of ecological karma, nor does it drive strategies aimed at limiting population size, but it's a conspicuous indicator of the presence of the deceased individuals' selfish thoughts and behavior. Such self-centered actions may have harmed the Earth and its creatures as well as other human beings, and it can be an occasion for the community to pause and reconsider its mores. It's an indirect mechanism that requires sensitivity to diagnose and wisdom to find solutions. I owe Bryan Boring Van Unen a debt of gratitude for explaining some of the nuances that weren't entirely clear to me when I read Pierre Madl's essay.

[129] Lewis, 26.

great majority of deforestation today is driven either directly or indirectly (i.e., clearing land to grow feed crops such as soybeans) by animal agriculture.

In systems where populations that cannot hunt or raise meat in sustainable conditions still demand to eat it, sacrifices are made. Humans' greed for land to raise animals for meat, and to raise the crops needed to feed them, have reduced the biomass of wild mammal species to only 4% of the Earth's total. We, ourselves, now comprise 36% of the biomass of all mammals, and the rest of it is mostly our cows and pigs. We have also done the same thing with birds: the biomass of domesticated birds, primarily chickens, outweighs the total of all wild birds by a factor of three to one. There are three chickens for each human being on the planet. Moreover, humans and livestock together now outweigh all other vertebrates, with the exception of fish.[130] It is likely that by the end of the present century, bio "diversity" will mainly consist of small, resistant generalist species such as rats, cockroaches, jellyfish, etc.

Animal agriculture is one of the prime drivers of "virgin" land clearance—and there's that ugly rape metaphor again, since there is no concept of virginity without its shadow of despoliation and the denial of self-willed development. Raising livestock as the predominant forms of vertebrate life on the land not only results in staggering degrees of soil, air, and water pollution, but also leads to the intentional and unintentional extermination of all other species that compete with food animals for space or are predators in their ecosystems

"Natural" and "free range beef" cattle are raised on the native habitats of other species, which are usually treated as varmints. Coyotes are poisoned with cyanide so they won't compete with ranchers, and wolves and bears are gunned down, sometimes even in their dens with their cubs and pups. The upscale "free range" meat that many consumers only buy for special occasions also provides a fig leaf for the bulk of the animal protein they consume, which—in most cases—comes from industrial animal agriculture operations.

---

[130] See Bar-On, Phillips, and Milo in PNAS.

It is well known by now that the majority of meat is produced in conditions that torment and degrade the commodity animals imprisoned within industrial facilities, and that the production of meat participates in various forms of environmental damage, including the production of excess greenhouse gases, water and land pollution, and excessive use of energy and land. Disentangling from this system is difficult. Most people do not have the opportunity either to raise livestock at home or to provision themselves through ethical hunting. Meat that has been procured from such sources can be difficult and very expensive to obtain, so it will come across as snobbish and entitled to tell others that you only eat the meat of "higher welfare" animals, rather than the kind that is most commonly available.

There are traditional cultures where people are able to self-sufficiently and sustainably provision themselves with meat. Their practices are not in any way comparable with industrial livestock production. There are also people living at the margins of industrial societies, such as in the small village where I live in Central Bohemia, who are able to provide all the meat they consume at home through their own small livestock and by hunting. Sadly, households like these are a rare exception. Also, even many vegetarians and vegans support industrial livestock operations when they feed their cats and dogs. This is my case, and I rue it.

The issues of animal agriculture and its impacts on the land, water, and wild species are all discussed at great length in other parts of this book, but I want to point out that our interactions with domestic animals and wildlife also lead us into other pitfalls. We increasingly face the consequences of engaging in intimate, bloody relations with both livestock and wildlife at a mass scale, in the form of "exotic" pathogens that afflict our species. It has been claimed that sixty-six percent of known infectious and parasitic diseases have their origin in zoonosis (transference between species).[131] This is the reason why scientists continually monitor the "viral chatter" in the key populations of bushmeat hunters and slaughterhouse

---

[131] See *Muséum Manifesto: Humans and Other Animals*.

workers: zoonotic viruses almost always leap to humans directly from slaughtered livestock or wildlife.[132]

The viral respiratory infection MERS, for instance, probably came to humans via camels, SARS was transmitted by Himalayan palm civets (a wild cat species) sold for meat in China's Guangdong province, Ebola most likely jumped from gorillas and chimpanzees, and Nipah virus is from bats. Campylobacter comes from poultry, Q fever comes from a variety of domesticated animals, hepatitis E is thought to have its reservoirs in deer and swine, and we have also had several novel influenza strains jump from farmed livestock. Both farmed and caged wild animals, and the "wet markets" where they are slaughtered and their carcasses are parceled out raw to customers, create excellent breeding grounds for diseases that have the potential for transmission to humans.[133]

Sometimes, wildlife and domestic animals are linked in surprising ways, as Natalie Glover reports for *The Guardian*: it's been theorized that African swine fever, which infected hog farms in China in 2018, dramatically reduced the supply of pork on worldwide markets because all infected animals had to be killed. This then drove a greater demand for "alternative meats," which included wild animals, "thus greatly increasing opportunities for human-coronavirus contact" as a team of researchers from China and the UK have claimed. With more wildlife entering the food chain, there is much greater opportunity for their viruses to infect people and domestic animals. Charlie Gardener, a conservationist from the University of Kent, points out that most of the world's biodiversity is found in the Global South, where ecosystems and wildlife have some of the weakest protection. His previous research in Madagascar revealed that when climate-induced natural disasters cut off people's sources of income, they would turn to other sources to make ends meet. For example, some farmers would turn to burning trees in the forest to produce charcoal, and then attempt to engage in slash-and-burn agriculture, while others would go to the coast to try their hand at fishing—but without skills and appropriate

---

[132] See Specht.
[133] Ibid.

equipment, they would "rely on destructive techniques like poison fishing."[134]

It's not only the poor who are responsible for the increase in poaching—in many cases, they are only the hunters who procure these commodities for others. As China and other Asian countries grow in wealth and power, the ability to purchase expensive "remedies" that cost the same per gram as gold becomes a marker of status. These practices are not dying out with the change of generations—young, urban professionals are among those who flaunt their consumption of wildlife products—and, with the expansion of general affluence, access is no longer limited to a thin stratum of elites. As Duncan Graham-Rowe writes:

> Traditional Asian medicine is on a collision course with wildlife preservation. The rhino and its horn are not alone: powdered tiger bone is used to treat rheumatism; the scales of the toothless, anteater-like pangolin are believed to reduce swelling and improve blood circulation; and *guilinggao*, a jelly derived from the shells of freshwater turtles, was used to treat smallpox in a nineteenth-century emperor, with little success—in Taiwan it is now reputed to cure cancer. It is a similar story for many other endangered species whose commercial use is restricted ...

He goes on to report:

> In 2008, a survey of nearly 1000 people from six cities across China found that 1.9% of respondents had consumed a medicine or tonic containing tiger within the past 12 months. If this represents national consumption, it would mean a user base of around 25 million people. In Vietnam, which is one of the largest markets for [Chinese Traditional Medicine] outside China, traditional remedies are sought after. If incomes were to increase, so too would consumption of products containing endangered species. This is hardly surprising ... given the perception that products such as rhino horn are capable of curing cancer.[135]

Early in the epidemic it was suggested the novel coronavirus first leaped to humans at a wet market in Wuhan, though conclusive evidence for this hypothesis is lacking. In any case, it hardly matters, because all of humani-

---

[134] See Gardener.
[135] See Graham-Rowe.

ty's intrusive processes are accelerating: the loss of habitat and exploitation of wildlife through hunting and trade increases the risk of "infectious spillover,"[136] and there will certainly be more zoonotic plagues in the future.

Research has already linked deforestation in the Amazon to increased zoonotic disease risk, finding that as habitat is lost, ecological dynamics are no longer as adept at regulating disease. There are good indications that restoring forests provides a protective function,[137] but, sadly, deforestation in Brazil[138]—as in many other places—has been greatly increasing in recent years. Apace with this, some of the traditional taboos that provided protection to certain species are eroding.[139] Perversely, the lockdowns and mobility restrictions imposed in response to the pandemic have also accelerated wildlife loss to poachers and traffickers, because this business—like so many others—increasingly moved online and therefore expanded its markets. In areas where shipping illegal animal products temporarily became more difficult, dealers simply stockpiled them, waiting for borders to reopen.[140]

Conflicts are inevitable as human settlements expand and as extractive industries and agriculture push animals into their last redoubts and then seize them. As habitat is lost, ecological dynamics are unbalanced, and the factors that regulate the spread of disease, such as predator and prey populations, are destabilized. Inger Anderson, the Executive Director of the United Nations Environmental Program, explains: "We should not blame the wild because viruses are everywhere—we get the cold, the flu—but we need to understand that prudent management of habitats and avoidance of habitat destruction is critical."[141]

We are facing clear choices and consequences, as environmental activist Vandana Shiva foretells:

> As we invade forest ecosystems, destroy the homes of species and manipulate plants and animals for profits, we create conditions for new

---

[136] See Cohen.

[137] See Nordseth. The team concluded that, if forests are just restored to levels mandated by the Brazilian Native Vegetation Protection Law, the transmission of hantavirus could be reduced by as much as 45% in Brazil's most populous region.

[138] According to the INPE Earth Observation satellite data supplied by the Brazilian government.

[139] See Joseph Dodds (2012), 6.

[140] See Abano and Chavez.

[141] See Rokhlin.

diseases. Over the past 50 years, 300 new pathogens have emerged. Scientific predictions indicate that if we do not stop this anthropogenic war against the earth and her species, in a hundred years we will have destroyed the very conditions that allowed humans to evolve and survive. Our extinction will follow that.[142]

Viruses are mediating factors in a biological dialectic where we bite into animals (as food, pet food, medicine, or by-kill) and then we are bitten back. This drives the evolution of all, as we merge into a complex community of species that develops new feedback processes. While the exchange is perhaps "natural" in one sense, the process has obvious dangers. People get sick and die, and the fear of this leads to irrational, violent, and scapegoating responses. For example, in early 2020, some people in Peru were setting fire to bats in their caves out of a belief that the animals might be spreading Covid. Himalayan palm civets were slaughtered en masse in China, because they had been a vector for the SARS outbreak in 2002.

Even the companion animals that bring joy to urbanites are not immune to the scapegoating impulse. In January 2022, the government of Hong Kong called for all pet hamsters to be surrendered because eleven of them had been discovered to harbor the Covid virus,[143] and in April and May of the same year, dogs and cats were collected for "bio-safety disposal" during the brutal lockdown imposed by the Chinese government on some neighborhoods in Shanghai in pursuit of their "zero Covid" policy.

So much for the bleak outlook for ecological buffers to contagion: even the vaccines intended to ward off diseases create ethical and ecological dilemmas. These dilemmas are situated in a cultural mythology of "production," that releases us from any sense of reciprocal relationship with ecosystems and the plant and animal species we interact with. Instead, it objectifies them, separates humans from other organisms, and puts us on top of food web with more and more of the strands out of it.[144]

While some may scoff or evince dismay at the use of endangered species in Traditional Chinese Medicine formulations, the current production protocol for vaccines also requires the killing of an increasingly endangered

---

[142] See Shiva.
[143] See Davidson.
[144] See Lewis, 125.

animal. To avoid any misunderstanding, this is true of all vaccines, not only those formulated for Covid. As humanity has scrambled to develop and mass-produce these vaccines, we have been rapidly crunching through the population of wild horseshoe crabs in the oceans.

After capture, the crabs are folded where their shells hinge, jabbed in the weak spot in the joint, and exsanguinated via steel needles. Their opaque light blue blood is then used in the vaccine manufacturing process to guarantee that the serums are free from dangerous contaminants. Sarah Zhang comments for *The Atlantic*: "So reliant is the modern biomedical industry on this blood that the disappearance of horseshoe crabs would instantly cripple it."[145] All medical supplies that come into contact with human blood have to be tested to make sure they are free of bacteria, and the tests are done with Limulus Amoebocyte Lysate (LAL) sourced from horseshoe crabs. This means not only every batch of vaccine serum, but also every syringe and vial used for administering them had to be tested first with LAL.[146]

This profligate cruelty was already present before the introduction of LAL to the pharmaceutical supply chain, but the previous victims were rabbits. The purity of all medical materials was ensured by injecting samples into rabbits. Laboratory workers then had to check the rabbits' temperatures every half hour to see if they rose, because a fever suggested bacterial contamination. This could then be confirmed by examining their blood under a microscope, since the cells had a tendency to clump around the toxin. The age of mass rabbit testing only ended in 1977, when the FDA allowed the huge colonies of lab rabbits to be replaced with Limulus Amoebocyte Lysate technology.

A synthetic substitute for horseshoe crab blood called "recombinant Factor C" was developed eighteen years ago, but pharmaceutical companies have been relying on suppliers protected by exclusive patents. Also, horseshoe crabs are cheaper, and they are not factored into calculations as worth saving, either for their own sake or for the sake of future human exploitation. The European Union allows the use of recombinant Factor C, but the

---

[145] See Zhang.
[146] See Sargent.

FDA has still not fully sanctioned its use. Eli Lilly has been lobbying the U.S. Pharmacopeia to update its guidelines, but so far they have declined.[147]

If horseshoe crab populations crash, the sea birds that feed on their eggs are also threatened, and the fibers of the aquatic web of life unravel.[148] At this point, at least one prominent vaccine manufacturer (Pfizer) is recommending repeating Covid booster shots every year—or even more frequently. As the virus mutates, pharmaceutical companies intend to develop new serums to annually (re)inoculate the nearly 8 billion humans on the planet, and there have even been proposals to vaccinate domestic animals in order to prevent them from becoming reservoirs for the pathogen.[149]

Naturally, horseshoe crabs are not the only species sacrificed to keep humans alive. Lab monkeys, who must be killed after they have been infected with the SARS-CoV-2 virus and used for various experiments, were suddenly in desperately short supply when the pandemic began, and their price rose dramatically. These commodified primates are now discussed as a "strategic reserve" that should be "stockpiled" for national security so another shortage doesn't arise; not only for current purposes, but for all other pharmaceutical research present and future.[150]

Even if we are comfortable considering wild organisms a "resource" humans should "stockpile" and use at will, what might happen if the horseshoe crabs are depleted? A horseshoe-crab holocaust will not bring an end to the new coronavirus, which is now endemic. Troubling questions arise of how new vaccines will be developed, and how the safety of old ones will

---

[147] See Zhang.

[148] See Carrie Arnold's report for *National Geographic* for a quick take on the issue, and Richard Gorman's original research article in *Frontiers in Marine Science* for a longer and much more complex analysis of different "stakeholders" in the debates over whether and how horseshoe crab blood should be used by the pharmaceutical industry.

[149] See Giordano. To my knowledge, vaccines against Covid intended for veterinary use have only been fully developed and used in Russia. There is widespread discussion of whether people will be expected to top up their antibodies every year or even more often. Experts have widely differing opinions on the recommended frequency of booster doses. Pfizer's CEO, Albert Bourla, told the BBC's medical editor in a video interview: "If we have to make a guess, based on everything I have seen so far, I would say that likely would be needed [sic] annual revaccinations to maintain very robust and very, very high levels of protection." In the meantime, in the US, the CDC has shortened the recommended interval for boosters and they say boosters can be administered to healthy individuals as soon as two months after the last dose. Andrew Pollard, the director of the Oxford Vaccine Group, and chief investigator for the clinical trials of the AstraZeneca vaccine speaks about "sustainability" as a limiting factor for ongoing vaccination, though he does not specify what, exactly, cannot be sustained. He told the BBC: "It really is not affordable, sustainable or probably even needed to vaccinate everyone on the planet every four to six months ... We haven't even managed to vaccinate everyone in Africa with one dose so we're certainly not going to get to a point where fourth doses for everyone is manageable." (See Walsh, Turner). Pollard has also stressed that targeting the "vulnerable" should be preferred over population-wide vaccination strategies. Occasionally, there are debates over whether the serum should be sent to countries where vaccination rates are in the single digits—or even lower—instead of attempting to get every European and North American boosted on a regular schedule.

[150] See Wee's article in *The New York Times*.

be maintained. Do we go back to torturing rabbits if they're cheaper than the synthetic alternatives? Are humans ever justified in wiping out entire species to provide for their own well-being? My father had a cynical saying; "Money talks, and bullshit walks," and by "bullshit" he meant everything that isn't money. As long as it's cheaper to use horseshoe crabs, they will be bled for us.

One might hope that, with the introduction of vaccines administered in pill or inhalable "mist" forms, and with more widespread use of pills to treat severe forms of the disease, the burden on horseshoe crabs and marine ecosystems would be eventually lessened. However, if governments insist on the use of vaccine "passports," they won't take it on faith that individuals have swallowed their medicine and not spat it out. Either the non-injectable vaccines will have to be administered under long and close supervision to ensure compliance, or the use of "passes" or QR codes as a means to separate the vaccinated from the unvaccinated will become obsolete. We shall see what priorities are expressed in these decisions: do we give the crabs and the ecosystems that depend on them a chance, or do we bleed them out and keep generating codes to confirm people's compliance? Or will the use of the more expensive recombinant Factor C eventually be mandated?

Some may be thinking: *who cares if they use up the horseshoe crabs—they're ugly. And we can farm, experiment on, and slaughter as many monkeys as we need. Taking care of human beings has to be the top priority and we'll have the luxury of caring about animals later.* Perhaps those people don't anticipate another pandemic for another century or so, but this is not a reasonable hope. The most notorious recent pandemic has all but passed out of living memory: the 1918-1920 Spanish Influenza. This virus claimed perhaps 100 million human lives, at a time when the world population numbered around 1.8 billion. More Americans were killed by this pathogen than in both world wars, plus the Korean and Vietnam Wars. Yet, this massive catastrophe is barely discussed compared to other historical events of the twentieth century.

But now, let me ask you: what were the most significant world events of 1968-1969? Events that most often come to mind are the assassinations of Martin Luther King and Robert Kennedy; the launch of ARPANET (the forerunner to today's internet); the Woodstock concert; the Apollo rocket launches and NASA's moon landing in the context of the US-Soviet space race; the invasion of Czechoslovakia by Soviet-led forces; the Tet Offensive in Vietnam and the introduction of the draft lottery; significant movements for greater rights for women, African Americans, Native Americans, and gay people; and student rebellions in multiple countries. Some lists mention the Chappaquiddick Affair, Charles Manson's murder cult, and the release of albums by the Beatles and other artists. It was a tense and chaotic period, pregnant with an air of revolutionary change tinged with both hope and dread.

However, one event that almost never makes it onto such lists was the Hong Kong flu. Official estimates say this virus may have killed up to 4 million people worldwide, though it's hard to be sure of the real figure, since there was relatively little testing. The world population then was 3.5 billion in 1968, but now it has grown to 8 billion. The official death toll for Covid in 2020 and 2021 is about 5.5 million. Proportionally, therefore, if we go with the higher estimated death toll, the Hong Kong flu was far more deadly—but no one blinked!

There was another pandemic influenza in 1957-58 that was not as deadly as the Hong Kong flu, but it, too, ran its two-year course without making much of an impact on historiography. It is also nearly certain that all the other coronaviruses familiar to humanity became weaker over time and now only cause "colds." One of the pandemic illnesses that probably developed similarly to what we witnessed at the beginning of the 2020s was the highly deadly 1889-90 epidemic of "Russian flu," which no one discusses much now. It is very likely that we will witness another pandemic illness with a similar or worse mortality rate within a few decades, because this is just part of the way the world works.

Our cultural memories of these events is weak, because plagues and pandemics aren't things humanity likes to remember. This is why it's hard to find public memorials to those who died in them. For example, while there are more than 3,000 monuments to the First World War in the United Kingdom, there isn't a single monument for the 228,000 Britons who died of the Spanish Flu. "As societies, we tend to remember wars, and we tend to remember great political struggles," said Bill Hirst, who teaches psychology at The New School for Social Research in New York. "Natural disasters are much lower down the list—they don't figure very much at all actually." The reason for this, according to Hirst, is that an event has to serve a purpose; that is, it has to be a part of a story that a society wants to tell about itself, and diseases rarely satisfy this condition.

Memorials are much more likely to be founded for those who created or delivered treatments for illness than for those who died from it.[151] Charles Eisenstein points out that governments and think tanks are nostalgic for the days when modern medicine and hygiene seemed to have the same power of defeating infectious diseases as the war machine showed in defeating the Nazis: when "nature itself succumbed, or so it seemed, to technological conquest and improvement. It recalls the days when our weapons worked and the world seemed indeed to be improving with each technology of control."[152] As Eisenstein had already pointed out in an essay on the Zika virus written on 2016, a virus or another pathogen fits into the "basic crisis response template of our culture." It's named as a single cause of the crisis, and it justifies the expansion of technologies of control into areas that previously had not been monitored and controlled.[153]

Olivia Humphreys notes that it rarely serves the interest of the powerful to reflect upon or commemorate a pandemic. Unlike in a war, there are no heroic deaths, and, even worse, they lay bare the flaws and weaknesses in a society. Any lessons that might be learned tend to require other improvements for which few want to pay: hiring more nurses even when they don't seem to be needed, improving sick pay, upgrading and maintaining ventilation systems, and others. The powerful would rather let the whole mess be quietly forgotten, and most people willingly do so, because of how painful and sad their experiences were.[154] In the end, they prefer to see

---

[151] Even the triumphalist narrative around Jonas Salk's polio vaccine omits a crucial contextual detail. As it turns out, the biggest risk factor for having a really ugly case of polio instead of just a mild flulike illness or diarrhea is not having tonsils, because this underappreciated organ provides the body's best defense against the poliovirus. In the mid-20th century, not only were tonsils almost always taken out in cases of tonsillitis (instead of at least trying antibiotics or other remedies first), but they were even taken out as a precautionary measure. Sometimes healthy children were shipped in busloads from rural areas to hospitals where they would all be subjected to tonsillectomies. Guess what happened to a lot of those kids? Yeah, you got it. Salk's vaccine *was* effective. But if so many people weren't missing their tonsils in the first place it would have been a remedy for a fairly rare syndrome in places where people are adequately nourished. Not surprisingly, the mass tonsillectomies have been consigned to the memory hole, like other large-scale medical mistakes. See Dwyer-Hemmings.

[152] See Eisenstein.

[153] Eisenstein, 6-7.

[154] See Humphreys.

themselves and their loved ones as protagonists who lost a "personal battle," and not as part of a statistic.

The threat of infectious disease, like the threat of terrorism, never really goes away. If there is going to be any significant reminder of the Covid-19 years, it's likely to hark back to some of the most antidemocratic and intrusive mechanisms of social control imposed during this period. These include (with variations from place to place): special states of emergency that allow enactments and expenditures without legistative debate or public scrutiny; the use of mandatory tracking technologies; non-medical personnel authorized to examine health records; suspension of freedom of assembly; military policing of civilians; pressure to eliminate cash purchases; censorship; compulsory medical treatments and the use of "passport" systems to monitor compliance; curfews; the slaughter of pets, livestock, and wildlife; the sacrifice of children's mental health; special new categories of crimes where the accused are not treated with due process of law; and the classification of activities on the basis of highly arbitrary rules (for example, you can leave home for this reason, but not that one, or you can walk outside with your dog, but not alone).[155]

With most of the special provisions now rolled back, we will see how many of these legacies will remain, and how little it will take to reactivate them for some other (surely very compelling) reason. Unfortunately, just like during the period of the USA PATRIOT Act, we have seen that too many people are willing to let elite actors and authorities treat their political rights as conditional privileges. If they lack the conviction that their rights are inalienable, people will not be motivated to demand or struggle for any improvements in their political or economic conditions. This is especially worrying to witness in anemic responses to the widespread crises in housing, energy, and inflation, as well as the greater crisis of the ongoing degradation of our ecosystems.

---

[155] Eisenstein, 15, 20-21.

We Didn't Start the Fire

Billy Joel once sang "We Didn't Start the Fire," a song whose lyrics are a litany of political and cultural events that took place between 1949 and 1989.[156] In that song, he suggests that the roots of present events stretch back further than most people are aware. "We didn't start the fire, it was always burning since the world's been turning" may be a dramatic exaggeration in the context of a mere four decades, but who deliberately set the fires that started to transform Earth's landscapes? Actually, it probably wasn't us: *Homo erectus* was the first human species to master the use of fire, between one million and about 300,000 years ago, and they were the first of our ancestors to become cooks.[157]

Physical traces of their campfires are scant, and it isn't clear how much their fires might have affected their habitats, but Neanderthals in the Pleistocene were already using fire to fateful effect. According to research pub-

---

[156] Billy Joel also doesn't mention the influenza epidemics of 1957-8 or 1968-9 in his list of 118 cultural, political, sporting, and scientific events that he thought deserved to make history.

[157] See evolutionary anthropologist Richard Wrangham's *Catching Fire: How Cooking Made Us Human* (2009). While some scientists dispute Wrangham's proposed timeline, it is clear the transition to cooking food increased the nutrition that was available, and it had profound influences on our faces and bodies, our brains, our use of time, and our behavior and social lives.
Pre-Neanderthal hominins already had advanced skills in working with fire, as evidenced by the placement of their hearths in Lazaret Cave in southeastern France. Analysis of smoke residue on the cave's surfaces shows they understood the behavior of fire, smoke, and air currents and optimized the hearth's location to take advantage of these factors (i.e., ensuring that air flow cleared most of the smoke out of the cave rather so they wouldn't choke on it). David Kindy, writing for *Smithsonian*, cites experts who stated that the hearth was placed first, and the rest of the space and the hominins' activities, including butchering, drying meat, and sleeping near the fire's warmth were organized around it.
Neanderthals were quite sophisticated in their foodways. Recent discoveries indicate that they used complex methods of food preparation and prepared a kind of pancake or flatbread. Burned remains of a meal thought to be about 70,000 years old have even been unearthed at a hearth in the Shanidar cave site in the Zagros Mountains north of Baghdad. Mixtures of seeds were soaked (probably in animals skins, since they lacked pottery) and then pounded to make the dough, and archaeologists assert that the taste of the cooked flatbread would have been nutty and palatable. See Geddes.

lished in *Science Advances*, Neanderthals transformed a mostly forested area into a fairly open landscape around 125,000 years ago. The question of whether they were deliberately influencing the biome with the use of fire has not been definitely answered; either way, the Neanderthals' settlement and activities preceded the change in vegetation. This suggests that the transformation of this habitat was caused by their activities, rather than by some other (natural) factor that made the sites attractive for settlement.[158]

Pre-*Homo sapiens* hominins may have bequeathed us environments they had a hand in landscaping, and this has profound implications for how we understand our behavior and our existence as a species. The fires have always been burning, and the baselines of "natural" landscape have always been shifting. As Karl Marx declared in an essay titled "The 18th Brumaire of Louis Bonaparte:"

> Men make their own history, but they do not make it as they please; they do not make it under self-selected circumstances, but under circumstances existing already, given and transmitted from the past. The tradition of all dead generations weighs like a nightmare on the brains of the living.[159]

The term "Anthropocene" is sometimes used to describe the age in which human activities began to act as a geological force that shapes the Earth's climate. Its use is contentious, and there are polemics over whether it should be applied to the period when human activities first began to shape the Earth's climate, or to save it for after the effects were accelerated by the Industrial Revolution.[160] The historian Dipesh Chakrabarty asserts we've long had a blind spot that prevents us from seeing how humans play a role in the planet's natural history: this is true for scholars (such as historians and philosophers) as well as for politicians and people in general. Acting unaware of our potential to function as a geological agent, we have unwittingly become one.

---

[158] See Bower.

[159] This text can be found at Marxists.org.

[160] Some thinkers, such as Donna Haraway and Bruno Latour, have even proposed the term "Capitalocene," as though Soviet and Chinese carbon emissions or other biocidal actions should be excused from humanity's sum total. Timothy Morton asserts that capitalism is, in any case, a symptom of the problem (of human hubris) than its root cause (23), and that what Marxist theory regards as "*nature*" is not actual trees and Arctic foxes but trees and foxes as they are metabolized by human economic relations. Use value isn't 'what things really are for,' but 'what things are for humans,'" which is an important distinction (26, emphasis in the original).

Sometimes, the workings of nature were attributed to a transcendent and inscrutable deity, who charges us with managing our own affairs in accordance with its commandments. But even after excluding supernatural causation from their analyses, idealist and materialist historians still called for the rejection of the crudely biological level of "impulses and appetites" from any understanding of historical processes, and they appealed for a focus on choices made by individuals and collective actors. Setting the tone for the socialist world, Joseph Stalin commented on the relatively unchanging geological conditions that allow for variety and change in political and economic systems, without exerting a determining influence on us, and without any awareness that we might exert a determining influence on them.[161]

Confronting climate science upends our understanding of ourselves, and puts us on the level of an inscrutably vast and powerful force, something not unlike an almighty god. Chakrabarty writes: "In unwittingly destroying the artificial but time-honored distinction between natural and human histories, climate scientists posit that the human being has become something much larger than the simple biological agent that he or she always has been. Humans now wield a geological force"[162] which is able to influence the planet's essential physical processes, and not in a positive way.

To individuals, this can seem unjust: we are charged with responsibility, but not endowed with the benefits we imagine should be available to a planet-shaping entity. Those already blessed with abundance are asked to live more modestly instead of enjoying what they already have; those who struggle are told there's nothing left for them. As when confronted with the enormity of a worldwide pandemic, we prefer to see ourselves as protagonists and not part of an immensity.

Chakrabarty acknowledges a deeper timescale to the geological transformations he describes, but he puts particular emphasis on the period after the Industrial Revolution. This was when the burning of fossil fuels became so pervasive that it could be described as a species-wide behavior.

---

[161] See Chakrabarty.
[162] Ibid.

Upon this innovation, people began to build what he terms the "mansion of modern freedoms," which offers the possibility of individuals or small groups to take shelter from human-made problems of "injustice, oppression, inequality, or even uniformity."[163]

Perversely, the more we create the possibility of fleeing such miseries by building on the ever-expanding edifice of unsustainable growth, the more they will become predominant conditions. We can observe this worldwide, as cities swell with slums filled with people who will have increasing difficulties procuring what they need to survive. They have diminishing chances of achieving any measure of happiness or dignity, a way of life that isn't hemmed in on all sides by abject misery. He cites the climatologist Mark Maslin, who concludes that, given the unlikelihood of an effective global political solution, "we must prepare for the worst and adapt."[164]

Where is the best place to begin when describing human-driven climate change? The "early anthropogenic hypothesis," proposed by climatologist William Ruddiman in 2003, states that humans began to transform life on Earth when they cut down forests 7,000 years ago. This resulted in more carbon dioxide being added to the atmosphere. There was also more methane in the atmosphere starting 5,000 years ago, when people began engaging in irrigated "wet" rice farming and keeping livestock. Ruddiman claims that the naturally warm Holocene climate should have cooled significantly over the past few thousand years, but it could not because of direct and indirect anthropogenic greenhouse gas production. Burning trees and plant matter would be considered direct production, while indirect production includes deforestation and tilling. The latter results in more soil runoff and thus larger delta areas that release, instead of sequester, gases.

Other researchers have challenged or built upon this core idea, citing evidence of created feedback loops in which the warmer atmosphere and oceans created more opportunities for ventilation of greenhouse gases. This was because of reduced ice coverage in circumpolar regions, which allowed the gases to emerge from wetlands. A further factor that prevented

---

[163] Ibid.
[164] Ibid, 15-16.

cooling is the lower solubility potential for carbon dioxide in warmer ocean water. William Ruddiman has suggested that cooling periods occurred during periods of global (human) pandemics, when population and activities were suppressed (along with human-caused increases in greenhouse gases),[165] which suggests they may be an element in planetary feedback cycles.

Critics have quibbled about how much of the pre-industrial "CO_2 anomaly" has been caused by deforestation versus climate feedback loops which, once initiated by whatever cause, became self-sustaining. Yet, there is still broad consensus that the effects of the Neolithic shift from a mobile and flexible lifestyle to a sedentary one—where people relied on a few staple crops and domesticated animal species—were cumulative and profound. "Although slow in developing, the climatic effect of these early agricultural factors by late in the Holocene rivaled that of the subsequent industrial portion."[166]

Humans' detrimental effects on large animal populations began long before the adoption of a settled agricultural way of life: this was a pattern that began deep in prehistory and then accelerated. In fact, until only 20,000 years ago, most mammals were larger than humans—but humans have always had a tendency to hunt the largest animals around.[167] Felisa Smith, an evolutionary biologist who researches the reduction in animals' populations and body sizes in the Late Quaternary period, claims that once hominins began migrating out of Africa, there were observable effects on other fauna everywhere. Population reduction, extinction, and smaller body sizes are a "signature of human impacts," particularly on the largest species, such as the gigantic prehistoric relatives of elephants, bears, and antelope.

It didn't take long: all of this can be observed within a few hundred to a thousand years at most. The timescales for any other types of extinction events are never this rapid, with the exception of the aftermath of the asteroid impact that killed the non-avian dinosaurs 65 million years ago.

---

[165] See Ruddiman.
[166] Ibid.
[167] See Ritchie for a very concise and well-illustrated presentation of extinction timelines for the past million years around the world.

Smith's research also demonstrates that, around 125,000 years ago, the average body size of African animals was only half that of animals found on other continents that had few to no hominins. While it could be expected that animals in Africa, which is one of the largest continents, would have a comparable body size to Asian and American fauna, their mean body size was only half as large.[168]

Human activities have not only affected animals, but also plants. A worldwide census of the number of trees, and comparisons of actual and potential plant biomass, all suggest that the total plant biomass (and therefore also the sum total of all biomass on Earth) has been reduced twofold, relative to its amount before human civilization began interfering with it. Previously, I described the disastrous replacement of wild animals by human and livestock biomass, but crops grown by humans only account for approximately 2% of total extant plant biomass.[169]

New technologies, including satellite photography and the recovery of food molecules or bacterial DNA trapped in dental plaque, enable more complex and nuanced timelines of humans' land use (and the diets that drive the management of land, plants, and animals) to emerge. Researchers working on the international collaborative ArchaeoGLOBE project tell us: "Recent discoveries are expanding our awareness of just how early, extensive and transformative humans' use of land has been."[170] Collaborative research in the ArchaeoGLOBE projects reveals that "human societies modified most of Earth's biosphere much earlier and more profoundly than we thought"—an insight with serious implications for how we understand humanity's relationship to nature and the planet. Hunter-gatherer populations had already significantly impacted the land by 10,000 years ago. By selectively harvesting and hunting certain species (sometimes to extirpation or extinction), or translocating them, and using fire to alter landscapes, "most of the terrestrial biosphere was already significantly influenced by human activities, *even before the domestication of plants and*

---

[168] See Bryce.
[169] See Bar-On, Phillips, and Milo.
[170] The ArchaeoGLOBE project brings together research crowdsourced from more than 250 contributing archaeologists whose work describes changing land use over the past 10,000 years. Although individual researchers have deep knowledge of the area and time period they focus on, they sometimes lack a comprehensive overview. This collaborative project aims at improving the pooled knowledge to date, for the benefit of all. See Stephens, Ellis, and Fuller's article in *Aeon*.

animals" (emphasis added by me). Then, over the next several thousand years, "Earth's terrestrial ecology was ... transformed by hunter-gatherers, farmers, and pastoralists—with more than half of regions assessed engaged in significant levels of agriculture or pastoralism" by 3,000 years before our present era.[171]

These changes did not take place in a triumphantly linear sweep towards a better way of life,[172] nor in a swift pivot at a certain point in time. Mostly, there were periods of trial and error with the management of plants, animals, landforms, and techniques, and it could sometimes take hundreds to thousands of years before a definitive transition—from hunting and gathering to sedentary farming—took place. The thresholds between one way and other were often hazy, and myths often evince an ambivalence about which way is better.

Transition Myths

Let us revisit three well-known Biblical myths that preserve prehistoric accounts of the Neolithic transition. The best-known one is the tale of Adam and Eve, who lived in a wonderful garden where they subsisted on the fruits of the land. After displeasing their god, they were sentenced to exile from their blessed condition: Adam was forced to perform hard labor as a farmer,[173] and Eve was punished with motherhood and submission to

---

[171] See Stephens, Ellis, and Fuller.

[172] Marshall Sahlins' essay "The Original Affluent Society," which arose from a symposium on "Man the Hunter" in 1966, was a challenge to the popular idea that a hunter-gatherer lifestyle was a constant struggle for survival with poor wretches constantly scrambling to get a few morsels of food while dangling over the brink of starvation. Instead, abundant ethnographic research indicated that among unsettled people, only a few hours of work were required to procure enough food. Surplus food and supplies couldn't be carried, so they aren't needed or wanted and this meant there was no opportunity for significant social inequality to arise. People's days were spent pleasantly, with intermittent and interwoven spells of work, rest, play, and socializing. No one had an aversion to work, and they showed cheerfulness and great courage when facing challenges or dangers. Hunter and gatherer populations that preceded agricultural communities and those who live adjacent to them today enjoy a varied diet, and better health and vitality, and they have fewer babies, which represents a lesser burden on women's well-being. Sahlins calls this the "Zen road to affluence" where human material wants are limited and few, and technical means are unchanging but adequate to provide for them. In the Western "Galbraithean" path to affluence, humans learn to want a lot, but they have limited means to acquire it. This will only eventually be remedied by industrial productivity–but at the price of forced participation in what we call the "rat race" and the loss of the original ease and leisure. For more, I recommend reading Graeber and Wengrow's (2021) *The Dawn of Everything*.

[173] Compare with verses from the Ramayana (ca. 7th -6th century BCE) recounted by Morton (38):
"In the Golden Age, agriculture was an abomination. In the Silver Age, impiety appeared in the form of agriculture. In the Golden Age, people lived on fruits and roots that were obtained without any labor. For the existence of sin in the form of cultivation, the lifespan of people became shortened."

By contrast with the story in Genesis, agriculture is the sin rather than the punishment. And, as Marshall Sahlins and others have argued, this is also demographically (historically) accurate. The recent obsession with gluten-free and "Paleo" diets, no matter what else we might think about them, also, in my opinion, represent an incipient recognition of the recognition that "give us this day our daily bread" was not such a good deal, considering what we got along with it.

And praying to the "Lord" of course reflects an ancestral obsession with bread, since the Old English word it derived from, *hlaford*, was a contraction of earlier *hlafweard* ("one who guards the loaves," from *hlaf* "bread, loaf" and *weard* "keeper, guardian"). *Weard*, like the modern English guard or ward(en), comes from the PIE root **wer-* "perceive, watch out for". See Etymology Online: "Lord." Etymology has thus preserved the memory of who indeed was doling out one's daily bread.

a patriarchal order. "I will make your pains in childbearing very severe; with painful labor you will give birth to children. Your desire will be for your husband, and he will rule over you." This is, indeed, a decent representation of the decline in female reproductive and social well-being after populations became sedentary.

Adam was chastised for taking his wife's guidance:

> Because you listened to your wife and ate fruit from the tree about which I commanded you, "You must not eat from it," cursed is the ground because of you; through painful toil you will eat food from it all the days of your life. It will produce thorns and thistles for you, and you will eat the plants of the field. By the sweat of your brow you will eat your food until you return to the ground, since from it you were taken; for dust you are and to dust you will return.

Essentially, Adam is supplied with a justification for resenting and punishing his wife, and this was given as a model for relations between all men and all women. Henceforth, human beings were denied the life of easy abundance once enjoyed by hunter-gatherers, because they had gained knowledge of new technologies that would ultimately create more pain and suffering. At a very real level illustrated by the archaeological record, Adam and Eve's fate was not individual but generalized to all of humanity: once some people begin claiming and fencing off land, there was ever less available for those who still remained hunter-gatherers. Ultimately, the lifestyle became unviable in the region of this tale's origin.

The second story is told about the next generation, who were born after Adam and Eve were driven out of the Garden of Eden. Their two sons are named Cain and Abel (Genesis 4:1). Abel was a shepherd, and Cain tilled the soil. As Richard Hess contends, Cain's name may actually be derived from *qyn*, a South Arabian word for "metalsmith." Clearly, there must have been a few generations between his parents' banishment from Eden and Cain's apprenticeship and mastery of metal-working. In any case, when it was time to bring sacrifices, Cain offered some of his harvest, and Abel brought lambs from his flock. Abel's meat was favored more, so Cain murdered him.

The tale can be understood as a metaphor of the victory of farmers, whose "sedentary lifestyle ... emerges victorious over the wandering lifestyle of the shepherd." This interpretation puts the story of Cain and Abel:

> "in conversation with what we know about the development of the agricultural revolution. Around 12,000 years ago, people in the Levant began farming, allowing them to grow their own food and produce surpluses. In turn, these surpluses allowed for population explosions, and the need to build cities to house these large populations, and to create governments to maintain them, etc." [174]

The replacement was not complete and unambiguous, though: Cain is punished for the fratricide by being forced to wander the earth. His sentence was carried out in the letter rather than the spirit of the judgement, since he settled in the land of Nod (נוֹד), which in Hebrew means "wandering." There, the former farmer built a city and became rich by doing wicked deeds, and his descendants[175] flourished with civilized arts. If Cain represented the progress brought by metallurgy—as represented by the farmer's plow—it also showed the dark side, as it became easier to kill and to build large impersonal agglomerations where wickedness could go unpunished.[176]

The third Biblical story describing a transition towards a settled way of life frames it as a positive evolution, rather than a punishment and a permanent curse on humanity. Jacob and Esau were brothers, twins who had struggled against each other ever since they were in their mother's womb. This primal conflict references not only sibling rivalry, but also the conflict between the older way of life represented by the hunter Esau and the farmer Jacob.

By this point, the farmers are considered to be the more virtuous group; herders' sacrifices are no longer believed to have a higher value. However, because Esau was the firstborn, he was due to inherit the family's "birthright, which included, among other things, being heir to the

---

[174] See Glaser.

[175] Besides the question of who taught Cain how to work with metal, we might also wonder who was living in these cities, and how he begat his descendants if his mother Eve was supposed to be the only other woman on Earth. This is one of the reasons my Sunday school teachers were constantly aggravated with me and told my parents they wanted me to stop asking questions.

[176] See Glaser.

Covenant between God and Abraham ... Esau was a skillful hunter and his father's favorite, but Jacob was a 'plain' man, dwelling in tents (Genesis 25:27), and the favorite of his mother. The Hebrew word for plain is the same word translated in other Scripture as perfect, upright, undefiled. The Bible affords the highest praise and blessing for Jacob: The LORD hath chosen Jacob unto Himself (Psalm 135:4)."[177]

Here is the story: Esau came in from the field, feeling faint, and asked his brother for some red stew (Genesis 25: 29-30). Jacob was crafty and asked Esau to sell him the birthright in exchange for the stew, knowing that his brother had little interest in the spiritual legacy. Esau agreed to the deal, replying: "I am at the point (about) to die: and what profit shall this birthright do to me?" (25:32-34) Was a man really going to die for skipping a single meal? Not likely, but either this indicates that he truly considered the birthright worthless, or perhaps it is intended to show that his nomadic lifestyle doesn't support him adequately—in other words, that hunters as such were a "dying" type. Whatever the case, the brothers made the bargain.

When their father Isaac was close to death, he would have to pass his blessing to Esau; however, Isaac didn't realize Jacob had already bought it. Isaac wanted Esau to go hunting so he could have a special meal before blessing him, but their mother overheard and helped Jacob disguise himself as Esau. Jacob then came in with the meal, while the real Esau was still away. Because the dying man had poor eyesight, he fell for the trick and blessed Jacob with the birthright. Esau was furious when he discovered what had happened, and Jacob had to flee to save himself.

While this may seem like a straightforward tale of an unscrupulous mother and son conspiring against an unfortunate son and their dying father, the blessing falling upon the farmer instead of the hunter is significant. Esau is called a profane (godless) person later in the scriptures (Hebrews 12:16), because even before they had been born, God knew that Esau's descendants would become enemies of Israel for generations to

---

[177] See Bible Study Tools.

come. God also knew Jacob was the kind of man he wanted to insert as an ancestor into the patrilineage of Jesus.[178]

A Litany of Baseline Shifts

We were never treated to historical, philological, or ethnological analysis at the Methodist Sunday school classes I was made to attend as a child. Instead, such stories were presented as moralistic warnings that we must fear God and obey his will. Even these oversimplified, moralistic interpretations, however, give us insight into ways humans process their environment and the forces which regulate their access to life's necessities. Thus, even the most stripped-down interpretations of the tales are relevant here.

Coming from an unexpected discipline, the ornithologist Carolos Botero and his team demonstrate that the geographical prevalence of human societies believing in "moralizing high gods"—defined as "supernatural beings believed to have created or govern all reality, intervene in human affairs, and enforce or support human morality"—can be predicted *with 91% accuracy*. Using rigorously and meticulously defined historical, social, and bioclimatic data from 583 societies, they assessed the potential effects of environmental forces, language, history, and culture on the global distribution of belief in moralizing high gods. Their analysis indicated that moralizing high gods are more likely to be found where people inhabit poorer environments, in which they experience more ecological risk or "duress." Specifically, this includes at least certain periods of restricted access to food and water.[179]

This team of biologists thought to analyze the data for humans because they were already well aware of the powerful correlation between cooperation and ecological uncertainty in nonhuman animals. For example, the stress of ecological uncertainty matches higher rates of cooperative breeding in birds, and higher rates of group living in mammal species. In other words, these animals benefit more from being sociable during lean periods

---

[178] Ibid.

[179] See Botero et al. What about the prophecies of the desert patriarchs? Hearing voices is increasingly accepted as occurring with a fair degree of frequency among human beings, but *the content of what the voices impart varies greatly by culture and individual psychological profiles*. Timothy Morton suggests that meeting the demands of "agrilogistics" was sufficiently stressful that it led to people hearing voices that seemed terrifying and commanding (87, emphasis and adjectives mine). See Clifton Parker.

than they lose from it during benign ones. However, when focusing on human societies, the researchers found a few more conditions that transcended environmental factors, accurately associated with beliefs in moralizing high gods. These include political "complexity" (the existence of jurisdictions outside the immediate community), the practice of animal husbandry, ownership of movable property, and a higher degree of compliance with norms.

The emerging picture is neither one of pure cultural transmission, nor of simple ecological determinism, but rather a complex mixture of social, cultural, and environmental influences. A shared belief in moralizing high gods can improve a group's ability to deal with environmental duress, and may therefore be ecologically adaptive.[180] Importantly, however, if the group is so successful at extracting scarce resources that they overshoot their territory's carrying capacity, they may then decide to wage "holy" wars against their neighbors in order to keep provisioning themselves.

Lifestyle changes of the types I've described can be jarring enough that they leave traces in myths for millennia afterward. When changes take place slowly, they can sometimes be imperceptible to eyewitnesses. This is referred to as "shifting baseline syndrome." A sense of things having been better in the past—more animals, more wilderness, fewer people, better food and so on—may be present, but shifting baseline syndrome is experienced more like a twinge in one's mind, rather than a sharp pain.[181]

Most adults alive today have seen very abrupt changes in the places where they life. When the baselines shift very suddenly, and people observe profound damage (whether natural or human-caused) inflicted on the land, there is a special kind of grief that arises. Various cultures have conceived of that grief, such as *uggianaqtuq* (an Inuit word that means "a

---

[180] Ibid.

[181] See Brooke Jarvis' article, where she cites a study published in 1995 by Peter H. Kahn and Batya Friedman, that summed up the way successive generations become used to environmental pollution by stating: "With each generation, the amount of environmental degradation increases, but each generation takes that amount as the norm." The shifting baselines may refer to pollution, changes in climate or weather, changes in local landscape features, or the variety, robustness, or size of animals and plants. However, each generation of people believes that what they're observing is normal. As an illustration, Jarvis describes photographs shown to the marine biologist Loren McClenachan. They showed fisherman over the course of many decades who posed holding up the fish they'd caught in the Florida Keys. "The fish got smaller and smaller, to the point where the prize catches were dwarfed by fish that in years past were piled up and ignored. But the smiles on the fishermen's faces stayed the same size. The world never feels fallen, because we grow accustomed to the fall."

friend acting strangely") or *koyaanisqqatsi* (a Hopi term that describes a state of life that is out of balance and disintegrating).[182]

Western discourses are only starting to recognize the need to describe these emotions: the neologism "solastalgia" (based on the terms solace, desolation, nostalgia, and the Latin *algia*, which means pain or sorrow) has been proposed by the environmental philosopher Glenn Albrecht. "If a person lacks solace or solitude in a much-loved place that is being desolated, then they will suffer distress. Solace is what provides 'heart's ease': it soothes the disturbed mind and brings that which was discordant back to harmony." Solastalgia is pain or distress related to an ongoing or increasing lack of solace, as well as a sense of desolation connected to deterioration of a place one considers to be their home or territory. It is chronic, and arises from an existential lived experience of witnessing ongoing negative changes, changes which feel like attacks on one's sense of belonging to a place.[183]

When someone says, "we needed this rain," it may be an expression of solastalgia over weather and climate. Many parts of the world are experiencing long-term droughts. People in older generations remember lusher vegetation, fuller rivers and streams, larger lakes and ponds. They are thus likely experiencing solastalgia. Until it rains, this all may be suppressed, and then they suddenly remember: *we needed that rain!*

If animals can grieve—and we know that some of them do—they must also have some form of solastalgia. That solastagia would perhaps manifest when they perceive disappearance or disruption of their habitats, or when they are so confounded by human-made light, noise, and pollution that they are unable to function in the ways they had before. Marine mammal researcher John Hilderbrand points out that over the past half century, the low-frequency noises made by shipping vessels have increased 32-fold. The

---

[182] See Albrecht, 36.

[183] Albrecht coined this term. He discusses it in many parts of his book, but see especially p. 38. He also provides a shorter explanation of the term on his blog, which may be of interest to those who would like to read about it without committing to an entire book. Solastalgia has been incorporated into academic disciplines including psychology, psychiatry, geography, public health, sociology, anthropology, literature, film, and environmental science, and it has also been adopted by artists working in many different media. Even governments have used it in assessing the human impacts of changes in landscapes.
Albrecht points out that Edvard Munch's famous painting *The Scream* was "indirectly a solastalgic personal response to global environmental impacts, as a result of the eruption of the volcano Krakatoa in Indonesia in 1883. The graphically depicted blood-red sky was a by-product of volcanic dust ejected into the global atmosphere ... Munch produced an archetypal, eco-apocalyptic response in the famous painting. In his journal of 1892, he wrote that he felt as if '... a great, infinite scream [had passed] through nature'" (Albrecht, 45).

largest whales can live for over a century: there are whales alive now which have experienced this increase, as well as witnessing the great reduction in the aquatic chorus of animals who once populated the waters. Humpback whales stop singing and orcas stop foraging. Crabs stop feeding, cuttlefish change colors, and other fish are more easily caught. To put this level of stress in perspective, Hildebrand comments:

> If I said that I'm going to increase the noise level in your office by 30 decibels, OSHA would come in and say you'd need to wear earplugs. We're conducting an experiment on marine animals by exposing them to these high levels of noise, and it's not an experiment we'd allow to be conducted on ourselves.[184]

Recently, population declines in organisms that inhabit the air, land, and sea have been taking place so swiftly that it's very distressing for observers. Birds, mammals, and amphibians are becoming extinct 1000 to 10,000 times faster than they did before humans began dominating the planet.[185] Those of us who are middle-aged or older can recall declines we have personally witnessed in animal, insect, or plant species in our bioregions.

If I seemed to have been taking the decline of horseshoe crab populations to heart in previous parts of this book, it's because I've witnessed it myself. I grew up on the North Shore of Long Island, within walking distance of a small sheltered bay where I spent much of my free time. In my childhood, these prehistoric creatures could almost always be seen cruis-

---

[184] Sometimes, the disruption to the natural world seems to be punitive sacrifice exacted upon it; a lashing out as revenge for the fates suffered by innocent people. Death came to thousands of humans from the skies, and those who grieve their loss are reciprocating and multiplying it because they haven't learned to mourn without shaking a fist.

"Every year on September 11, the sky above New York City is pierced by two columns of intense blue light. This annual art installation, known as Tribute in Light, commemorates the terrorist attacks of 2001, with the ascending beams standing in for the fallen Twin Towers. Each is produced by 44 xenon bulbs with 7,000-watt intensities. Their light can be seen from 60 miles away. From closer up, onlookers often notice small flecks, dancing amid the beams like gentle flurries of snow. Those flecks are birds. Thousands of them.

This annual ritual unfortunately occurs during the autumn migratory season, when billions of small songbirds undertake long flights through North American skies. Navigating under cover of darkness, they fly in such large numbers that they show up on radar. By analyzing meteorological radar images, Benjamin Van Doren showed that Tribute in Light, across seven nights of operation, waylaid about 1.1 million birds. The beams reach so high that even at altitudes of several miles, passing birds are drawn into them. Warblers and other small species congregate within the light at up to 150 times their normal density levels. They circle slowly, as if trapped in an incorporeal cage. They call frequently and intensely. They occasionally crash into nearby buildings.

Migrations are grueling affairs that push small birds to their physiological limit. Even a night-long detour can sap their energy reserves to fatal effect. So whenever 1,000 or more birds are caught within Tribute in Light, the bulbs are turned off for 20 minutes to let the birds regain their bearing. But that's just one source of light among many, and though intense and vertical, it shines only once a year. At other times, light pours out of sports stadiums and tourist attractions, oil rigs and office buildings. It pushes back the dark and pulls in migrating birds." See Yong

[185] International Union for the Conservation of Nature Red List: "Species Extinction—The Facts." The IUCN points out that unlike the previous five known extinction waves in geological history, the present one has been caused almost entirely by a single species—ours.

ing along the sand in shallow waters. Then, during the nights of the full or new moons in May or June, they would swarm out of the water, using their long tails to flip themselves, or else floating or walking up onto the shore. The soft clacking of the legs and carapaces of these glistening multitudes was a lively counterpoint to the hum and whisper of the soft waves of the Long Island Sound.

The males scope out females with one or more of their ten eyes, then they hook themselves to a female's shell. The females crawl up onto the shore, pulling their mates along, and then the males fertilize the eggs laid into the sand of the intertidal zone. After the spawning rituals end, they all then tumble or glide back into the depths. This scene played out for more than 450 million years, during which time Earth witnessed several major ice ages, the formation and breaking up of the supercontinent Pangaea, and the evolution and destruction of the dinosaurs. But now it's becoming rare even to see their dead shells wash up.

While this species of horseshoe crabs is specific to certain coastal areas, many people across the world remember how a summer bicycle ride inevitably meant bugs in our eyes, nose, and mouth; a summer drive always meant later scrubbing their splattered bodies off our car windshields. According to entomologists Francisco Sánchez-Bayo and Kris Wyckhuys, insect populations began declining at the beginning of the 20th century. That process then accelerated mid-century, and it reached truly "alarming proportions" over the last two decades. At present, more than 40% of insect species are currently in decline, and a third are endangered. They report that insects' rate of extinction is eight times faster than that of mammals, birds and reptiles, and the best data available indicates the total body mass of the world's insects is declining by a "precipitous" 2.5% a year. As much as they may seem like pests at times, insects are ubiquitous: they are the most varied and abundant animals on Earth, and together outweigh humanity by 17 times. Moreover, they are "essential for the proper functioning of all ecosystems, the researchers say, as food for other creatures, pollinators and recyclers of nutrients."[186] Human activity—including urbanization, the removal of habitat such as trees and shrubs to make way for agricul-

---

[186] See Sánchez-Bayo and Wyckhuys cited in Carrington.

ture, climate change, and the heavy use of increasingly devastating pesticides—is to blame, and this is happening worldwide.

A 2014 report by World Wildlife Fund estimated that the numbers of animals living on the land and in marine ecosystems have faced equal rates of decline, but of course there is variation among types and species. Predatory fish—the large species that people most frequently eat—have declined around 75% over the past hundred years, while their prey species have actually increased. (And that's despite the fact that these smaller fish are used for fish meal, oil, and other products.)[187] At present, 82 % of the species of fish exploited by fisheries are below sustainable yield levels, and 87% of these are in the "very bad" category, which means their biomass is less than 20% of what would be needed for maximal sustainable fishery catches. Even animals such as the common octopus, previously thought to have high reproductive rates, are not equal to the pressure from overfishing.[188] A review of 14,705 individual surveys in 87 countries shows that coral reef cover has decreased by more than half since the 1950s, due to the effects of ocean warming, as well as of overfishing, pollution, and new diseases.[189] Freshwater fish may be in even more trouble: a global assessment found that populations of migratory freshwater fish declined 76 % between 1970 and 2016. Worse, this data may not depict the entire extent of the threat to them: much information is missing from tropical regions, where fish are overexploited, as well as being forced to cope with habitat loss, habitat degradation, and climate change.[190]

Zoologists have warned that amphibians (frogs, toads, and salamanders) are threatened worldwide by pathogens capable of devastating their global populations. Many species have gone into steep decline, and at least 100 have become extinct due to a fungal disease called chytrid (chytridiomycosis) over the past thirty years. However, there is another type of pathogen, called ranaviruses, that interacts with the various forms of chytrid, causing much worse effects than the either pathogen could on its own. As bad as it

---

[187] See Christensen et al.
[188] See Samurović.
[189] See Greenfield.
[190] See Lovgren.

is when species disappear, the overall amphibian numbers are also of concern because of the loss of their contribution to ecosystems. Tadpoles eat algae, which reduces the potential for algal blooms, and adult frogs eat mosquitos, which can spread diseases of concern to humans. Amphibians also serve as food for other animals, such as birds.[191]

Bird populations are also in continual and accelerating decline. Threats such as domestic cats, collisions with buildings, declining insect populations (probably largely due to pesticides), and increasingly erratic weather and storms have contributed to their attrition. Information on bird populations is collected by volunteer bird watchers, as well as by radar weather data which is able to record the biomass of migrating birds. An analysis of both sources indicates that the biomass of birds migrating in the spring dropped by 14 percent over the last 11 years. Multiple independent lines of evidence indicate that the overall avian population of North American has declined by 29% since 1970. That's more than one in four birds, across species groups including songbirds, long-distance migratory birds, and even "common" birds like sparrows.[192]

Bird communities have declined in almost all ecological zones, with grassland birds having decreased by 53% over the past 50 years. For some species, the numbers are even worse: six out of every ten wood thrushes, three out of every four eastern meadowlarks and nine out of every ten evening grosbeaks have vanished.[193] Some of the factors driving bird population crises are linked to climate change phenomena. For instance, bird watchers in some American states have reported entire flocks of migrating birds falling out of the sky—dead—in the wake of unusually large and ferocious wildfires in 2020. The necessity of changing migration routes to avoid the blazes was one factor, but the birds also must cope with changing habits in the insects they feed on, which are also driven by changes in climate and weather, as well as changes in their habitat. Migration routes developed over long time spans—in concert with factors such as weather patterns and the availability of food sources—are becoming impossible to

---

[191] See McKie.
[192] See Daniel Becker, cited in Ansari, and also see Weston, and Newton. I owe Brendan Myers a debt of gratitude for these three references, which I found in a draft of his forthcoming work *The Circle of Life is Broken*. Also see Holden.
[193] See Dubow.

navigate. "The fact that we're finding hundreds of these birds dying, just kind of falling out of the sky is extremely alarming ... The volume of carcasses that we have found has literally given me chills," one student from New Mexico State University told a *Guardian* reporter in 2020.

There are also combined effects, such as the loss of seed-spreading species of animals impacting the ability of plants to reproduce in their habitats. Animals that eat fruits and then spread seeds in little fertilizer packets of droppings "offer an all-inclusive transportation service for half the world's flora." University of York biologist Chris D. Thomas has observed that two thirds of all animal species are living somewhere they didn't live fifty years ago, and he predicts that the overlap between "historical" distribution with new habitat ranges will decrease to nearly zero in the next century.[194] As the animals die off or migrate as a result of climate change and other anthropogenic factors, the plants are left behind. For example, they may need to shift to a different temperature range up or down a mountain by a few tens of meters per year. The speed at which suitable climate zones move across the landscape has become faster, and therefore more challenging for plants to keep up with, since they cannot walk, crawl, fly, or swim to new locations.[195]

The logic of exploiting whatever is lower on the Great Chain of Being didn't stop when it reached humanity. The history of colonialism is a history of the displacement of people who were ranked lower—in either biological or theological terms—from their traditional homelands, for the capture of commodifiable "resources" or to acquisition of land for growing commodity crops. The process is now coming full circle. Glenn Albrecht elegantly illustrates this in an interview with a man whose ancestors had fled environmental disaster in England to seek a new life in New South Wales, Australia:

> One of the reasons they left the north of England was on the physician's recommendation because they were suffering from respiratory problems and consumption ... The child mortality rate was pretty high ... They had steam engines roaring past the house and black smoke and soot. Yes, it's gone round in a big circle. It took a hundred and fifty

---

[194] Cited by White, 38.
[195] See Kimbrough.

years, they came here to get away from it, and they did. They said what a wonderful country it is and it's caught up, the industrial revolution's caught us again, we've got the same trouble. Where do we go? Patagonia or somewhere?[196]

As we move into what looks like a sixth mass extinction event, let's not get too comfortable[197] with the idea that this only affects creatures that humans may think rank lower than themselves. According to a report based on the largest such study ever undertaken, in 750 locations in 43 countries, which was published in *The Lancet Planetary Health*, five million people die every year due to abnormal temperatures, accounting for 9.43% of global annual deaths.[198] According to a study published in 2019 in the European Heart Journal, 8.8 million people (including 800,000 Europeans) are killed each year by air pollution, mostly caused by burning fossil fuels. Another study claimed that one out of five deaths worldwide, and one out of three in eastern Asia, were caused by air pollution in 2018.[199] Additionally, the Food and Agriculture Organization (FAO) estimates that 5 million children die every year from hunger, while (in 2018) 159 million children suffer from stunted growth and 50 million were experiencing acute malnutrition. Worldwide hunger had been declining for a while, but it has been resurgent recently.[200]

To put these figures into the context of social and political priorities, it took two years for the official global death toll from Covid-19 to reach 5.5 million. Yet where's the news coverage of the millions of the victims of climate change and air pollution? Where are the desperate polemics that we could be doing something about this but aren't? Where are the Facebook profile frames? Where is the blaming, shaming, and scapegoating? Oddly, there is only an uncomfortable silence.

---

[196] Albrecht, 52.

[197] Actually, maybe it won't be comfortable at all. In his forthcoming work, Brendan Myers warns of a great diminishment in the satisfaction of our most basic biological need—breathing. "... since the year 2000, the global average atmospheric concentration of carbon dioxide has risen by an average of twenty parts per million (ppm) every year; this is the fastest rate of increase in the last 800,000 years. In May of 2018, the Mauna Loa Atmospheric Baseline 10 Observatory detected a concentration of 411.25 ppm, the highest ever recorded up to that time. In the 19th century, before the industrial revolution, global CO_2 concentration was about 280 ppm during warm periods, and about 180 during ice ages; the current rising trend is 100 times faster than any rising trend since the end of the last ice age, around 11,700 years ago. The significance of these facts is not only that CO_2 has heat-retention properties which contribute to a global greenhouse effect. A human being exposed to CO_2 levels of 2,000 ppm or higher will experience nausea, headaches, disorientation, and insomnia. If that level became the global average, then we would lose the cognitive capacity to sustain civilization. At 5,000 ppm or higher, we die."

[198] See Ferreira writing for *Vice* for a simpler presentation, and Zhao et. al. for the original article.

[199] Cited by Solnit, 69.

[200] Cited by Eisenstein, 18.

The idea that we are separate from what we consume, and from the life forms that populate the lands we live in, is based in delusion. We must keep in mind that the accelerated pace of our activities is destroying ecosystems, creating massive losses of biodiversity, and—as if that were not reason enough to reconsider our behavior—also threatening our continued existence.

The French structuralist anthropologist Levi-Strauss famously proclaimed "animals are good to think with," by which he meant they provided humans with rich material for comparison and contrast that we then use to structure our mental and social lives. Some of the earliest cave art depicts animals, humans, and humans who seem to be dressed as animals or are in an animal trance. Societies have used insights gained from animals to emulate them or to set themselves apart. They have found metaphors for birth, death, initiations into clans or other social groups (often styled after animals), and for many other rites and mysteries.

We are killing them in unprecedented numbers. The declines are visible everywhere, but we are failing to draw the obvious conclusion. They not only share, but also constitute, our physical world in the most material, real ways. In addition, as many traditional cultures and as the Freudians have pointed out, they participate in a porous flow between our inner and outer worlds. As we kill them, we kill off vital parts of ourselves, mentally, physically, socially, and spiritually.

What is the value, as compared with the market price, of salamanders, wolves, free-range bison, rhesus macaques, horseshoe crabs, and all the other organisms that are enmeshed with them in their ecosystems? Aldo Leopold remarked: "The last word in ignorance is the man who says of an animal or plant: 'what good is it?'"

Are the cynics right that "money talks, and bullshit walks"? I would hate to think so. As Gregory Bateson poignantly remarked in his book, *Mind and Nature*:

> What is the pattern which connects the crab to the lobster and the orchid to the primrose and all four of them to me? And me to you? And the two of us to the mysterious universe unfolding around us?[201]

---

[201] Bateson, 8.

Unheimlich Maneuvers[202]

In *The Structural Study of Myth* (1955), Claude Levi-Strauss proclaimed: "mythical thought always progresses from the awareness of oppositions towards their resolution." The stories we are examining mediate just such a resolution, that of the relationship between humans and the land. The crucial realization is that the two are intrinsically woven together. As we saw in the tale of Sir Gawain and Lady Ragnelle, it is the lack of awareness of this interwoven state which provides space for dramatic tension in stories before the two elements are reconciled. This ambiguous, liminal space of unawareness is where subtle messages are sent and received.

Ideas or individual and collective fantasies about animals tell us much about ourselves and the relationships we try to have with these creatures. However, they can also reflect realities that aren't so easily accessible in our ordinary states of mind. Joseph Dodds puts it like this: "it is likely that on at least some level the animal ambassadors in our patients' dreams reflect the effects of the ecological crisis, as the 'hyperobject' of climate change impacts our minds, individually and collectively."[203]

Any animal might be the bearer of an ecological message when interpreted with a mythic mindset. In particular, the unexpected appearance of

---

[202] As anyone who has visited a restaurant knows, the Heimlich maneuver, which is named after the thoracic surgeon Dr. Henry Heimlich, consists of abdominal thrusts applied to someone who is choking to help them disgorge something stuck in their throat. *Unheimlich* maneuvers are the sometimes involuntary experiences through which something that has been repressed (stuck) in the psyche comes up to the surface of awareness. Hopefully, these too have a beneficial effect.

[203] Joseph Dodds (2012) "Animal Totems and Taboos," 4.

deer often heralds a parting of a veil between the sensed and the intuited, as well as the the individual and the ecological. I have already discussed the otherworldly symbolism of the color white, and I illustrated the curses and taboos with which the figure of the white deer is hedged. Also, in an earlier part of the book, I suggested one reason deer are associated with the dead and ancestral lore may be that, thanks to the longevity of hunting tales, deer have long been associated with ancient lifestyles. This means that when a deer—*in particular one that is white*—unexpectedly appears, it can be interpreted as a symbol of something extraordinary that has faded from our world, and it seems to present an invitation to take on a perilous quest. One who encounters the animal may have a feeling of being in the presence of something both disturbingly alien and all too familiar, which is what psychologists call the "uncanny."

The Uncanny and the *Unheimlich*

The concept of the uncanny was most famously developed by Sigmund Freud and the psychoanalytical tradition, and it has been adopted into literary scholarship for analyzing works that deal with fear, horror, the supernatural, and themes belonging to Gothic and fantastical genres. In Freud's classic 1919 treatise on the uncanny (*unheimlich* in German), he first discusses the contemporary definition of *heimlich* (native, familiar, and domestic), and then refers to Daniel Sanders' 1860 dictionary of the German language, which provides some of the older definitions of *heimlich* that had become obsolete. Previously, in addition to the connotations of the family and the home, *heimlich* also referred to domestic or tamed animals. Bearing the latter definition in mind, it is clear that the sudden and unexpected appearance of a deer is much more *un*heimlich than the sudden appearance of, for instance, an escaped sheep.

What does this feel like? With a poet's knack of dreaming while he is awake and sharing the vision, Ted Hughes' 1973 poem, titled "Roe Deer," seems a late echo of the theme of a sacred messenger's irruption into the contemporary world (even if the message is no longer entirely legible): the recipient knows that he has been called, but doesn't know how to respond.

Hughes is traveling along a road "in the dawn-dirty light," a liminal time of day, and it was additionally during "the biggest snow of the year." The big flakes swirling around seem to create conditions where objects and their surroundings disintegrate in "all ways." Two darkly silhouetted deer suddenly appear:

> They happened into my dimension
> The moment I was arriving just there.

Why wasn't Hughes in his own dimension just before the deer came into view? Perhaps he had been distracted by thoughts or memories, and the unexpected appearance of the animals in the road before him brought him back to presence in his body and the place itself. It felt to Hughes as if the deer were there seeking him, expecting him to "remember some password or sign." Each element present (deer, trees, the poet himself) was no longer what it was supposed to be: everything was both "disintegrating" and full of potential. However, it was just a fleeting moment, and the "dawn inspiration" that had drawn the veil between this sensitive, open awareness and a more ordinary one was closed again by snow, and mundane reality was reasserted.[204]

Something was extraordinary about the deer's appearance during the snowstorm and about the haunting way they regarded him. Recalling Baudelaire, Hughes is approaching Nature through forests filled with *symbols observing him*, communicating by means that can seem equally clear and obscure. Something opened up here between the poet and the deer. He doesn't say just what it is, but this sudden flash of awareness of a sentience in which he, the deer, and possibly some broader field participate seemed to be the revelation.

When what we take for "ordinary" conditions disintegrate, this potential can be revealed. I, too, once had an uncanny experience with an apparition of a deer, on a dark evening in November when the trees were bare of leaves. I was driving my children home from a nearby village where we had been visiting friends, and I had just rounded a very dangerous bend in the road. For some reason, my eyes drifted upwards to where the trees' naked

---

[204] From *A Ted Hughes Bestiary*, 103.

branches met over the road, and I was surprised to see what looked like the head of a stag clearly outlined by the branches, with a kind of a wreath around it.

I hit the brakes to get a better look at this unusual sight, and just at that moment a magnificent stag (of flesh and blood) leapt out of the tangle on the right. It passed directly in front of my car and bounded to the other side. Had I not seen the uncanny vision and braked for it, we would have had a painful and possibly fatal collision with the animal.

I drive along this road nearly every day, and I have looked above the road many times for the shape of a stag's head in the branches, but I have never seen it again. The most restrained interpretive framework is that there was a connection between my unconscious mind and the deadly danger in the immediate environment: my brain needed to see a legible symbol in order to justify the reflexive action of smashing down the brake pedal. But—I suspect there is more to this.

The *Heimlich* and *Unheimlich*

Returning to the discussion of Freud's pair of terms, it is very curious that *heimlich* was also used sometimes to refer to things that are secret or concealed, such a clandestine love affair, and the *"heimlich* art" was magic. That is: folk magic and charms, not church magic or formal ceremonial magic. *Heimlich* thus gives the impression of a contronym: a word that has exactly opposite meanings, because it refers both to "that which is familiar and congenial, and ... that which is concealed and kept out of sight." Freud comments:

> *Unheimlich* is only used customarily, we are told, as the contrary of the first signification [i.e., the domestic, familiar, and cozy], and not of the second [that which is hidden] ... we notice that Schelling says something which throws quite a new light on the concept of the "uncanny," one which we had certainly not awaited. According to him, everything is uncanny that ought to have remained hidden and secret, and yet comes to light.

He then cites the entry from Grimm's dictionary, which states *unheimlich* means free from ghostly influences, and then he arrives at the crux of the paradox: "Thus, *heimlich* is a word the meaning of which develops towards an ambivalence, until it finally coincides with its opposite, *unheimlich*. *Unheimlich* is in some way or other a sub-species of *heimlich*."[205] So rather than being a true contronym, we see that *heimlich* is so capacious that it contains its opposite, which is only partially concealed, or rather "estranged" through the process of repression.

Timothy Morton applies a similar nested understanding of the concepts of *heimlich* and *unheimlich*, stating that the most familiar places seem to have the deepest secrets. Many genres of literature and film (including Gothic, horror and folk horror, mystery, and other related styles) use tropes of people who are drawn into events that cause them to look deeper into the hidden aspects of a place, one which seems tranquil but conceals dark secrets. However, he claims, ecological awareness—*as such*—is dark-uncanny, or weird: "it has a twisted, looping form,"[206] because there is always so much that we are unaware of right where we are, no matter where that is.

How capacious is our home—I mean, in the broadest possible sense of the world that everyone calls home? As I already discussed in a footnote in "The Nature of Myth, The Myth of Nature," the word ecology was coined by Ernst Haeckel from the Greek *oikos* (house, household) and *logia* (discourse). However, the term ecology contains a fundamental ambivalence: is it the *logos* of *oikos* (meaning the logical system of the environment) or the *oikos* of *logos* (the house that embraces human logic, or the intellectual system)? As Pierre Madl points out, "the former assumes a human rational and logical imposition on the universe, while the latter suggests human acceptance of the universe as the way it operates."

The relevance of psychoanalytic modeling to understanding ecology is particularly evident in the case of "elemental catastrophes" (i.e., floods, epidemics, etc.), because this tradition habitually views mind and environment as looped or intertwined. The Scientific Revolution crowned us with victory prematurely. We believed that we would no longer be at Nature's whim, at the mercy of plagues, droughts and failed harvests, or catastrophic storms and fires; and we no longer ascribed them to Divine

---

[205] Freud, 2-4, emphases in the original.
[206] Morton, 11; 4.

whims or punishments. We believed that, if we understood the causes of these events through science, we could manipulate them through technology and help more people survive and prosper.[207] And, as I have already discussed at length, we have mostly failed to appreciate how our species bears some of the responsibility for increasingly inhospitable conditions on Earth.

As I wrote in the context of pandemics, people show very little ability or even willingness to grapple with natural disasters. Such disasters are often ignored in historical retrospection, and only rarely memorialized. We prefer clear narratives with victors and heroes in them: protagonists, not mass villains or mass victims. But Nature doesn't provide these: "Nature is both reassuring and terrifying, an ambivalent, uncanny terrain. Thought and earth move together, become destabilized, flow and erupt."[208] As participants in a force of nature, we are terrifyingly *depersonalized*.

Psychoanalytical theory and Timothy Morton's understanding of Object Oriented Ontology (OOO) both allow space for the dance between symbols, mind(s), and reality. There can be no banishing of a certain magical principle: reality is always-already both mysterious and magical, "because beings withdraw and because beings influence each other aesthetically, which is to say at a distance."[209] The thrill of meeting an uncanny apparition is like the chill that runs down our spine when, as the folk tradition has it, "someone is walking on our grave." This is because the uncanny arises as an effect, when the boundaries we have set "between human and nonhuman, and living and dead, are threatened, blurred, or erased." The apparition of a vulnerable, mutant deer that stands out brightly and distinctly from its surroundings is a reminder of the flexible seams between what Félix Guattari calls the "three ecologies of mind, nature, and society, with flows and feedbacks circulating and undulating between human and nonhuman, semiotic and material, individual and collective, organic and technological, living, and non-living."[210]

---

[207] See Merchant, 737. It is interesting to note, as Timothy Morton ruefully does on p. 14 of *Dark Ecology*, that insurance companies still refer to such events as "acts of God"—despite the large helping hand humanity provides in giving rise to them (via global warming, destruction of biodiversity, etc.) The crucial distinction is that they were not directly caused by the individual policyholder as a sole actor.

[208] Joseph Dodds (2020), 3.

[209] Morton, 17.

[210] Joseph Dodds (2020), 1.

Paradoxically, irrational dreams and uncanny (*unheimlich*) visions bring us into an expanded realm of the *heimisch*, the known-and-familiar. This process does not take place through habituation (because such apparitions are rare), but through an inspired resolution of the tension between the artificially separated pair. It's a mediation between psyche, symbol, and the other beings with whom we share space. It occurs in a way the constitutes worlds: territories and relationships between independent—yet interconnected—beings contained within them.[211]

Expanding Our Awareness

How does an expanded ecological awareness arise? In Hughes' poetic vision, it was the "disintegration" effect of snow that blurred the boundaries between the commonplace and the extraordinary. Such an awareness can also foster practical realization. For example, in the case of my encounter with the stag that leapt into the road in front of my car, it was evident people's roads have encroached on the deer's territory, not the other way around.

At times, divisions between the world of physical objects that move in space, and deeper, underlying powers or realities can seem very clearly defined; however, our experiences in dreams show us they are not so distant. For this reason, people have long attempted to cultivate dreams that would bring wisdom: either in symbolic form, or through contact with gods or spirits able to communicate with the unconscious mind.

The ancient Elysian oracles involved white stags in their myths and symbolism, using them to solicit supernatural guidance. This is evidenced by Brut the Trojan's account of visiting the island of Leogrecia, where he received a moon-oracle message while sleeping on a newly-flayed hide of a white hart whose blood had been poured on the sacrificial fire.[212] Fortunately, such practices are not required: images, symbols, and metaphors can appear spontaneously. They also appear when cultivated by more humane methods, such as meditating on a particular image or a verse before drifting off to sleep, or by trance, "journeying," or lucid dreaming tech-

---

[211] Joseph Dodds (2012), 3-4.
[212] Graves, 217.

niques. Sometimes, the symbol is a living animal. If its appearance is unexpected and seems numinous, it can facilitate a flash of recognition that something has come bearing a message. The next important thing is to interpret it.

Humans have a powerful ability to transmit and receive symbolic messages: it is simply one of our faculties, such as walking, swimming, or singing. This may come more easily to some than to others, but it is hardly the preserve of specialists (e.g., shamans, psychoanalysts, professional artists). This is a skill that can be trained through attention to all forms of what Briana Saussy calls the sacred arts, which include stories, poetry, visual and media arts, live performances, and rituals of every kind. In his originally unpublished notebooks, Friedrich Nietzsche called the drive toward the formation of metaphors "the most fundamental human drive." However, he thought of this mental function, which "finds its discharge in myth and art," as a kind of irrationality that is suppressed by rational, truth-seeking acts and concept formation. This drive "continually manifests an ardent desire to refashion the world which presents itself to waking man so that it will be as colorful, irregular, lacking in results and coherence, charming, and eternally new as the world of dreams."[213]

This libidinous metaphor-making impulse is embedded in language just as much as in the mind, and it is not only pleasurable but also very functional. Philosopher Owen Barfield observed that, contrary to what many would expect, metaphor conveys more aliveness and allows for more meanings to emerge than literal descriptions. "The fact that it does not work like this says something important about metaphors—that they might be powerful transformational enchantments ... and something even more important about the universe in general: if 'aliveness' encapsulates it better, *then the whole thing is probably alive.*"[214]

Meanings can be multivalent, shifty, and tied to personal stories and interpretations, which is all the more reason to see them as messages that come from a living matrix. When associations are too rote (long things = penises for dogmatic Freudians; something dark is a "shadow" for Jun-

---

[213] See Alwan.
[214] White, 65.

gians; a white chicken feather that falls across your path is an angelic message for New Age Christians), it can be a sign of the recipient not looking closely enough at the context of what is being presented. This reduces the agency and power of who ever or whatever may be trying to communicate something, a message imbued with more transformative power than a few schemes or stories we've already memorized and look for.

Not seeing beyond ourselves can also hamper our ability to heal. As shamanic practitioner and medical anthropologist Alberto Villodo has pointed out, we never heal ourselves from within our own stories.[215] There needs to be an element or motif that emerges from a larger field, one we were not aware of, and whose appearance or transformation surprises us.

Meaning-making through metaphors is omnipresent in folk stories, myths, and classic fairy tales. Many have criticized the popular fairy tales over the past half century for their focus on marriage as a goal or end state for young female characters, which is entirely justified from a social perspective. Stories for young people where the relationship patterns are more diverse have been welcomed by parents and others who are tired of the old "princess bride" monoculture for girls. However, as philosopher Wes Alwan points out, the traditional psychological conception of libido is far more all-embracing and all-pervading than romantic love, and it deserves to be recognized as a force that, paradoxically, roots a person more firmly in reality.

While Nietzsche thought making metaphors was a fundamental drive, Freud saw libido as the first impulse which precedes the act of metaphor-making. In dreams and fantasies, "certain ideas or images become imbued with meaning and emotional resonance," because libido has become attached to them. This libido soon meets with obstacles that are either imposed by reality or by conscience, which makes it "jump, associatively, from one idea to another like it (metaphor) or to another contiguous with it (metonymy)."

However, it is not only what we want that changes: because we can't always get what we want, or at least not right away, libido must work on the psyche itself. We therefore "alter ourselves to the extent that we can't alter

---

[215] See White, 144; 213.

the world according to our wishes. It is the history of our particular course of love that tells us how and why we became who we are. Love is character."[216] A popular formulation of this idea is found in the quote "What you get by reaching your goals is not nearly so important as what you become by reaching them." Who is the author of this nugget of wisdom that is often cited in self-help memes and even in books? Attributions include Henry David Thoreau and Johann Wolfgang von Goethe, but the real source seems to be the motivational speaker Zig Ziglar.[217] The idea he conveys in this formulation has escaped its pedigree and established itself as a piece of feral folklore with the borrowed haloes of intellectual heroes. And that's wonderful: the camouflage allows it to thrive and proliferate.

One of the most courageous responses to fear—be that fear of the unknown, fear of an uncanny blending of conditions and categories, or fear of anything else—is to reach out with love and to be open to receiving it. A love which is not mere sentiment or possessive attachment, but an active process of creative engagement. This isn't just being open to reading symbols or receiving "messages"—it means merging with the field in which messages are transmitted. Love of the world around us may be innate, as I will discuss in the context of Edward O. Wilson's "biophilia hypothesis" in a subsequent chapter. As Sophie Strand so eloquently describes in her essay "Make It A Love Story," an ecstatic eroticism is all-pervasive in the living world:

> The forest is densely particulate—with mildew, with spores, with mothdust from wing beats, with water molecules, with slow ropes of sunlight strained and frayed through the pine needles. A ghost pipe glistens against the shadows, still in curled supplication to the Russala mycelia that feeds her spectral body. Nearby the underground fungi of the Russala fruits: the waxy red mushroom wears a hat of bleached leaves it has pushed up from under. I think of the "parasitic relation-

---

[216] Ibid. Also see Marina Warner who, in her characterization of wonder tales, (a broader category of stories than fairy tales), writes that a certain series of transformations is typical: "After wonder, consolation; after inquiry, resolution; after shapeshifting or metamorphosis, the happy ending," Warner (1994), 6. And this is one of the reasons why these stories are so important: they model the character traits and behavior that lead to improvement in one's relationships and life conditions. As the famous quote (spuriously) attributed to Albert Einstein says: "If you want your children to be intelligent, read them fairy tales. If you want them to be more intelligent, read them more fairy tales."

[217] See Quote Investigator, "What You Get By Reaching Your Goals ... "

ship" between the ghost pipe and its fungal partner. I think of all the strands of mycelium pooling and looping below my feet. Kissing into elm trees. Sucking in sugar and dispensing minerals. Always hand holding. Always interrogative, inter-species, constituting a lovemaking that doesn't strictly belong to just the fungi or plants or trees or bacteria involved.

When a being that is constituted by a mutualism mates with another being constituted by a mutualism how many beings are making love? How many species create a reproductive event? … The world is plush with love. Anarchic love that wears no face. Love that bites and pricks and explodes morphologies. Love that turns our own bodies into a meshwork of molecular eroticisms. Love that needs no nuclear couple … Sometimes you have to write yourself into another body. An ecosystem of bodies … I have not been inside a love story. I have been a love story: my very body a clamorous, complicated interplay of beings disagreeing, singing, swooning, and melting together. I don't know where the love goes. But I know that every time I breathe out, it overflows.[218]

If we are mentally predisposed to love and take pleasure in participating in the world through our senses, the blocks imposed on this are cultural, which means they are mutable. And the dysfunctions experienced when individuals or cultures are prevented from immediate engagement can therefore be healed.

---

[218] See Sophie Strand, *The Flowering Wand: Rewilding the Sacred Masculine* (2022).

The Hart-Breaking Work of Erring Stag Genes[219]

White deer are rare, but they can be found haunting the wild. They are more likely to appear where their movement is constrained by natural factors—such as lakes and rivers—or by human constructions such as highways, tall fences, and similar. Most of the animals are leucistic (that is, they have reduced pigmentation, but unlike a true albino their eyes, hooves, and noses have normal coloration instead of being pink) or piebald (a creature that has large white splotches on an otherwise brown coat). And, confusingly, some wildlife biologists and hunters refer to the leucistic animals as "piebald," even if their entire coat is white.

True albinos are considerably rarer than the former two types. However, what they all have in common is vulnerability: when they shine so brightly against their surroundings, they are more visible to predators and poach-

---
[219] With apologies to Dave Eggers.

ers, particularly at night. This is why these animals are sometimes called "Judas deer" by hunters: they reveal the location of their herds. In addition to their luminous pelts, these deer may have additional handicaps that decrease their chances of survival, such as partial or complete blindness, deafness, or endocrine abnormalities. Most don't survive their first year, unless they are assisted by people in a managed ecosystem.

Humans play a strong role in bringing these mutants to life, even if we are largely unaware of it. This is because the rare, recessive genes that create leucistic, piebald, or albino coats are more likely to propagate when there has been inbreeding, and this happens when humans have divided up their habitat and prevented normal gene flow. We see a kind of symbolic prefiguring of this in the story of Peredur when he is asked to kill a one-horned stag that is harming the best trees in the forest, killing every animal he meets, and causing the other creatures to die of hunger on the island where he lives. Additionally, the stag causes drought by drinking up the fish pond every night, leaving the fish exposed so that they die before the water refills.

Of course, it is unrealistic that a single monstrous animal could destroy so much of a habitat and exterminate so many other animals. In this story, it also seems that causes and effects have been reversed, which is not surprising on a magical island where many typical symbols and relationships are inverted. However, the element of a tightly constrained natural range (because this beast lives in a forest on an island) rings true. And while it is absurd to imagine one animal could damage the land to such an extent, a general overpopulation of deer is indeed a very destructive force.

A superb example of the proliferation of mutants is the population of white deer that has arisen on the premises of the old Seneca Munitions Depot, in the Finger Lakes region of New York State. The 10,600 acres of the nuclear munition storage facility are tightly enclosed by high fences topped with barbed wire. This means that animals from the surrounding lands couldn't get in, and those that lived inside the enclosure couldn't get out. The result was a considerable degree of inbreeding among the confined deer. Since 1951, base commanders have restricted the hunting of white deer, other than culling protocols to prevent them from outnumbering the brown ones (which were also culled to prevent overpopulation).

The result has been the largest known population of white deer on Earth, living in a herd that has comprised up to 300 leucistic and 500-600 brown animals.[220]

Seeing a white deer may be a harbinger of good luck or adventure to a person who sees it,[221] but killing it is supremely unlucky in many cultures. For example, many Native traditions of North America consider such animals to be endowed with special powers, and in some places in Africa, there are taboos on killing white gazelles. In many traditions, as well as in some of the stories presented in this book, only a righteous king may kill the white deer as his royal prerogative, but ordinary hunters may not. It is possible that this seeming paradox is related to ancient customs in which a king is required to commit various kinds of taboo acts in order to concentrate "poison" within himself. Then, if a disaster strikes or seems to be impending, his sacrifice removes this poison, appeases the gods, and restores harmony.[222]

The protection of white deer in the wild is sometimes enshrined in laws, such as in several American states or regions defined politically or in other ways (such as according to the prevalence of chronic wasting disease in the deer population). The desire in some cultures to protect the deer because it is connected to otherworldly forces, or taboos that have either a general or a personal nature (as in the case of an Irish *geas*) are not universal. There are people who simply find the animals beautiful and hate to contemplate them being killed, so they lobby for their protection. However, these views are not shared by some hunters and wildlife biologists, who believe that appeals to sentiment or tradition lack practicality and good judgement. They argue that letting the mutant deer survive and breed will result in weaker overall health for the herd. In some places, state and wildlife-management agencies actively encourage hunters to legally harvest albino deer in order to improve the genetic stock.[223]

---

[220] See Carl Mrozek's article for CBS.

[221] See Dunk.

[222] See Eisenstein, 120.

[223] See Faulkner. Professional wilderness managers (an oxymoron if there ever was one!) find their work hampered by what they refer to as the "Bambi complex," a prevalent mindset that regards nature as a steady state, and wild animals as cute, tame outdoor pets. Alongside this, there is a corresponding resistance to forest-management tools such as culling overpopulation and using fire for controlled burns (see Schulz).

These creatures, which in conditions unaffected by human activities would be vanishingly rare, hold a mirror up to our stewardship. Their presence suggests a state of ecological disruption, pointing to our past violations of the balance of nature and a ghostly foretoken of the future. The deer is fey: marked by death and doomed to die early. Like an uncanny vision or a dream, here a message is struggling to surface. Often, there is only a feeling that one ought not to kill the white deer for a trophy, but the "why" is usually unarticulated, or it is considered a matter of sentimentality and appreciation for beauty. If the animal is killed, its message falls silent: people will once again pass into complete obliviousness, not noting their effects on the landscape that sustains the deer's prey and thus themselves. In other words: don't shoot the messenger, or there may be a terrible price to pay.

There is a story related by a contemporary Lenape storyteller, which has some common themes with the legend of St. Hubertus I recounted in the chapter on myth and literature. This hunter encounters a special deer, and after exchanging gazes filled with understanding, he realizes there are larger spiritual forces that must be respected, that this particular deer is a messenger, and that it is necessary to respect life and give proper offerings.

> In the season of bow hunting, in the year 1970, we went scouting, in particular, for the "legendary" White Deer. For many thousands of years, on what we now refer to as the Delmarva Peninsula, there had been "talk" of the White Deer, not only with the Original peoples, but among the settlers and many generations of mixed bloods, thereafter.
>
> Hunters have told of having "the same dream" of becoming the one who would capture this magnificent four legged creature. They misinterpret the meaning of their dream, not understanding that the dream is for teaching a life lesson.
>
> ... On this day, I went with great trepidation, in search of this spirit, with my husband but only desired to see this creature, for myself. I did not wish to bring this spirit harm and was determined, if we were to see this great White Deer, I would persuade my husband to take no aim.

... we came to the edge of the field at the same time as the great White Deer. My husband became silent and nothing was exchanged between him, me and the great White Deer except looks. The great White Deer did not challenge and showed no fear, but in these precious moments, my husband became a great hunter—a man who now understood he must respect the life of the four legged creatures.

After this encounter, he grew to understand he could no longer take the life of any creature, without making an offering to the Great Spirit. ... As he stood, on the edge of the woodland, he looked directly at my husband and directly toward me. He looked back at my husband and held his gaze. His eyes were stern, but not accusing. When great White Deer was sure my husband understood, he turned back into the woods as quickly and silently as he had appeared.[224]

"Shall We Fit Them With Precious Collars?"

But let us turn now to discussing deer and mutations in a completely different context. In 2020, there was a intense interest in determining whether the new coronavirus had first jumped to human beings from "exotic" species such as bats or pangolins, as well as an obsession with tracing viral occurrence in animal populations. That obsession led to a panic over a mink farm where the infected animals were killed and buried. Then, the dead animals rose up out of their graves due to sloppy grave-digging. However, there is another less "exotic" animal species—far more prevalent and closer at hand—which also hosts the virus.

It has been known for a long time that deer can also serve as hosts for pathogens of concern to humanity, such as bovine tuberculosis, Q fever, chlamydiosis, leptospirosis, campylobacterosis, salmonellosis, and giardiasis. In September 2020, computer models suggested the SARS-CoV-2 virus could bind to and enter deer cells, but no one took much notice. Then, the suspicion was confirmed in a survey of white-tailed deer in the Northeast

---

[224] See Deborah Russell. She adds, after telling the story: "Many tribes and indigenous peoples throughout the world, have this same or similar Holy story. It is one story of wisdom, one that is valid and validated as a truth of our great history. Among native people are the following tribes which relate sightings of the great White Deer; Seneca, Chickasaw, Roanoke, Algonquin, Nanticoke and Pocomoke tribes. Curious enough, in Kamakura, Japan, the "legend of the White Deer" relates to a priest, who saw the White Deer in a cave called 'Byakurokudo' (bya-koo-rok-doh).

Although there are many deer which have white markings and there are albino deer, they are not the great White Deer that is described, above. The great White Deer is not a folk tale, although native people, like all cultures, have stories about animals that were told simply for entertainment and mainly for children. These stories usually teach a lesson or have some moral implication."

and Midwest: 40% of the animals had antibodies suggesting they had been, or still were, infected with the virus. This was trivial in comparison to what a team sampling deer in Iowa between November 2020 and January 2021 found: up to 80% of the deer they examined tested positive. At the peak of the surge, one of the researchers stated, the prevalence of the virus in deer was effectively 50 to 100 times the prevalence in human residents of Iowa at the time.

While the novel coronavirus doesn't seem to make deer sick, this indicates that they have the potential to be a very significant reservoir for it (which means that mutations are likely to arise), and the deer can spread it to humans and domestic animals, both directly and indirectly.[225] White-tailed deer are the most abundant large mammal in North America, and their US population alone may number some 30 million. If tens of millions of deer are functioning as a viral reservoir, the novel coronavirus will never be eradicated, and no radical containment strategies can be successful. The deer often live in close proximity to people, and they come into direct contact with hunters, motorists, wildlife management officers, field researchers, and people engaging in recreation and tourism. There has also been speculation that water sources can also be contaminated with the virus, though this theory is as yet unproven. Such a means of transmission would be more likely between deer and grazing livestock than domestic pets.[226] There is no indication that deer were the first animal to spread the new coronavirus to people, but there is every reason to believe that we will be passing it back and forth in our shared environment, probably perpetually.

The reason why there are more white deer roaming the land than might be expected is the same reason why we'll have to expect the virus to pass freely to ourselves and our livestock: we have removed most of the deer's natural predators from their ecosystems. This results in overpopulation, which has further effects on vegetation (as they overgraze certain species, such as grasses and trees). This, then, affects the habitat afforded to other

---

[225] See the articles by Doucleff for NPR and Shannon, Gresham, and Barton for *The Conversation*.

[226] See Doucleff. The "lack of fire" refers to the abandonment of the older Indigenous practice of creating controlled burns that benefited forests and wildlife. On the transmissibility of coronaviruses between wild ruminants and domestic cattle, and on feces as a source of infection, see Alekseev et al.

species, as well as other ecological factors such as soil erosion. The overpopulation of white-tailed deer has burdened every landscape east of the Mississippi River, and the damage they cause has been overlooked, or even accepted as "natural." In the opinion of three of the editors at Nature.org, "no other threat to forested habitats is greater at this point in time—not lack of fire, not habitat conversion, not climate change. Only invasive exotic insects and disease have been comparable in magnitude."[227]

The absence of predators is a significant cause of the destructive effects of overpopulation. The reintroduction of predators would not only reduce the absolute numbers of deer, but it would also affect their behavior. When predators inhabit a landscape, the prey animals have to be cautious, and they try to keep on the move in order to avoid ambush. This provides a degree of protection to the plants and other organisms that benefit from a habitat without overabundant deer.[228]

Let us look back to the old myths of emperors putting gold collars on white deer to show that the animals were under their protection, and to Lisel Muller's poem, which echoes this motif. I believe she asks the question "shall we fit them with precious collars?" because she wants people to face the fact that the animals have no other option than to consider us their Caesars. No one else can protect them from us, and no one is now protecting us from them.

When we lost the ability to speak to the animals, it led us to ruin their habitats; with the enchantment that once bound us together broken, all that remains is their desperation and our rising fear. The poet is calling us to accountability. She leaves us with the ominous feeling that the animals are closing in us, and they will have the last word.

---

[227] See Pursell, Weldy, and White

[228] See Mentzer. Also see the paper by Darimont et al., which offers a powerful rejoinder to those who say that killing predators is natural or desirable human behavior. In their abstract, the authors state: "Our global survey ... revealed that humans kill adult prey, the reproductive capital of populations, at much higher median rates than other predators (up to 14 times higher), with particularly intense exploitation of terrestrial carnivores and fishes. Given this competitive dominance, impacts on predators, and other unique predatory behavior, we suggest that humans function as an unsustainable 'super predator,' which —unless additionally constrained by managers—will continue to alter ecological and evolutionary processes globally."

Loathly Ladies & the Men Who Love Them

The hart, he loves the high wood;
The hare, she loves the hill.
The knight, he loves his bright sword,
And the lady loves her will.[229]

A loathly lady is a distinctive archetypal figure in English, Welsh, and Irish literature. She shapeshifts from young and fair to and old and unattractive, blighted, or even bestial or monstrous. The way she is received by an unsuspecting young male ruler or adept for the throne—such as a prince or a highborn knight—defines the relationship he is to have with the land during his reign. Passing the test she gives him is, in fact, one of the qualifications to rule.

Medieval Irish tales such as "Sovranty Hag" from the *Coir Anman* manuscript and "Adventures of the Sons of Eochaid Mugmedón" in the *Book of Ballymote* offer typical examples; so does the story told by the character Alisoun in the "Wife of Bath's Tale" from Geoffrey Chaucer's *Canterbury Tales*. Typically, the plot of these stories contains the following sequential ele-

---

[229] Traditional Mother Goose rhyme.

ments: first, there is a transgression upon which judgment is pronounced. The sentence, however, is often suspended. A riddle is posed, and then the loathly lady makes her appearance and selects the lover she wants. After the riddle is solved, a marriage takes place between the hero and the lady, whom he must willingly embrace and please on their wedding night. In the marriage chamber, she presents a beautiful countenance, and after the consummation of their union, the lands and the moral milieu of the realm are restored to their correct order.[230]

The story of Gawain and Ragnelle is a quintessential example of this type of story. The crucial aspect of the loathly lady is that she partakes of both aspects of divine mystery described by the German theologian Rudolf Otto: the *mysterium fascinans* (the aspect of divinity that is beautiful and intriguing) and the *mysterium tremendum* (its polar opposite: the "terrifying, repulsive, and yet inspiring end of the numinous spectrum").[231] Her possession of both of these traits, and her ability to shift their appearance at will, show us that these female characters are much more than ordinary women: there is a religious dimension to their interactions with their mortal partners.

A great number of these stories feature deer,[232] and the deer often functions as a symbol of the relationship between the king or a noble adept and

---

[230] See Heiniger, 315-18; 320. She goes on to describe how the shapeshifting Sovereignty Hag was divided into two fixed figures during the Celtic Revival. She says that James Joyce drew upon the myths in his monumental Ulysses, but with the twist that the loathly lady would grant artistic, rather than territorial, sovereignty to deserving young (male) artists. The frustration that the protagonist Stephen Dedalus experiences is a result of failing to grasp the paradox of the interrelated figures of hag and lovely lady, who are personified in his mother, May Dedalus. May is overloaded with associations not only as Stephen's biological mother, but also as "Mother Church" and "Mother Ireland" and by the dualistic virgin/whore and physical/ethereal associations that the Church-dominated Irish culture struggled with at the time. As Heiniger points out, the artist's mission is to overcome these divisions, because "only by complete submission and abandonment to the repulsive other can the hero find fulfilment and gratification." When Stephen fails to embrace the love of all the multifarious Mother figures, he is haunted by loathly ladies that appear everywhere around him, but he never meets Molly Bloom, the character who best personifies the complete archetype. Dedalus experiences a breakthrough in understanding, but does not produce a literary work on its basis—except for four lines of poetry that describe a prostitute clad in "rancid rags" who seems to shift into a mythical moon goddess (i.e., she seems to be a loathly lady).

There is also a deep connection with the Irish *aisling* tradition, in which a mystic dream or vision of an otherworldly representative of Sovereignty, a *speir-bhean* (sky woman) appears to the hero. The tradition is possibly of very great antiquity, and is preserved in folk stories, poetry, Grail romances where Sovereignty wears the faces of both Grail Maiden and Loathly Lady, and in medieval romances. She often leads the hero directly to the Otherworld, and pours into his cup. And she would ask poets to appeal to Ireland's exiled heroes to come and save her from marriage to an unworthy husband (Matthews, 59, 64, 69). The theme was also taken up in 18th and 19th-century poetry, in which a love for the land and desire for political self-determination was expressed in coded ballads. Any more open expression of Irish patriotism could be punished by death or exile. See O'Donoghue (2022), 109.

[231] See Hunter, 12. Otto may have been describing the Christian god in these terms, but he himself opened the doors to wider applications of the theory when he described the *mysterium tremendum* with an orderly and rational "Apollonian element" and the *mysterum fascinans* with the chaotic and irrepressible "Dionysian element."

[232] There are also strong traces of deer, or perhaps a cult where priestesses represented their goddesses or another important aspect of the land, in many female characters' names that are variations of Elen/Helen. Examples include Elen from the dream of Macsen Wledig, Elaine of Astolat (Tennyson's "Lady of Shalott"), and Ellyne or Elene from Libeaus Desconus (here, she is the partner of Gingalain, who is the son of Gawain and a forest fay named Blanchemal—a Flower Bride name, which is a motif I will discus later on). Gingalain's attributed arms display a white unicorn, which, as I have already mentioned, is a beast that sometimes overlaps with white deer in myths and legends.

the lady of the land. Sometimes, we are told there is a white deer that is supposed to be preserved; or, alternately, it appears to provoke a hero to a challenge and it can only slain by the "right" man, who is able to meet the Otherworldly challenges it guides him to—perhaps because he is the intended recipient of its message.

The story of Gereint and Enid, which is one of the three Welsh romances associated with the *Mabinogion*, is a complex story which I will simplify, focusing on the symbolism of the deer as a promise of a balanced relationship between a man and a woman, and of the two of them with their lands. Bear in mind that in this complex story, each figure has at least one counterpart, so that the Gwenhwyfar's maid is her double; the dwarf represents his lord, the earl; Gereint is taking on Gwalchmai's duties, and Enid represents the goddess of sovereignty. However, since they are all imperfect copies, they have to make mistakes and learn from them.

Gereint and Enid

On Whit Tuesday, one of Arthur's foresters arrived and delivered a report of an unusual stag. He tells the king: "It is pure white, and out of arrogance and pride in its lordliness it will travel with no other animal." Arthur gave orders for it to be hunted, after the custom of his father Uther. His queen, Gwenhwyfar, said she wanted to watch the hunt. Gwalchmai (i.e., Gawain) suggested whoever succeeded in cutting off the stag's head should present it to his lover as a gift. Queen Gwenhwyfar rose late on the day of the hunt and set out to observe the action, attended only by her maid.

When they encountered a richly-dressed woman, a knight, and a dwarf in the woods, the dwarf insulted the queen's maid. A knight named Gereint arrived to defend the maid, and it was decided that he would formally redress the insult to Queen Gwenhwyfar's honor by challenging the earl (who was the dwarf's master) in a joust. In order to participate in this event, which was part of a large festival that had been planned beforehand, Gereint had to bring along a lady in whose honor he would compete. Not having another lady on hand, Gereint asked if he could represent Enid, the daughter of the poor family who had given him lodging. Gereint defeated the earl in the joust, which redeemed Gwenhwyfar's honor, and he arranged for Enid's family's property and titles to be restored. This uplifted Enid socially, making her fit to join courtly society.

Meanwhile, many others were out hunting the white hart. Arthur's hound cornered it, and Arthur slew and beheaded the creature. Back at the court, there were disputes over who should receive the head to give to his lover, but Gwenhwyfar made everyone wait until Gereint returned. When he returned to the court accompanied by Enid, he was royally thanked, and Enid was presented with the stag's head and with elegant clothing from the queen's own wardrobe.

Despite the early potential he showed for chivalrous behavior, after their marriage Gereint proved to be a selfish husband who didn't listen to his wife and didn't seem to like her much, and he dominated and humiliated her. Further adventures followed, and then came a fateful encounter with an otherworldly woman in a misty orchard. He had a change in heart and finally regarded Enid as a true, worthy, equal partner. At the end of their wandering, Gereint and Enid returned to their own lands—which he had now proven himself worthy of administering—and ruled wisely and well thenceforth.[233]

Sadhbh

A contrast to this story of a wife who was found, lost, and then found again is in the Irish tale of Sadhbh, the partner of Fionn mac Cumhail and mother of Oisín. Inverting the order of the plot elements, Sadhbh was lost, found, and then lost again. Also, in this story, the deer needed to be protected rather than hunted down. Like St. Winifred, Sadhbh was also threatened by an aggressive suitor: Fear Doirich, a wicked druid who was one of the Tuatha Dé Danann. Enraged that she rejected his advances, he enchanted the maiden so she looked like a doe. She remained in this form for three years, until one of Fear Doirich's servants took pity on her and told her that if she entered the castle of the Fianna warriors, she would be free from his master's power.

---

[233] Matthews, 135-40; 148. She provides the most important takeaway from the story: "Gereint is rightful lord not only of his own lands, but also of the inner realms belonging to Sovereignty. The seal of his association is set by Enid, Gereint's wife and Sovereignty's representative" (148).

On her journey to Fionn's dwelling she encountered the master's hounds, and he expected them to bring her down, but they did not harm her because they recognized that she was a human enchanted into animal form—just as they were. Sadhbh was restored to her proper form as a lovely maiden once she got inside the castle, and she married Fionn.

Fionn was so enamored of his bride that he neglected all of his other activities, including hunting. Sadhbh became pregnant, and he was overjoyed. However, one day while her husband was at war against the Vikings, Sadhbh was lured away from their home by an illusion created by the wicked Fear Doirich. He struck her with a hazel wand and turned her back into a deer. After Fionn returned home, he searched for Sadhbh for seven years in vain. She was not found, but at the end of this period, a wild boy was discovered in the forest by his faithful hounds, who then immediately went to protect the boy. Fionn recognized his features in the child's face and realized that he must be the child of his lost wife. He named his son Oisín (Young Deer), and the boy grew up to become the greatest of all the Fianna warriors. Sadhbh was never found, and legends tell that she still wanders Ireland's forests.[234]

Arianrhod, Goewin, and the Maidens of the Wells

In Gereint and Enid, the deer had been legitimately taken by Arthur; in the tale, his right to rule is not contested. However, the blessing conferred by the deer's head cannot be transferred automatically. Gereint had proven himself worthy of receiving it through some of his acts; still, he had much to learn about respecting women, and his wife likewise required some personal growth so she could be an equal partner to her husband. This is the proper course of events—tutelary figures put characters on the right path, and they corrected their mindsets and conduct when they erred. However, when a deer is killed by an unworthy hunter and/or maidens are raped, this act is often a symbol of improper attitudes or moral failings not only of

---

[234] The Whiteboys (an underground organization that defended tenant farmers' rights to subsistence farming and opposed exorbitant rents, tithe collection, excessive priests' dues, evictions, and other forms of oppression in 18th century Ireland) invoked Sadhbh as "Queen Sadhbh" as their queen of sovereignty. They issued eviction notices in her name against English and English-sympathetic Irish landlords.

the perpetrator, but also of the king (when the two are not the same). Gawain and Ragnelle provide an example of this theme with the deer woven in, but we also find a fine example without a deer in the story told in the Fourth part of the *Mabinogion*.

In this tale, King Math fab Mathonwy could not rest without dying unless his feet were held in the lap of a maiden or unless he was at war.[235] In other words, the king needed to be connected to the sovereignty of the land, personified in this maiden, whom he had a duty to protect. The alternative was either endless bloody strife or his own death.

Math had a pretty girl named Goewin for his foot maiden, and his nephew Gilfaethwy desired her. Gilfaethwy's brother, Gwydion, created a pretext for a war between the north and south, which meant Math had to leave his court and his foot-maiden. While he was away, the youths assaulted Goewin, and Gilfaethwy raped her in the king's bed. Learning of the crime upon his return, Math punished his nephews by turning them into a series of paired animals, and each time the alternately-sexed nephews would have to mate and bear young together, before being transformed into the next set of beasts.

Math married Goewin, making her his queen to relieve her of the shame of what happened. However, the king still needed a virgin to hold his feet. Gwydion brought his sister Arianrhod before him as a candidate. As a test of her virginity, Math bade her step over his magician's rod. She didn't pass the test: she immediately gave birth to a boy, Dylan ail Don (his father was Don, a sea god), who fled to the sea, and then to a blob-like entity that eventually becomes Lleu Llaw Gyffes. Arianrod was humiliated both by the ritual test and also the forced births. Dylan was then killed by another uncle, and Arianrhod placed curses or destinies (*tynghedau*) upon Lleu in an attempt to deny him the three most important attributes of masculine identity: a name, weapons, and a wife.

This story can be read in many ways, but one of them is that a king's duty in peacetime is to protect the bearers of sovereignty (like Goewin) who are

---

[235] Why did he have to have his feet grounded in a maiden's lap? I find a hint in Seán Pádraig O'Donoghue's *Courting the Wild Queen*: "The sacred King is the tree to which people tie their colored ribbons and weave them in the dance. But if the tree is not rooted in the land, then it will topple—so also, if disconnected from the land, the King falls." (26) The maiden's lap was a symbolic threshold to her generative organs: the womb/tomb of the goddess the king was symbolically wed to, and the burial mound he would be placed within after his life of service had ended.

the source of king's power, but not to insist on their own rules about purity (as he did with Arianrhod).

Failing to protect the representatives of the land's sovereignty can have dire consequences for the entire kingdom, as we see in the anonymously-authored *Elucidation*, which was composed as a prologue to Chrétien de Troyes' *Peredur*. The second part of the text describes how Maidens of the Wells used to serve food and drinks to all visitors until the wicked king Amangon, who was responsible for protecting them, raped them and stole their cups. Afterward, the land became a wasteland, and the Castle of the Rich Fisherman was lost. King Arthur's knights do not manage to find the Maidens of the Wells, but they defend some other maidens, who turn out to be the descendants of the Maidens of the Wells and their rapists. Eventually, the knights find the castle, but it is not released from enchantment until the right questions are asked when the knights behold the Grail. The land is restored, for a time, but a new generation brews up new trouble.[236]

Ragnelle

Briana Saussy's retelling of Sir Gawain and Lady Ragnelle, which I presented in its entirety earlier in this book, has the dual transgression of a rape and the killing of a white deer as the events that set the story into motion. Her version takes some of its elements from the anonymously-authored *Weddynge of Sir Gawen and Dame Ragnell* and others from Chaucer's "Wife of Bath's Tale." Like Chaucer's story, Saussy's also has a knight as the rapist. However, Chaucer doesn't name the victim of this crime, and she neither speaks for herself nor reappears in the narrative, so the crime against her is not redressed directly. Nor is the guilty knight executed as expected: the queen orders his date with the executioner's axe to be delayed for a year and a day—on the condition that he correctly answers the riddle of what women want when his period of grace ends. This is how the character of Alisoun (the "Wife of Bath") narrates the part where the knight delivers his answer to the queen and her ladies:

---

[236] See Grigsby, 2002, 208-9. I commented earlier that I also see a parallel between the Maidens of the Wells and St. Winifred. After Winifred's uncle restores her head to its rightful place, a spring healing spring appears. No doubt, the spring long pre-dates the story of the saint, and her severed head also harks back to oracular motifs I discussed previously.
At the same time, the Christian story of pious martyrdom undermines the older connection between women's self-determination and the well-being of the land. While the violation of the maidens caused the land to turn into a wasteland, in the Christian legend it's the violence against Winifred that brought the spring into being.

"My liege and lady, in general," said he,
"A woman wants the self-same sovereignty
Over her husband as over her lover,
And master him; he must not be above her.
That is your greatest wish, whether you kill
Or spare me; please yourself. I wait your will."

The queen spares him. Perhaps, this was a teachable moment for her court and the rest of the subjects. But the story wasn't over until the knight's actions matched his fine words: as in other versions, he granted his bride freedom in choosing her own appearance on their wedding night. Once this is done, he ends up with a wife who has all the most charming qualities a woman could possess. Alisoun wants her companions to take a lesson from this, and she concludes:

So they lived ever after to the end
In perfect bliss; and may Christ Jesus send
Us husbands meek and young and fresh in bed,
And grace to overbid them when we wed.
And—Jesu hear my prayer!—cut short the lives
Of those who won't be governed by their wives;
And all old, angry niggards of their pence,
God send them soon a very pestilence![237]

Scholars have long debated to what extent Chaucer was extolling or lampooning self-sovereign wives, and some interrogate the conceptions of crimes against women, and what options existed for justice or reparations for bodily harm in the Middle Ages.[238] As intriguing as this all of is, however, I'm more interested in peeling back these layers of the tale to find older motifs.

There was an aspect to Ragnelle's story that wasn't brought forward by either Chaucer or Saussy: the man who violated the moral code wasn't just some creep hanging out in a dark part of the woods. When his name is provided in the *Weddynge of Sir Gawen and Dame Ragnell*, it's Sir Gromer

---

[237] Chaucer, 286; 292. Despite the reference to a "land brim-full of fairy folk," this story is lacking in supernatural elements. Additionally, Arthur's queen is not named.

[238] For example, Carissa M. Harris offers a very good analysis of these contexts the *Open Access Companion to the Canterbury Tales*. However, I want to leave these interpretations of loathly lady motif aside, because they represent a degradation of her status from (The) Sovereignty, a goddess who grants privileges to men at her whim and pleasure, into a figure who must simper and sing her own praises in order to achieve equality in a domestic relationship.

Somer Joure—but this isn't a name like yours and mine. It means "Man of the Summer's Day" or perhaps "Gentleman of the Summer Solstice." And what's more, this allegorical figure was Ragnelle's brother.[239] Sir Gromer and Ragnelle do not have the most cordial sibling relationship, and what seems to be cooperation (he poses the riddle to Arthur, and she provides the answer on the proviso that Arthur gives her Gawain as a bridegroom) was more likely her winning move in the struggle between them.

There are many puzzles in Sir Gromer Somer Joure's name. First, Gromer[240] suggests a young person of fairly low rank in a medieval household, but Arthur seems to treat him with the dignity of a knight and uses the honorific Sir. Like the Green Knight who lays down a challenge in another famous story featuring the duo of Arthur and Gawain, this figure has a very otherworldly aspect to him, and he strikes fear into those who encounter him. The courtesy he is afforded in conversation, and the Joure in his name, both evoke French romances, in which newcomers to a court are almost always perceived as superior to the English locals in looks, accomplishments, martial prowess, and courtly manners. However, this encounter does not take place at court, and Gromer's manners would leave a lot to be desired if it had.

The formidable knight, who is fully armed, threatens to kill the unarmed king, and the king counters him by saying he would become a social outcast if he did. Gromer doesn't seem to care at all about what courtly society might think of him: he has a serious grievance with Arthur, and he's of a mind to settle it on his own terms. This odd juxtaposition of a character with a name that is both "low" and celestial, who is described as a "quaynte

---

[239] Bugge, 200. See "The Wedding of Sir Gawain and Dame Ragnelle" edited by Thomas Hahn for a version of the story in sixteenth-century Middle English (based on a text held at Oxford's Bodleian Library). This is the story I refer to here that has Sir Gromer Somer Joure in it, and, as Bugge points out, names are one of the elements in stories that tend to remain stable over time, so it is likely that he is one of the most ancient aspects of it.
While the story seems to have been committed to writing later than the *Canterbury Tales*, some of the motifs appear to be of great antiquity. Not only the Sun/Earth duo, but also Sir Gromer Somer Joure's claim that he owns the rights to the animals in the forest (such as the hart Arthur slew), that he has been robbed of his ownership of certain lands, and the assertion that the king's head is forfeit if he cannot answer the riddle he poses. Essentially, Arthur and Gawain are forced to acknowledge deeper forces that could punish humans for taking that which they had no right to—and of course, here the final straw was the killing of "a great hartt and a fayre." The king gave chase, and "att the last to the dere he lett flye / And smote hym sore and sewerly [surely]" (lines 23 and 40-41 in Hahn's edition). By contrast with his moral status in Gereint and Enid, Arthur is not worthy of making the kill in this tale.
It would be fair to point out that the narrator in Saussy's version speaks of Ragnelle as "my sister," but she doesn't let us know what sort of sibling Ragnelle might have. Certainly though, this sibling seems to have more sympathy and compassion for Ragnelle than Gromer Somer Joure shows in the *Weddynge*.

[240] I'm grateful to Stephen P. Bare for helping me find etymological sources on this puzzling name. "Man" is not an exact translation of Gromer, which seems to be derived from the Old English, probably OE *grŏm*, *grōma*, and cognate with "groom," in the sense of a boy or young servant who tends to horses, and whose rank is lower than a yeoman's but higher than a page's. There is also the connotation of "a man of low station, or a worthless man." See Middle English Compendium: *grǫm*.

gnome,"[241] and who displays crude manners along with his swaggering airs of superiority, suggests that the figure is more than he seems. He is probably a supernatural being of some kind:[242] one who cannot be imposed upon to behave nicely, but who can lay charges upon or kill men—even kings—at will.

Gromer complains to Arthur that he has been aggrieved with him for a long time already, even before the king poached the white deer. Arthur promises that he will give him whatever he wants in exchange for his life. Gromer states his lack of interest in obtaining new lands or gold—it is made clear in the text that he and his sister Ragnelle are already very wealthy. When Ragnelle appears in the forest, despite her monstrous physical attributes, she is richly clothed and has many fine adornments sparkling with gold and gemstones—and she even carries a lute! When she arrives in church on her wedding day, her attire is even finer.

Arthur's shooting of the white deer may have provoked this confrontation, but Gromer had no recourse for it until Arthur entered the realm where the Gentleman of the Summer Solstice reigned supreme. To make things more complicated, the person who held the last (illegitimate) title to the land wasn't Arthur—it was Gawain—because the king had transferred the land to him. Clearly, Gromer's claim to the land is older than Arthur's (or Gawain's), and it seems to have been a form of allodial title—a type of ownership where the holder's unlimited rights to the land were underwritten "by the grace of God and the Sun."[243]

Allodial lands were usually acquired by their owners through inheritance, and held through their occupancy and defense of the property. These owners were not subject to any feudal obligations, such as rent, service, or even the acknowledgement of a higher human authority. Another key element for our story is that allodial titleholders also enjoyed the right to hunt freely on their land. For all of these reasons, custom granted the owner of an allodium equal status with any prince, regardless of their title

---

[241] Etymology Online provides some archaic meanings for "quaint," which come from the French *cointe* or *cwointe*—a very relevant association for this tale. It did not have the modern connotations of something that is picturesque and charming, like a "quaint seaside village". Some of the period associations are: clever, arrogant, proud, and elegant. The Middle English *queintise* refers to wisdom or knowledge—but also to cunning or deceit.

[242] See Classen, 143-44.

[243] Perhaps this doubling of the guarantors was enshrined during a transitional phase that allowed the pact to conform to both Pagan and Christian beliefs.

or the size of their holdings. This explains Sir Gromer Somer Joure's haughty attitude: naturally, the Gentleman of the Summer Solstice held his land by the grace of the Sun, which was a higher authority than the monarch's. Thus, he was justified in treating Arthur as his equal within the bounds of his own territory.

Twenty years after the Norman invasion, there were no more allodial titles to land in England, so Gromer's claim was very quaint (in all the senses mentioned in the footnote) for audiences hearing this story hundreds of years after the Normans had transferred all lands to the Crown. Regardless, they surely understood the logic behind it. Crucially, Arthur does *not* dispute Gromer's account of what happened. One of the ambiguities here is why the king submits to the challenge, instead of settling the matter in a more typical way. Because he has been caught in two transgressions, it seems that his sense of honor demands that he try to solve the riddle, even if failure might cost his life.

All these issues pale before the question of who is actually the rightful owner of the land. We can see that the relationship between Gromer and his sister Ragnelle is not very harmonious. Ragnelle knows about the riddle Arthur was charged with solving, and she knows the answer to it—and I argue that this is because it's *her riddle*.[244] If Gromer took the riddle from her, was he even the rightful owner of the land to begin with?

Ragnelle outfoxes her brother. He was poised to take blood revenge for the illegal seizure of his land, but she not only helped the thieves escape punishment, but also married the one that held the current title to the property. On her wedding night, she seems to be exulting over this, saying that Gawain has given her "the sovereynté / Of alle his body and goodes, sycurly."[245]

Gromer grumbles that he'd like to see Ragnelle burn in a fire for her treachery, but he doesn't protest her act of securing the right to "his" land any more than Arthur had protested Gromer's more ancient and legitimate claim to it.

---

[244] While this may seem like a bold claim, and by stating it I disagree with Bugge (201) that Gromer owns the riddle, the principal substantiation I offer is the fact that in all the other loathly lady stories the riddler is female. The role of riddler is also typical for guardians to a threshold to the "otherworld" (see Matthews, 209), and of course it is Ragnelle (and not her churlish brother) who initiates Gawain into the secret of Sovereignty—which also supports the idea that she is the true guardian spirit of the land.

[245] For more of this line of analysis, see Sheryl L. Forste-Grupp.

Why should Ragnelle be immolated and not destroyed in some other way in her brother's violent fantasies? Compared with hanging, drowning in a lake, or beheading, immolation was costly because of the fuel required. However, in the later Middle Ages, this was the preferred, and sometimes even prescribed, form of capital punishment for traitors, heretics, and witches: in other words, for those who seriously challenged the secular and religious order. Perhaps the bard who composed these lyrics took inspiration from the *De heretico comburendo* ("Regarding the burning of heretics" in Latin), a law mainly intended to be used against the proto-Protestant Lollard sect, passed earlier in the same century when this poem was written. It was enacted by Parliament under King Henry IV, in order to provide for the public burning of those who were convicted of heresy, not only "sacrilegious and dangerous to souls," but also "seditious and treasonable." In other words, Gromer was prescribing the worst penalty a woman could be condemned to at that time, for the most serious kinds of crimes.[246]

From Sovereignty Goddesses to Solar Gods

Perhaps this was part of the "languaging" of the period—putting things in dramatic, contemporary terms to heighten the drama of the story. Saying such a thing, especially about a sibling, had to express a great deal of anger. For those hearing the story, it could conjure macabre images of condemned Lollards they'd seen writhing in flames. However, there is likely more to this story than mere medieval family drama. If Sir Gromer Somer Joure represented summer and the sun, his sister—an equal and complementary figure who has an ancient magic in or upon her—would represent winter and the earth.

Many of the most ancient sacred sites in Britain were appropriated from cults of goddesses and transferred to the cult of a solar god, who was part of a way of life that featured significantly more violence. If Ragnelle has taken the land back—not only from the Lord of the Summer Solstice, but also from Arthur, the champion of Christianity, who was its next heir—she

---

[246] Malory's unfaithful Guinevere was also supposed to be burned at the stake for treason. Some believe that Malory may be the true author of the Weddynge, but there isn't adequate evidence for the claim. Whether or not Malory put these words in Gromer's mouth, it is still true that both the *Weddynge* and *Le Mort d'Arthur* have this dramatic trope in common.

is the heroine of a story that is much more subversive than the typical "war of the sexes" many of the commenters on Chaucer's work suggest. Instead, she is inverting the triumph of the cults which put women into submissive positions and turned land from places that embodied sacred stories into territory to be fought over, stolen, and traded. This goes much deeper than ordinary heresy.

As John Grigsby documents extensively in his doctoral dissertation, sacred monuments such as Stonehenge, Avebury henge, the Sanctuary, Woodhenge, Thornborough, Bryn Celli Ddu, Barclodiad y Gawres and Yeavering were aligned to the position of the Milky Way and the rising and setting of certain stars and constellations—most notably, Crux/the Southern Cross, Cassiopeia, and Orion, or sometimes to the winter solstice.[247] The yards outside of the mounds and barrows were places where stellar "shows" could be observed by large crowds,[248] and their inner sanctums were places where people could immerse themselves in flows of life-giving energies in order to participate in sacred dramas of renewal.

Serving as both womb and tomb, the inner, chthonic shrines were also connected to the starry realms above and to the spirit roads. Many cultures have considered the Milky Way to be a route for souls that are entering or leaving the world, and sometimes the Great Rift or the diamond (lozenge) shape of the constellation of Crux has been considered a sky goddess's vulva. This, too, was one of the alignments used by Neolithic architects, as well as artists working in many other media in this period. The connection between womb and sky was made using white quartz crystals, which were placed on the exteriors of structures and around henges and burial monuments. Of course, the stones used to unite earth and sky were of terrestrial origin, but they had an enticing shine to them. It's also likely that people were taking advantage of the stones' property of triboluminescence: when

---

[247] Grigsby (2018), 3.

[248] Many people apparently believe that monuments like Stonehenge were constructed so that ancient astronomers could figure out when the solstices are going to occur. This is wrong: nothing so grand, and which required so much labor, would have been needed for this purpose. It is also nearly certain that the site was meant to serve large numbers of people who would have been milling around instead of just a handful of astronomer-priests. John Grigsby writes: "To reduce the 'window of use' of a henge or passage grave to a single moment of sunrise or sunset is to misapply what anthropology and ethnology tells us. We might better see the whole Stonehenge environs, for example, as a 'ceremonial landscape' in which different sites might be used on different hours of the night, or different days/nights or even different seasons; the setting of the sun at the midwinter solstice might be witnessed by hundreds of people stood along the Avenue, for a few minutes a day, for the 5 days of the solstice—yet other celestial happenings, such as the rising of the Milky Way after sunset might be witnessed nightly for months. Such rituals may have been less a gathering of elites focusing on a single moment once a year, than the equivalent of, say, a modern music-festival, with large groups of people moving from 'stage' to 'stage.'" Grigsby (2018), 130.

two pieces of quartz are rubbed together in an absolutely dark chamber, they emit a small amount of light, like stars underground.

As the Neolithic Revolution progressed, it created many hardships including famines, pestilence, and feedback loops of environmental damage and crop failures.[249] The growing sedentary populations were not only making unsustainable demands on their ecosystems, but also creating new forms of social organization. Thanks to agricultural surpluses, societies were increasingly stratified, and chiefs became kings interested in expanding and augmenting their kingdoms, power, and glory. For this, the large "surplus" population of young men who were not needed for agricultural work came in handy as a warrior caste. When metalworking technologies became more advanced, there were more riches to be won, as well as more effective and deadly weapons to use in their taking.[250] There was not only earthly glory to be had after successfully raiding others' lands: any reluctance to engage in warfare could be countered by the promise of a glorious afterlife for warriors and a lesser glory for virtuous women (who might be allowed to act as their cup bearers in the next life.)[251]

These ecological and social changes may have led to uncertainty about the potency of deities who were believed to provide for the yearly cycles, or perhaps doubt of those who officiated at rituals that aimed at bringing in a reliable and sufficient abundance.

Another change has been theorised as causing deep alarm: a phenomenon called the precession of the equinoxes or axial precession. This phenomenon creates an apparent shift in the heavens, so that the places where stars were rising and setting changed. It may have been impercep-

---

[249] It's worth contemplating that major changes in agriculture are often precipitated by dramatic changes or fluctuations in climate. As I will discuss in the next to last chapter, the retreat of the last Ice Age led to Mesolithic permaculture, which coexisted in many places alongside grain farming, but then declined in a period of dramatic cooling. The "Little Ice Age" of the 17th century resulted in massive failures in Europe's grain harvests and inspired the cultivation of potatoes and other New World crops, and surges in cereal farming across Europe occurred as reactions to severe climate fluctuations over the course of millennia. See Paschall.

[250] This is likely why many "Golden Age" or Eden-type myths describe a world innocent of both the plow and the sword, which are two sides of the same blade.

[251] See Artisson (2021), 71-72. Also consider the resonance of how in the *aisling* visions of Sovereignty there is a royal, otherworldly woman who fills the hero's cup—perhaps a late Neolithic or Bronze Age motif. However, as Christian themes work their way deeper into the story material and become structuring elements, the maiden with the cup is no longer the incentive and prize offered to the hero, but a mere cup-bearer or messenger (Matthews, 75). Anyone who is in doubt about the lower position of a cup-bearer might investigate the myth of Ganymede, Zeus' winsome cup-bearer, who became the prototype for *paiderastia*, a relationship between an older and a younger male where there was love and pleasure, but also inequality between them. When the young boy becomes a mature man, he takes on the role of the active, dominant participant in affairs that he will have with adolescents who will take the passive, subordinate role. Robert B. Koehl has argued that pederasty was institutionalized as a rite of passage into military service in the Late Minoan period, and that cups such as the "Chieftain Cup" were one of the gifts given to the young initiates. I do not know how far back the origins of this specific social institution reach back beyond this period, or how widespread they may have been in other Bronze Age cultures.

tible over a lifetime, but it would have been quite evident over the course of the thousands of years during which so many astronomically-aligned structures were built. Some of the constellations known to earlier builders were eventually swallowed up by the horizon, never to appear again in places like Britain. One of these was Crux, whose appearance on the horizon seems to have been an important focus of not only architecture, but also of rites performed within them.[252]

The axial precession cycle is roughly 26,000 years long, so there may have been an ongoing sense of the most fundamental things failing to work as they used to. As Robin Artisson theorizes in *The House of the Giantess*:

> As it turns out, the Neolithic cultures and their religious interiors, being so dependent on the shifting night-sky of stars, contained the seeds of their own downfall. It wasn't just the ecological and sociological issues they faced as they grew into massive agricultural-based and complex societies. It was something more fundamental, tied to the Gods, to the stars and the shifting of the sky itself. Their native religions were shaken and subverted by the changing night skies—and this, after a point, left them vulnerable to new cultures that had new religions—religions that rejected the stars as Gods and instead focused on something that was more reliable: The Sun.[253]

He argues that frustration grew as the old system was beginning to fail. Then, at a point when people's confidence was particularly low, they encountered aggressive new ideologies or cultural complexes from Bronze Age cultures, such as the Yamna (or Pit Grave) Culture from the Pontic Steppe, which glamorized war, looting, conquest, and masculine heroics.

---

[252] Grigsby provides plentiful evidence for a complex of "obscene" dance that has been observed in cultures ranging from Japan (the "whirling, heavenly woman" Uzume) to Ancient Greece (Baubo, whose name means belly/womb, a headless old woman whose facial features are on her chest, who reveals her vulva to Demeter on the Bridge of Jests), and elsewhere, including Aditi in India and Nut and Hathor in Egypt. The basic plot of the sidereal story was that at the midwinter solstice the rising of Orion heralds the appearance of Crux, which "dances" upon the horizon just before the Sun rises at the same place. Crux was sited at the base of the Milky Way—which was lying upon the Earth's horizon. The union of earth and sky was thus understood as a heavenly goddess who was lying in coitus with an earth god, and together they (re)create the sun as their child, which would then grow stronger and provide for another year's abundance. Young sun priestesses may have performed dances wearing sun discs on their bellies and string skirts that revealed their genitals for rites that were intended to facilitate/participate in this cosmic drama. See Grigsby (2018), 122-3; 199; 216.

[253] Artisson (2021), 36. There is a detailed discussion of when and how the shifts in culture and religion came about in the Neolithic and then the Bronze Age in Artisson's work, and in John Grigsby's thesis, which Artisson uses as a primary source material. All that is crucial to understand here is that the earlier religions were concerned with creating ritual sites with alignments to twin hills, and often with rivers. Their entrances were positioned so that there was homology between the Milky Way, or certain stars and constellations and the gap between two hills and/or site entrances, and—often—with nearby rivers, which were probably where people usually disposed of their dead. The ritual sites functioned as otherworldly places shared by the living and the dead, where the forces of the sky, the land, and the water were aligned. They were at once in the belly of the great mother, who was sometimes styled as a cow, and among the stars, as symbolized by the use of quartz stones around the outsides of the structures or the henges.

Despite what might be expected, Neolithic cultures were not usually violently attacked and subjugated, but instead transformed through contact with other cultures. As populations blended over time, they adopted the newcomers' material culture, way of life, and ideologies—including their patriarchal religion and patterns of relations. Chthonic (underworld womb/tomb) and stellar cults lost prestige, and they were sidelined in favor of religious focus on the sun and on heavenly realms.

For instance, the Bell Beaker culture—which arrived in Neolithic Britain from the Iberian Peninsula—featured a solar god, and burials of the dead in which bodies were positioned to face the sunrise. The Bell Beaker culture arrived around the time when Crux was disappearing through the southern horizon. Perhaps, then, while the Neolithic Britons were facing crises of various kinds, they offered attractive models for emulation. The immigrants had finely wrought metal accessories, they went on quests and adventures, they accumulated wealth, and they may have thus seemed more rewarded by their solar god, who was styled as a slayer of chthonic forces such as snakes and dragons—old symbols for the Earth's regenerative forces.[254] The new god sent the old ones down to where *he* didn't shine—the depths of the underworld—and he reigned over life on earth from on high. Though that sun-god had to consign himself to their realm each night, he reemerged in the morning, victorious again.

Many sacred sites were remodeled in a way that appears to reflect the subjugation of the Neolithic goddesses with their aspects and forms—which ranged from the sun itself, to the Milky Way, to the giver of rivers, to a cosmic cow, to an Earth womb. With the prestige of the old cults in disrepute, the old goddesses, rites, and priesthoods may have been viewed with suspicion. During a period fraught by disruptive changes to local climates, crop growth, and even the stars, it may have seemed necessary to put the older powers under the control of the new ones. Thus, the Bronze

---

[254] See Artisson (2021), 98, and for comparisons between European, Vedic, and East Asian versions of several of the motifs I discuss in this chapter, see Ananda Coomaraswamy's "On the Loathly Bride." Coomaraswamy's approach is marked by the generalizing tendencies of mid-20th century mythologists as well as by his commitment to the universalizing "perennial philosophy," and should be considered a starting point for more in-depth research into any of the myths. What I found of greatest interest in his work are his comments on mythic archetype in the loathly lady stories being a marriage between a sun god and an earth goddess, and the detailed examples he provides for the latter's earlier chthonic and ophidian (snakelike) aspects.

Age solar god was not "killed" every year (he was now eternal), and he had the power to command the Earth to produce crops at his pleasure.

The remodeling of Stonehenge around 2,500 BCE provides an excellent illustration of this transition, because its original orientation to the Milky Way and the winter solstice was eclipsed by new structures focused to the summer solstice. Five massive trilithons (three stones that form a kind of "gateway") were erected in a horseshoe shape, with the largest trilithon standing at the center of the formation. This was done right at the center of the old burial monument; the open "arms" of the horseshoe shape faced the rising summer solstice sun, as befits a site for the worship of a solar deity. More Welsh bluestones were imported to stand inside the trilithons, as though they were a council of the land powers that would witness the rites, and possibly also a rapprochement of the political powers of East and West. A massive "altar stone" was put in front of the largest trilithon.

Uniquely, as part of this updated ritual structure, a huge ring of sandstone blocks (sarsens) sealed the center. This ring sealed the ancient dead kings and the powers of the land inside. On the five days around the summer solstice, the sun gradually shone on each one of these lithic elements, subjecting them to his majesty and light in an explicit triumph of the "Gentleman of the Summer Solstice" over the older goddess cults.

Guinevere and Gwyn ap Nudd

Many millennia passed between these transitions and the first written stories bearing the loathly lady motif. Regardless, a powerful resonance or reverberation is eminent between the themes, and there are certainly other elements of Neolithic culture preserved as late as into the medieval age.[255]

A possible link appears in the rich and varied lore relating the motif of the loathly lady and the requirement that kings must wed a female repre-

---

[255] For example, mounds appearing in legends as gateways to Otherworldly sites. We see this theme in Peredur, with the Woman of the Mound, and in a tale told by the "Black Oppressor" who tells the story, at the point of Peredur's sword, of how he lost his eye:

"There is a mound called the Mound of Mourning, and in the mound there is a cairn, and in the cairn there is a serpent, and in the serpent's tail there is a stone. And these are the attributes of the stone: whoever holds it in his hand will have as much gold as he wishes in the other hand. And I lost my eye fighting that serpent ... " (See Parker). The serpent, of course, like dragons, is an old symbol for the indwelling fertile powers of the land.

In the tale of Gawain and the Green Knight, the knight's "Green Chapel" is often understood to be a prehistoric burial mound, since it is a round hillock with an entrance on one side, located by the side of a brook.

sentation of Sovereignty before they are invested with their full powers.[256] The Matter of Britain—the corpus of medieval literature from medieval Britain and Brittany discussing legendary kings and heroes, particularly King Arthur and his court—is replete with stories of generous yet fickle goddesses of the land and men who accept her challenges to rule under her auspices. In others words, the loathly ladies and the men who love them.

At the core of such stories is a need for a change of leadership, driven by the questions of who holds the land and by what mystical right.[257] Often, this need is made evident by the state of the land itself, revealed as under wicked enchantment or plagued by supernatural beings. The land is blasted, dried, infertile. Human relationships may be distressed, and sometimes both the land and the people suffer together. In stories with Fisher King figures in them, such as *Perceval* or *Parzival*, the old ruler suffers from a wound from which he cannot heal but from which he also cannot die. In parallel, the woes of the land seem also incurable, and the solution for both the king and the land is for a suitably virtuous successor to take over.

According to later versions of the Arthurian tales, King Arthur's reign either ended because of an incestuous union with his half-sister (resulting in an ill-begotten son named Mordred), or because Guinevere was having an affair with Lancelot (who is a relative newcomer in the stories). In Malory's *Le Morte d'Arthur*, Arthur's willful blindness to his wife's love affair caused him to lose the confidence of his knights. To regain their confidence, Arthur sentenced her to burn at the stake; Lancelot rescued her and they escaped together. Ultimately, Guinevere ends up in a nunnery. In another late tale, the 15th century *La Tavola Ritonda*, a romance about Tristan written in the medieval Tuscan language, the queen perishes when she

---

[256] I have also wondered if this isn't an underlying reason for some of the white American sexual fetishization of Native American women, and the validating claims of a Native female ancestor, such as the groan-inducing "my great-grandmother was a Cherokee princess." The Cherokee, of course, did not have princesses, but those who had any awareness of their customs might have noted that they reckoned kinship through maternal lines; women owned all the houses and fields; they could marry and divorce as they pleased; and clan mothers often served as magistrates—which may have seemed like very royal prerogatives—especially in the eyes of descendants of Europe's lower classes. In their imagination, marriage into a putative "royal" line would make kings of these descendants of European peasants–if anyone was willing to take their tales seriously.

Certainly, conquest itself is a motivation for "sexy Indian squaw" costumes, or other styles of representation that make Native women look like sex objects served up for the Euro-American male gaze, and there is an ugly triumphalism in "Indian" sports mascots, and a Victorian-age notion of social evolution in the background of children's "Indian" camps. However, I believe it's at least possible that for generations who grew up with at least a modicum of guilt over settler violence and land theft might like to ease their minds a little by imagining that some Native women—darling, sexy Disney Pocahontases—welcomed their ancestors, and by blending their bloodlines, they offered legitimation to the newcomers' claims upon the land that they know had been stolen.

[257] See Matthews, 13.

hears that Arthur was slain by Mordred. All these versions bear a heavy influence of patriarchal Christian and Classical motifs.

Just as over time Arthur becomes more Christian, Guinevere's originally very otherworldly character becomes more earthly and fallible: she is increasingly a foil and a liability, rather than the source of his sovereignty. The older conceptions point to something else. In them, we see not a queen demeaned, imperfect, or sinful, but rather one who represents a goddess with imparting access to the sacred powers of the land. Going back even further, we see she also imparts the mysteries of life, death, and rebirth. Thus, her role in arranging for the king's replacement was an obvious and necessary function.

Her story is archetypal rather than individual; thus, the king accepting her, mating with her, and then facing inevitable betrayal by a younger and more virile successor are each part of a self-evident sequence of events. Because of the difference in status between an immortal and a mortal being, a figure of her stature would be portrayed as beyond the usual social mores, beyond good and evil, "for she alone bestows sovereignty upon her chosen champion, selecting and discarding her candidates with impunity."[258] King Arthur, himself much more than mere charismatic warlord, was thus mated with a figure of far greater antiquity than himself. This put a stamp of legitimacy upon his rule exceeding anything he could have accomplished on his own.

Philology indicates the likelihood of an association between Arthur's queen and ancient Otherworldly powers. As we recall from "Is it Wyrd, Is it White, Is it Promised to the Night?" the color white has many associations with death. Guinevere's name derives from the Proto-Celtic *Windo*, which refers to that which is white, pale, or holy, and *Sebara*, which means a magical or supernatural being.[259] So, of course, this fickle figure is much more than an earthly spouse who might be judged by the conventions of men. In her more supernatural aspect, Guinevere was a late echo of the

---

[258] Matthews and Matthews, 288.

[259] This older proposed etymology is shared by Artisson in *An Carow Gwyn* (p. 109). Also see Matthews and Matthews, 175, though these two authors only repeat the claim that "some scholars" have traced a root derivation from "white phantom or fairy" without committing to this interpretation themselves. The queen's name is considered equivalent to the Irish Findabair, and Gwynn = Fionn. Consider for a moment that the Irish word *fia* means both "wild" and "deer," and *Fianna* is white. Thus, Fionn Mac Cuhhail is the "white" leader of the Fianna, the band of warriors whose name derives from *fia* ("wild" and "deer") and we've made a perfect circle of all the main themes in this book.

"White Queen of Spirits who ... had earlier been worshiped as the divine entity that tribal kings had to enter into a sacred marriage with, to justify their rule over the land and people."[260]

Gwynfa is a Welsh word for paradise, and Lorna Smithers points out that the ruler of the dead, Gwyn ap Nudd, whose first name means "White, Blessed, Holy," is the type of deity who, like Guinevere/*Windo*Sebara*, probably participates in the tradition where deities' names are eponymous with their realms. Familiar examples from other mythical traditions include Hades, Hel, Psyche, Luna and Oceanus, who all shared their names with their domains or areas of influence.[261]

An additional attribute of Guinevere appears in the eleventh-century *Vita Gildae* by Caradoc of Llancarfan. She was abducted by Melwas of the Summer Country, who keeps her in his realm until Arthur comes to rescue her. The story is reworked about a century later, and in a poem titled (in English) "The Dialogue of Melwas and Gwenhwyfar," her abductor addresses her as *"Gwenhwyfar of the deer's shape."*[262]

As for Gwyn ap Nudd, he is incorporated into the Arthurian tales in *How Culhwch Won Olwen*, which was one of the earliest known Arthurian romances, and was included in Charlotte Guest's *Mabinogion*. The story of *How Culhwch Won Olwen* has resonances with the theme of a solar conqueror contending with forces of darkness for access to a fair goddess named Creiddylad.[263] Gwyn here serves not only as the king of the dead (and therefore, in medieval texts as a lord of infernal forces), but also as a figuration of winter. Gwyn contends with Gwythr (summer) to take Creiddylad for his own. However, Gwyn doesn't play fairly: he seizes the maiden

---

[260] Artisson (2018), 110.

[261] See Smithers, who also traces Gwyn's gradual loss of status. While he was once a god of Annwfyn and lord of the dead he was demonized in the Middle Ages as a fiendish huntsman, and his role was "punitive as he was subsumed within Christianity's doctrine of fear and control as a devilish figure. Charles Squire writes, "Gwyn ... his game is man ... the "mighty hunter," not of deer, but of men's souls, riding his demon horse, and cheering on his demon hound to the fearful chase'. John Rhys notes, 'What Gwyn hunts are the souls of those who are dying; but Christianity has greatly narrowed his hunting ground, as his quarry can now only be souls of notoriously wicked men.'" This is a prototype of the "Wild Hunt" motif. Also see Matthews and Matthews, 157.

[262] Matthews and Matthews, 175-6, emphasis added by me. Caitlín Matthews also suggests that there are faint echoes in the story of Gereint and Enid of Gwenhwyfar's abduction by Melwas because the responsibility for an insult to the queen was with the earl Edern ap Nudd, the "Eternal Son of Night."

[263] According to Caitlín Matthews, Creiddylad was an example of a "Flower Bride"—an otherworldly maiden of "unearthly beauty who will succeed to the Goddess of Sovereignty, and for whose hand many men fight"(220). By keeping her imprisoned, Arthur—in this story—is preventing her maturation into a queenly Sovereignty figure. Certainly, in some stories he and his queen occupy the positions of justified ruler and otherworldly queen, and they also feature in dozens of stories where she is abducted and he has to rescue her (see Matthews, 291-2) but the very Christian overlay here emphasizes that these older traditions are to be suppressed in favor of the new ones.

from Gwythr by force and takes her to Annwfn, his kingdom of the dead, which has the effect of bringing winter to the land.[264]

Gwythr was determined to win her back, so he musters an army and storms into Annwfn, where he was defeated. Here's where the story no longer resembles an ancient cyclical figuration of the seasons: King Arthur intervenes and prevails over Gwyn. Arthur then binds Gwyn and Gwythr to do battle for Creiddylad every Calan Mai until Judgement Day, when the winner can take her—just before the Christian powers achieve their ultimate victory.

Lorna Smithers points out that Gwyn couldn't be completely destroyed, because he contains the dead spirits of Annwfn within his powers or his realm. He is the only one who can control them and prevent them from rampaging. Since he cannot be eliminated, he has to be held in check with an equal and opposing force (Gwythr). However, the framing is triumphally Christian. While the ancient cycle was restored after a fashion, it was done so in submission to Arthur's will: "the purpose is to display Arthur's control over these two old seasonal gods"—and over Creiddylad as well. Smithers notes that Arthur getting the best of Gwyn was a:

> primary step in the destruction of Brythonic Paganism and the assertion of Christianity. Gwyn's mythos had to be erased and reconfigured in a new literature documenting his defeat and replacement by Arthur as a protector of Britain who fights against the 'devils' of Annwfn.[265]

Blodeuwedd and Other Figures

The unfaithful otherworldly wife motif is by no means limited to Arthurian tales. Another faithless bride can be found in the Welsh story about Blodeuwedd's betrayal of Lleu Llaw Gyffes.[266] This tale is told in the Fourth Branch of the Mabinogi, the tale including Math fab Mathonwy and his requirement of a foot-maiden that I discussed earlier. Lleu's mother Arianrhod had put a *tynged* (fate, destiny or obligation, similar to an Irish *geas*) upon him, which forbade him to take a human wife. In re-

---

[264] These are themes that could well have come from sources as ancient as the old star stories that told of the turning of the seasons.

[265] See Smithers. I have paraphrased and abridged her excellent retelling of the tale.

[266] Lleu is considered to be the Welsh equivalent of the Irish god Lugh. Earlier generations of scholars attempted to classify him/them as a solar deity, but this identification is probably ill-founded.

sponse, his uncles Gwydion and Math fashion a bride for him out of the blossoms of meadowsweet, broom, and oak. Her name is Blodeuwedd, which means "Flower-Faced," as it is a composite of *blodeu* (flowering, blooming) and *gwedd* (face, appearance).

This ruse doesn't serve Lleu very well, because who owns the spring flowers? No one: they are simply there to please themselves. While he is away from home, Blodeuwedd takes Gronw Pebr, the ruler of Penllyn, as her lover, and they conspire to kill Lleu. This is not an easy matter, because Lleu has enchantments upon him that prevent him from being killed during the day, during the night, while indoors or outdoors, while riding or walking, while clothed or while naked. He also cannot be slain by any lawfully-made weapon. Therefore, it's only possible to kill him at dusk, wrapped in a net, with one foot atop a cauldron and one on a black goat, next to a riverbank and using a spear that was forged over the course of a year only during the hours that everyone was supposed to be attending Mass.

When the fateful weapon strikes him, Lleu does not die but rather changes into an eagle and flies away. His uncle Gwydion finds him and transforms him back into his human form. Gwydion and Math then nurse him back to health so he can take his lands back from Gronw and Blodeuwedd. As a punishment, Gwydion transforms Blodeuwedd into an owl, which is said to be hated by all the other birds.[267]

Lleu survived this attempt on his life, and his wife is punished, but many stories in the British Isles tell of kings who weren't so lucky. Comparison shows that "a suspiciously high number of Celtic kings and heroes" die in incidents where there is a sexual context. King Conchobar of Ulster, for instance, dies at a ford when he is showing his "nakedness" to a group of women. Cú Roí dies in bed with his wife, with her head in her lap, and Cumhaill, the father of Fionn, could only be killed while he was sleeping with his wife; also, like Cú Roí, he would have to be killed with his own sword. Accordingly, "to protect him from death, on the night of his wedding … seven marriage chambers are constructed around the bridal bed, but still his enemy, Arca the Black, the king's fisher, who has hidden in the inner room, is able to kill him," while he's engaging in "the act of love." John

---

[267] Ragnelle, too, compares herself to an owl when she is in her "loathly" aspect. John Bugge points out that owls were considered ugly, oversexed, and an ill omen of death, as well as being classified as "unclean" in Leviticus (203-4).

Grigsby raises the interesting question of whether the slaying of a Sovereignty-empowered king was at one time done while he was in coitus with a priestess.[268]

A very secular ballad featuring a betraying figure—*Adam Bell, Clym of the Cloughe, and Wyllyam of Cloudeslee*, has been dated to the 16th century, though perhaps it could be much older. This work is best known today as Child Ballad 116 (the Child Ballads are traditional English and Scottish ballads collected and anthologized by Francis James Child in the 19th century). The tale recounted in the ballad is of the three outlaws named in its title. Wyllyam is a family man and misses his wife and children while he is away

---

[268] Grigsby (2003), 40.
There is a cluster of themes hidden within the word "stag," which touch upon virility and death blows. "Stag" is derived from the PIE root *stegh-*, which means "to stick, prick, sting." In Old English, *stagga* already takes on the meaning of "stag" that we know today, and Old Danish has *stag* meaning "point." In Old Norse, *stong* is a stick or pole. The word "stang" (referring to a forked stick used in some traditions of witchcraft) is naturally also a derivate. The verb "to stagger" was introduced in the mid-15th century, and it comes from the same source, perhaps through a Scandinavian branch of development (such as the Old Danish *stagra* or Old Norse *stakra* "to push, shove, cause to reel" also "to stumble, stagger," perhaps even by hitting with a stick, as suggested by the Germanic *stakon-* "a stake." See the definitions of "stag" and "stagger" at www.etymology.com.
The animal boasts a magnificent (or, one could say, "staggering") rack of multi-pointed antlers. However, the parallel between its natural weapons, and the idea of blows inflicted with a long, pointed implement causing an unsteady gait or stumbling seems like a nice attempt at invoking the desired result of a hunt: hunters striking at their prey and causing it to wobble on its feet and then collapse. The hunted animal must die, yet it is celebrated for its virility while alive.
The masculine exuberance of modern "stag" parties also seems like a ritual that uses ribaldry to invoke the abundant, satisfying sex that the groom-to-be hopes he will enjoy in his marriage. However, paradoxically, the stag's antlers have also long been the symbol of a cuckold. The connection sometimes drawn to Ovid's account to Actaeon who was turned into a stag by Diana doesn't make sense for a lot of reasons (see McEachern, 616-17). Perhaps the precursor was the rampaging of the 12th century Byzantine emperor Andronicus I Comnenus (who was generally known for cruelty and depravity). It is said that after Andronicus raped his subjects' wives he would hang horns on the outside of their houses. This signified the compensatory hunting rights he granted to these men. See McEachern, 615; El Organillo. References from the Middle Ages sometimes layer on associations with the Devil, perhaps also out of a reflexive habit of associating him with other horned figures (Pan, Dionysus, satyrs, etc.) Another association between antlers ("horns") and cuckolds came from the Charlton Horn Fair, held on St. Luke's Day at Cuckold's Point. This spot is situated at a sharp bend in the Thames River in southeast London that was once marked by a post topped with a pair of horns. The Horn Fair drew upon an already-established symbolism rather than creating it, and it's likely that the putative origin story for the fair was composed in accordance with the common practices.
It was told that King John was out hunting and stopped to rest at a miller's house. He was greeted by the miller's pretty wife, and their acquaintance had just advanced to the point where he was kissing her when the miller returned home. He drew his dagger, threatening to kill them, but King John revealed who he was, and the miller asked for a different form of compensation. He received a large land grant and also the right to hold a fair every year on 18 October (St Luke's Day). Out of envy or contempt, the miller's neighbors dubbed the river boundary of the miller's new land Cuckold's Point and they wore horns to his fair to mock him.
The fair was most popular in the 18th century, and it was famous for ribald activities and entertainments. Visitors carried or wore horns and all the vendors decorated their stalls with horns of all shapes and sizes. Even the gingerbread men sold there had horns. See Oxford Reference; Swift. The word "cuckold," of course, has nothing to do with deer—it refers to the cuckoo, who leaves her eggs in another bird's nest to the detriment of that family.

from home with Adam and Clym.[269] His friends tried to dissuade him from visiting home, but he goes despite their warnings. Wyllyam is greeted affectionately by his wife, Alice, and their children. However, there is someone else in their home: an old woman the family had taken in out of charity. This ungrateful guest betrays Wyllyam to the Sheriff and Magistrate of Carlisle, for which she is rewarded with a red dress. Further adventures ensue, in which Alice proves her loyalty time and again, and when it seems that King John will see Wyllyam and Adam hanged at last, his queen intervenes by asking for mercy for the condemned men as a wedding gift she had been promised but had not yet named.

After this, the men are offered chances to display their skills and psychological fitness, and they win due honors. As Zteve T. Evans argues, Wyllyam, his family, and his friends have all benefited from the coordinated action of the three female characters. Alice was warm and alluring, and his choice to see her and their children endangered him. Then, it was the old woman's betrayal which initiates the events which bring about the improvement in his circumstances. The Queen enters the story as the outlaws' savior (much as the queen did for the knight in the "Wife of Bath's Tale"), and then she also becomes their benefactress. The coincidence of this being a wedding gift could not be more striking: this is an echo of a sacred marriage, though it is now done by proxy with a commoner rather than directly with a man destined to rule.

---

[269] Sadly, there are no deer in this outlaw ballad. For a murder ballad that has a "milk white hind," see "The Famous Flower of Serving Men," published by Laurence Price in 1656. In its middle stanzas, a king goes out hunting and encounters a white hind in the wood. She leads him on a long and difficult chase, and the king becomes afraid of her:
Oh what is this, how can it be?
Such a hind as this I ne'er did see
Such a hind as this was never born
I fear she'll do me deadly harm.
Undaunted, he draws his sword to kill her, but she vanishes before he can. The king finds his attention drawn to a grave, and a dove that cries tears of blood alights there and tells him the story of the murder of his beloved servant's husband and child, which he avenges. There is not a loathly lady in this secular story, but the king's lover had been serving him disguised as a young man, which is an interesting twist. I owe a debt of gratitude to Scarlet Loring for drawing my attention to this haunting song.
J. G. McKay's 1932 article "The Deer-Cult and the Deer-Goddess Cult of the Ancient Caledeonians" raises the possibility that there was a connection between deer-women and outlaws in Scotland. He speculates on ancient cults led by priestesses who wore antlers and were associated not only with deer but also with a giant Cailleach figure. Folklore attributed to them the power of changing into grey hinds. (Why grey? Were they perhaps reindeer? As I mentioned previously, reindeer only died out in Scotland in the 13th century.) When hunters gave chase, the deer women might reveal their human form to avoid being struck by weapons, and in some stories they married these hunters. Their sympathies seem to have been with the common people and outlaws, and were generally against the aristocracy who "represent some invading and conquering race, who had promulgated game-laws and arrogated to themselves the right to hunt." (McKay, 159). The notions that an ancient deer priestess order once guarded access to venison and fish, and that when they were refused their ancient tribute and role in regulating the take they became enemies of the new rulers, are very intriguing. But McKay seems to raise more questions than he is able to answer in this article.

Even though there is no magic, and the characters in this story are not supernatural, Evans remarks that the three women's actions work toward the same goal. It is even possible to view Alice, the Old Woman, and the Queen as "aspects of a kind of triple goddess looking after William and his family and friends."[270] Of the three, the wicked old woman is the most puzzling figure: she seems selfish and treacherous, but the blessings could not have been won if she had not pushed the plot along. Taken as a whole, complete figure, these three each correspond to aspects of the loathly lady, as well as pointing to older mysteries.[271]

Sovereignty and the Earth

Sovereignty, embodied in divine or semi-divine female characters in British myths and legends, is portrayed in three stages. In her youthful form, she's a Flower Bride who must be wooed and won. At maturity, whether or not she is married, she appears as a Sovereign Queen who embodies hospitality and generosity, who must be defended from insults and abductions, and who inspires heroes to go on quests. Finally, there is the "admonitory" figure who scolds and harangues her proteges.[272] Good examples of the admonitory female appear in the early 13th century version of the Perceval cycle called *Perlesvaus*. Here, Guinevere scolds Arthur for failing to keep a strong court, and she sends him out on adventures to win back his glory. He eventually wins a crown and a war horse while on a pilgrimage to Avalon, and a maiden similar to the "black maidens" in other stories reproaches him:

---

[270] See Evans.

[271] The splitting of deities is also known in Indian, Nordic, and Classical mythology, among many others. Sometimes the mysteries of coming into life and exiting it can be assigned to three "sister" deities, such as the Norns, the Graeae (the "grey women" who shared one eye and one tooth among them), the Roman Moirae (Lachesis, Atropos, and Clotho), and the Matres and Matronae of northwestern Europe.

Goddesses who have triple forms but are not obviously mother figures, such as Hekate—referred to as "triple-sounding, triple-headed, triple-voiced ... triple-pointed, triple-faced, triple-necked" (etc.)—in the Greek Magical Papyri) may be considered powerful in three realms. This particular enigmatic Titaness was believed to have power in the realms of sky, earth, and sea, and it brings to mind the Neolithic goddess whose realms were the underworld, the starry sky, and the life-giving rivers. With later syncretisms we can observe the conflation of Hekate with other goddesses (notably Diana and Luna or Proserpine, who made up the *Diva triformis*). The concept is also preserved in the Roman goddess who was considered equivalent to Hekate and called Trivia (*tri* = three; *via* = paths, because she was associated with crossroads, especially three-way crossroads, which again suggests power in three realms.) At other times and places, a goddess might represent different life stages, such as in the cult of Hera in Stymphalos.

In the 20th century, we encounter the enormously influential theory of a Maiden/Mother/Crone goddess who mirrors the phases of the Moon as developed by Robert Graves, Marija Gimbutas, and others who helped shape a distinctive modern theology that became prominent in Wicca and other Neopagan faiths.

[272] Matthews 296-7, emphases in the original.

"Sire, you have won ... this golden crown and this war-horse, for which you should rejoice indeed, so long as you are valiant enough to defend the land of the finest lady on earth, who is now dead ..."
To whom did the land belong? asked the king. *And what was the name of the queen whose crown I see?*
"Sire, the king's name was Arthur, and he was the finest in the world, but many people say that he is dead; and the crown belonged to Queen Guinevere, who is now dead and buried."

Guinevere isn't an immortal being in this tale, even though she still retains these sovereignty-granting prerogatives. This role is further underscored later, when Madeglans of Oriande appears at Arthur's court. He demands that the Round Table and his right to rule be given him, as Guinevere's closest kinsman. Now that she is deceased, her widowed husband had no more right to it—unless he weds Madeglans's sister Jandree and renounces Christianity.[273]

Loathly ladies partake of threatening and boon-granting natures in one mysterious, shape-shifting body, but not every story drinking from these old wells is so economical. Sometimes, separate stories with the same character illustrate their different natures, as in the conflicting and overlapping versions of the Arthurian tales. At other times (as in the ballad of Adam Bell), there are three apparently different figures who assist the hero. In other cases, their essential and underlying unity comes through in characters who are given very similar or identical names, with only slightly different parentage or other personal details, as is sometimes done with Queen Guinevere, and also with Isolt.[274]

In ancient and in modern times, the Earth is often styled as Mother. This is a venerable tradition, but it has certain conceptual limitations, especially in regards to the relationship human leaders have with the land. In contrast, loathly ladies require the human partner to develop a more complex relationship with her than the one between infants and their mothers. Exclusive focus on the maternal "providing" aspect is fraught with the potential for leading to an uncouth "gimme" approach from supplicants. We can

---

[273] You may recall the theme of Christianity putting a stop to the old cycles in the previous discussions of Creiddylad and Gwyn, and of the Hungarian miracle stag Csodaszarvas.
[274] See Matthews, 289; 291; 294; 296.

witness this problem in the world's wealthiest people, who seem always begging for even more "abundance," because human appetites can be insatiable.

As Joseph Dodds writes, "The phrase '[M]other Earth' suggests our experience with nature relates to the (m)other of infancy, including not only feelings of love and being held, but fantasies of an infinitely giving Earth-breast we feel entitled to suck on with ever increasing intensity without limit. Responses to ecological crises include rage, envy, destructiveness, and paranoid attempts at omnipotent control"—for "the breast is not only a provider of nutrition, but a place into which we expel unbearable states of mind."[275] What is missing from the simple greedy infant/abundant mother dyad, which turns the infant into a squalling ball of fury when it can't have everything it wants, is an honest reckoning. Also, it excludes the fact that life is taken away from us just as easily as it is granted.

Giving attention to the human mothers around us, we can notice that giving life and caring for offspring are only two aspects of the complex and lifelong relationship between a mother and her child. Others include teaching children through words, passed-on lore, and example, as well as protecting or defending children from danger. Many cultures acknowledge the complexity of these relationships through myths of goddesses, such as Kali Ma (Mother Kali), who both births and devours her offspring. The Christian(ized) *pieta* image, that of a mother holding her dead son, also reflects the idea of a mother not only as one who gives birth, but a caretaker of the dead. This aspect is echoed very nicely in the Czech verb *pochovat*, which means both to cradle a child in one's arms and to bury a person.

A healthy relationship with Nature cannot be based in expectations that it will always show only its most pleasing face, endlessly providing for our growing numbers and growing appetites. The earth is a complex and self-regulating system possessing its own intelligences. It is communicating with us, speaking in messages as subtle as small shifts in temperature and as obvious as massive wildfires. Its moods can seem capricious or cruel, alternating between beautiful and bountiful and dangerous and barren. It cycles through seasons with the face of a Flower Bride and with the face of

---

[275] Joseph Dodds (2020), 123.

a wintery hag. Ancient kings had to give up the dualistic thinking when faced with the Loathly Lady's riddle, and to be ready to "accept the feminine authority of Fate that he and his people were subject to."[276]

John Beckett writes:

> The land and the king are one! This concept is older than Arthur is even supposed to be. The king ruled the land, but he did not own the land. The land is an entity of its own, represented by the concept of sovereignty and the Goddess of Sovereignty. The king was joined to the land in sacred marriage and their fates were intertwined. If the king ruled wisely and justly, the land and the people would prosper. If the king ruled poorly, Sovereignty would withdraw her blessing, the land would go barren, the people would suffer, and the king would be replaced – perhaps peacefully, perhaps violently, and perhaps in a sacrifice where his blood was offered to restore the fertility of the land.[277]

While instituting a divine kingship—with or without sacrifices—would be difficult to implement today, and is a likely a terrible idea for many reasons, I believe we can apply this concept of partnering with the land in ways relevant to our lives. John Beckett interprets Sovereignty as "both the right to rule and the obligation to rule rightly. And that brings us to the key question ... who controls your sovereignty? Who is king of your life, and are you flourishing under that king's rule? Does your life honor the inherent dignity and worth that is yours simply by right of being alive?"

Rather than yielding sovereignty to others who use and abuse us (advertisers, politicians, producers of all kinds of PR and propaganda, or unhealthy relationships, among other usurpers), we can place ourselves in the role of the sovereign actor who vows to care for their people, and who draws upon the expertise of other members of the community.[278] Choices we make can be made under a vow to strive to live more lightly, with less encumbrance to ourselves (clutter, guilt, procrastination, obligations that

---

[276] See Artisson (2018), 111. Also see Bugge, 205.

[277] John Beckett's essay on Sovereignty can be found at Patheos Pagan.
Seán Pádraig O'Donoghue points out in his most recent work that in ancient Ireland, the king's role in bringing nourishment to his subjects was made extremely explicit: people would suck on the king's nipples. If he failed in his duties, betraying his land or his people, his nipples would be cut off and his body was tossed into a bog. This was not a "sacrifice" of the failed king's vital powers—it was a form of containment. His corpse was exposed to the preservative action of the bog's tannins because they would stall his body's decomposition and thus hinder his rebirth. This is in contrast with the burial of a good king, who is "buried with his ancestors beneath the Hollow Hills, held in the arms of his Wild Lover as his body dissolves into Hers and he prepares to be born again among his people." (2022), 26; 108.

[278] Another way to think of exercising sound judgment based in moderation and an understanding of one's own mind and of "the nature of things" is through the development of sophrosyne, which I will discuss in a subsequent chapter.

serve no good purpose). We can prioritize actions and relationships which help us, those around us, and the land to flourish.

We should try to set our household (*oikos*) and lands into order before asking for more favors. A ruler empowered by sovereignty acknowledges indebtedness to the land and receives its blessings under an obligation to serve it. True sovereigns don't conquer and dominate (this is the shadow archetype of the Tyrant). They serve life, and they honor reciprocal sovereignty in all the members of their community. They thus heal the separation between persons, between the people and the land, and between matter and spirit.

The true coronation of a sovereign being "marks the emergence of the unconscious into consciousness, the crystallization of chaos into order, the transcendence of compulsion into choice ... No longer the vassals of fear, we can bring order to the kingdom and build an international society on the love already shining through the cracks of the world of separation."[279]

To bring these themes to their conclusion, it is no wonder that deer often function as symbols of sovereignty, because the stag provides a very powerful model of leadership. Seán Padráig O'Donoghue relates an encounter that helped him see why this noble animal is considered a worthy example to follow. At a time just before the rutting season, he visited

> ... the remnant forest these herds call home, seeking to understand the ways of my ancestors. I prayed beneath an Oak at the edge of a field, and then rounded the bend to a thicket, where a Stag came out to meet me—barrel-chested and with antlers as wide as my arm span. He raised his head high and cantered across the field—first showing his power, then trying to lead me away from the herd, and then circling it to mark a protective boundary. I sat still, and soon he did too, resting beneath a tree while the does and the younger bucks grazed. In the way of the wild, when he knew his kin were safe, he relaxed into calm presence. I understood then that it was the Stag who taught us what a chieftain was—not the other way around. This was the authentic expression of sovereignty that Suibhne tried to hold onto in the face of the model of leadership that came with Christianity—a model that sought to make

---

[279] Eisenstein, 39-40.

the king and the chieftain enforcers of the rigid laws in a book written in a distant desert, as interpreted by Latin-speaking theologians.[280]

Like the deer encountered by O'Donoghue and the Lenape storyteller Deborah Russell, sovereignty is perceptive, and it is protective, but it isn't boastful, and it's certainly not narcissistic. To quote O'Donoghue again,

> People now tend to speak of sovereignty as being individual and personal—our right to control our own bodies and lives. But the individual rational actor is an invention of capitalism, a concept that severs our connections to land and community. In reality, our bodies and our minds are ecologies—communities of myriad beings coming together and giving rise to a more or less shared consciousness—and are completely interdependent with the humans and other-than-humans who share our landscape.

This is the "enchantment" alluded to by Lisel Mueller when she writes of a lost age when animals and people were in communication. The figure of the righteous king, or—by extension, anyone who is sovereign within a community of beings reliant upon each other in infinitely complex webs of relation—does not relish pomp or splendor, nor the power to give arbitrary orders and engage in self-aggrandizement and exploitation.

The sovereign's duty was to uphold the natural order, and to provide nourishment for his people. By taking the noble stag as an emblem and

---

[280] O'Donoghue (2021) 81. Suibhne, whose name is also written in English as Sweeney, and who is called "mad," was one of the last Pagan kings in Ireland. He was cursed by a saint for struggling against those who were building a church on his family's sacred land. The next time he went into battle, he went mad from the war trumpets and other sounds and took refuge in the wilderness. It is said that he lived in the trees and grew feathers. Later, he became a monk and wrote lyric poetry in the Irish language. As a bookend to the nursery rhyme "The hart he loves the high wood ... " I used at the opening to this chapter, here is an English translation of a fragment from one of his poems:

I prefer the re-
echoing of the belling of a Stag
among the peaks
to that arrogant horn,

Those unharnessed runners
from glen to glen!
Nobody tames
that royal blood,
each one aloof,
on its rightful summit,
antlered, watchful.

This abbreviated account of Suibhne's life and the verses (above) translated by Seamus Heaney are on p. 80 of O'Donoghue's book. Madness that drives one to live in the wild is also a recurring motif in Celtic and Arthurian legends. In *Owain*, the titular hero forgets to honor a promise he made to the Sovereignty figure of the Lady of the Fountain to return to her after three months. She appears unexpectedly and takes back a ring that had been a token of his faith, and this causes him to remember that he had broken his word. Maddened by shame and remorse, he flees the company of the court and spends a period among the beasts, where he can "regard the wonders of creation and understand [his] own relationship with plant and animal life" until he is cured. See *The Mabinogion*: Owain ap Urien; and Matthews, 113-14.

model—after the fashion of kings of old—we can also cherish our mortal lives and loves, and realize others will carry on after us. We can teach others to to build relations with the sacred, living land and the many other beings who share it with them.

Hubris and the Green Wall

Hubris (ὕβρις /hýbris) is a term familiar to many from ancient Greek literature, but the concept is recognizable in stories from many times and places. The Collins Dictionary defines hubris as pride or arrogance; and (in Greek tragedy) an excess of ambition, pride, etc., ultimately causing the transgressor's ruin. Merriam-Webster adds "overconfidence" to the nuances of the word, and explains that the ancient Greeks

> considered hubris a dangerous character flaw capable of provoking the wrath of the gods. In classical Greek tragedy, hubris was often a fatal shortcoming that brought about the fall of the tragic hero. Typically, overconfidence led the hero to attempt to overstep the boundaries of human limitations and assume a godlike status, and the gods inevitably humbled the offender with a sharp reminder of their mortality.[281]

Early usage of the word in a Greek context referred to wanton violence, insolence or outrage.[282] Specifically, in ancient Athens, it referred to the intentional use of violence for the purpose of humiliating or degrading the target, typically for pleasure or gratification. In modern terms, the crimes covered by this category include assault and battery, sexual assault, or the

---

[281] See Collins Dictionary. The Encyclopaedia Britannica entry on hubris discusses how the concept sometimes overlaps with the idea of the tragic flaw (hamartia) of figures in myth and history, such as Ajax, Oedipus, or Xerxes in Herodotus's history of the Persian Wars.
[282] See Etymology Online: "Hubris."

theft of public property or the property of religious institutions. Over time, a semantic shift took place, and hubris acquired the definition of "overweening presumption that leads a person to disregard the divinely fixed limits on human action in an ordered cosmos."[283]

The consequences for acts of hubris were social disgrace for both the victim and the perpetrator, and even the risk of a kind of curse: violating the limits given by the natural order dissolves one's identity, and even sometimes "exposes one to monstrousness."[284] Briana Saussy's story of Gawain and Ragnelle provides a perfect illustration of all of these themes, as we see that the maiden fled into the forest and became monstrous after the knight raped her. He was executed, thus perpetuating the violence, and the land became hostile, stingy, and incapable of supporting human life as a consequence.

The Ecology of Bad Ideas

There is an ecology of bad ideas, just as there is an ecology of weeds.[285] Our ancestors were adaptable and inventive, and they did everything possible to ensure that they would be provided for. They expanded their range out of the original African homeland into just about every part of Earth—except for Antarctica (until recently) and the depths of the sea (for now). In general, the only real check to expansion has been other human societies, those capable of repelling an invasion of territory they considered their own.[286]

Part of what facilitated humans' remarkable expansion and adaptations has been the degree and variety of cooperative behavior. As research by Botero et al. and by other zoologists indicates, cooperation allows various species of fauna to push themselves into regions that otherwise couldn't support them as solitary organisms. As this became a kind of "second nature" for our hominin ancestors, rules and norms came to replace previous limits imposed by natural conditions. Those limits were increasingly treat-

---

[283] See Encyclopaedia Britannica: "Hubris."
[284] *Muséum Manifesto: Facing the Limits*, 70.
[285] Gregory Bateson, quoted by Guattari, 27.
[286] *Muséum Manifesto: Facing the Limits*, 73.

ed with suspicion and hostility, and rejected on principle. As these habits became routine, people became overconfident in their powers.

Eventually, some who lived in the harshest landscapes developed doctrines about transcendent deities who are harsh, moralizing, and concerned with minutiae of our manners and behavior, while also granting us superiority and mastery over nature. When we are given (have taken) this right to dominion, nature is then externalized and alienated.

On the human side, there remained a form of spirit posited to be transcendent and eternal. This, in its turn, was later replaced in the dyad with a more secular notion of mind. Part of the process of both religious and secular education was to train us to identify with the eternal spirit/mind, while in turn treating matter, bodies, nature, or any beings lower on the Great Chain (even human beings) as resources to be exploited for the glory of oneself, one's king, or the God who sanctioned all of this. This resulted in the belief that meaning, and the justification for actions, always comes from a *higher* source, not from a lower "resource."

After the adoption of Bronze Age solar gods, and apace with the spread of social hierarchy as a norm, more and more peoples began to prioritize violent conquest and exploitation of others. Raising themselves up above their peers with palaces and ostentatious displays, as well with standing armies (and the wealth required to maintain them), led to ever-increasing and ever more unsustainable demands on the land. They asked solar and heaven-dwelling deities to aid and glorify their rule, and they imposed strict and moralizing religions on the people to ensure their cooperation.

Levels of consumption that are greater than it is possible to supply sustainably often leads to an economic, social, or military conflict. This is still true today, though often the conflicts are often out of sight and therefore out of mind.

Dualism in philosophical, theological, and scientific thinking intensified again during the West's Enlightenment. This moment shifted one half of the dyad from the theological conception of spirit to that of mind, likewise set in superior opposition to the body or the material world. For instance, René Descartes' dualism of mind and body proposed that "there is a great difference between mind and body, inasmuch as body is by nature always divisible, and the mind is entirely indivisible … the mind or soul of man is entirely different from the body." This was revolutionary, because it undermined truth claims put forth by secular and religious authorities in the Age of Absolutism. Despite Descartes' devout intention to naturalize a belief in God, immortal souls, and an afterlife in which souls are punished and rewarded, disembodied transcendent reason discarded theology in favor of mechanistic political and economic theories in the centuries to follow. Now, even parts of the world that didn't embrace Christian hegemony or the Enlightenment (such as the communist states in Asia) are affected by this dualism.

We have conceived of "nature" as something separate from ourselves. By believing that only what's in our brains or the biological organisms of our bodies are real, we mistrust our experiences of the body and the world around us. This leads to our modern insistence on mediating our experiences of the living world through technology.[287] What's left over is just "imagination," or symptoms of mental illness.

Necrophilia and Transhumanism

At its extreme, the dualistic antipathy toward life itself can verge into what the psychologist and social philosopher Erich Fromm described as "necrophilia." He was not referring to a sexual fetish for dead bodies, but a love of

> all that does not grow, all that is mechanical. The necrophilous person is driven by the desire to transform the organic into the inorganic, to approach life mechanically, as if all living persons were things ... Memory, rather than experience—having, rather than being—is what counts. The necrophilous person ... loves control, and in the act of controlling he kills life.[288]

For Fromm, deadening one's perception and pain were also necrophilic behaviors. "Transhumanist" fantasies, which dream of using technology to free individuals not only from injury and death, but also from old age and the constraints of a physical body, are surely one of the most necrophilic phenomena ever to appear. This worldview looks at computers and robots

---

[287] Paraphrased from White, p. 24.
[288] Fromm is quoted by Glenn Albrecht, 88.

not as tools to accomplish tasks, but as ideals that human beings fall short of and ought to strive to resemble. Here is a characterization of this way of thinking:

> ... the entirety of our personalities, thoughts, feelings, and memories [are] merely a result of an operating system and various programs running in our skull. Many people ponder if a personality could be downloaded as data to a computer, or if a computer could, given the right sequence of 1's and 0's gain conscious self-awareness, or even a soul. Transhumanists can hardly wait for a new bodiless age where personalities live in a digital cloud and can be downloaded in to a variety of human or robot bodies. The implications of this are highly dualistic, a kind of sci-fi Gnosticism. The body is thought to be something that restricts. An imperfection that prevents us from reaching the potential of pure mind or spirit.[289]

NBICs (nanotechnologies, biotechnologies, information technology and cognitive sciences) promise men and women the opportunity to defy death's promise of oblivion. Unsurprisingly, enterprises selling the idea that technology can provide physical perfection and mental immortality to those who can pay, or offering to rescue a few elites from a dying planet, enjoy considerable patronage from Big Tech corporations. This is more than just paid flattery for tech-bro oligarchs: to the extent that people believe that these technologies are extensions of themselves, they are creating (or perhaps simply refashioning) cosmologies.[290] These necrophilic cosmologies have not only grown out of older ones that contributed to killing the animals, plants, and the ecosystems that keep us alive, but they even rob death of its juicy, fertile power of recycling nutrients to provide the conditions for new life to emerge.

Necrophilia isn't only the preserve of the financial and technical elite. At a more popular level, there is a kind of mental derangement instilled by politicians, economists, and journalists who promote

> a vicious ideology of extreme competition that pits us against each other, encourages us to fear and mistrust each other and weakens the social bonds that make our lives worth living. The story of our competi-

---

[289] See Freeman.
[290] See Hui.

tive, self-maximizing nature has been told so often and with such persuasive power that we have accepted it as an account of who we really are. It has changed our perception of ourselves. Our perceptions, in turn, change the way we behave.[291]

Mistrustful, but with their appetites awakened, people become ungrateful and discontented: most of those who live in consumer capitalist societies are dissatisfied with their present material conditions. After a certain point, countries with rising standards of living do not always enjoy rising standards of happiness (the controversial Easterlin paradox), and when people in "developed" countries are asked how much income a person needs to be rich, the answer is usually about twice the amount that they are currently earning. Everyone compares themselves to others (this is explicitly encouraged), and measures themself against media presentations of a good, desirable lifestyle. Nearly everyone feels that they are coming up short, and many feel ashamed, as though they had failed.

The idea that enough "growth" can or should accommodate everyone's access to ever-expanding excess is underwritten by an impossible assumption of infinitely expanding finite material means. It seems to dangle the impossible carrot of "someday, we'll all get there" ahead of individuals and collectives, which mindlessly race after it.[292] The cultures of industrial societies tend to focus on material culture alien to the local environment: having enough (which means having more than most other people), means having something that costs more (to someone, somewhere) than what is easily provided for locally.[293]

Othering Nature

It's a long walk down the road from earlier cosmologies which favored connection to the perverse and pathological mental states many live in now. Glenn Albrecht proposes four stages through which experience of

---

[291] See Monbiot (2017) "How do we get out of this mess?"

[292] *Muséum Manifesto: Facing the Limits*, 80.

[293] Strang, 33. Gary Snyder contrasts "ecosystem-based cultures" and "biosphere cultures." The former refers to societies whose life and economies are centered in terms of natural regions and watersheds, and the latter are societies that discovered (seven or eight thousand years ago, in a few places) "that it was 'profitable' to spill over into another drainage, another watershed, another people's territory, and steal away its resources, natural or human. Thus, the Roman Empire would strip whole provinces for the benefit of the capital, and villa-owning Roman aristocrats would have huge slave-operated farms in the south using giant wheeled plows. Southern Italy never recovered" (46).

nature and life moves, ranging from a primal connection to complete detachment. "First nature" is where there is "a complete merging of self and the body with the greater forces of the Earth." Anthropologist Veronica Strang provides an example of this in Australian Aboriginal culture:

> Social and environmental sustainability are so closely integrated that they cannot be imagined independently. The close identification between clan groups and their local environments frames each part of Nature as an aspect of the self, incorporating and embodying Nature within human "being" in a seamless relationship between spiritual, social and physical existence. The intimacy of sensory experience in hunting and gathering, and the close-grained knowledge that supports it, reaffirm the projection of the self into the local environment as internalised aspects of social identity. In effect, the material world is not alienated and objectified, but is bound into a subjective co-identification. Nature is not merely "near"... it is integral to the self.[294]

Then, there is "'second nature,' where humans are still partially connected to first nature but forge their own technologically mediated Earth." Nature is framed as "other" to oneself, and it becomes expendable in relation to other needs and desires.[295] As this continues, the Earth is increasingly unable to supply what they demand; people become frustrated and angry, and they eventually withdraw from engagement with it and begin engaging in necrophiliac thinking and behavior. During the second stage, human cultures and languages undergo "extinction events,"[296] as words and concepts fall out of use and then become alien. For example, there has been a gradual removal of "nature words" such as *acorn, newt, fern, bluebell, blackberry,* and *kingfisher* from children's dictionaries in England, in favor of terms like *bullet-point, chatroom,* and *broadband.*[297]

Third nature is where "whatever nature is, it is no longer normally part of a totally technologically mediated human experience. There is a story of engagement, alienation, and then separation of humans from nature taking place here." These include Elon Musk, transhumanists who dream of

---

[294] Strang, 48.
[295] Ibid, 51.
[296] Albrecht, 68. The rest of the quotes relating to the four stages of separation and reconnection are also on this page.
[297] See *The Lost Words*, written by Robert Macfarlane and illustrated by Jackie Morris. This collaboration between a poet and a painter is what they call a "spell book," and it represents an attempt to conjure these disappearing animals and plants back into children's minds.

eternal AI afterlives, "long-termers" who are willing to sacrifice people alive now for the "vast and glorious" potential of humanity's future,[298] and all those who have gone numb or who are trying to anesthetize themselves into an unfeeling stupor with drugs.

Consider: where are all the other species in AI? The otters and kingfishers and blackberries—are they going to be present as flat simulations, or did the architects of the future worlds decide we no longer need them? The loss of direct experience and its replacement by technological mediation is far more than just aesthetic: our human minds have been shaped in relation to countless other-than-human intelligences. Losing them, cashing them in, and sacrificing them means also losing ourselves. As Robin Artisson wrote:

> Long before we became so entangled with our human social world and so mentally separated from the other-than-human world, human and animal co-created and co-shaped one another. Humans and the land co-created and co-shaped one another. We are foolish if we imagine that our dream of separation from Nature has caused these older bonds to cease functioning. They are still here, aching inside of us like a dream devalued and ignored. Every being, every phenomenon in our world of experience represents a pre-existing relationship, or a potential for new relationship, an opportunity for change, transformation, and co-creation. Thus, every time a being vanishes from our world, every time a family of animals goes extinct, or a family of plants vanishes, the range of transformative and insightful creative potential that our entities might express is forever lessened. We are forever diminished, whether or not we consciously realize this. The more of the world we destroy, the more of ourselves we destroy and degrade.[299]

---

[298] Let me get more specific about what kind of racist, eugenic dystopia these people advocating for: In the pursuit of this "vast and glorious potential," longtermists argue:

"we must not 'fritter ... away' our resources on such things as solving global poverty. It is for this goal that we should consider implementing a global surveillance system, keep pre-emptive war on the table, and focus more on superintelligent machines than saving people in the Global South from the devastating effects of climate change (mostly caused by the Global North). In fact, Beckstead has even argued that, for the sake of attaining this goal, we should actually prioritise the lives of people in rich countries over those in poor countries, since influencing the long-term future is of 'overwhelming importance', and the former are more likely to influence the long-term future than the latter. To quote a passage from Beckstead's 2013 PhD dissertation, which Ord enthusiastically praises as one of the most important contributions to the longtermist literature:

"Saving lives in poor countries may have significantly smaller ripple effects than saving and improving lives in rich countries. Why? Richer countries have substantially more innovation, and their workers are much more economically productive. [Consequently,] it now seems more plausible to me that saving a life in a rich country is substantially more important than saving a life in a poor country, other things being equal.

"This is just the tip of the iceberg ..." (See Torres).

[299] Artisson (2018), 47-8.

"Third nature" is a painful form of slow dismemberment that can be numbed with drugs and ideologies, but cannot be healed using its own logic and means. This is like the Fisher King, whose generative powers have been destroyed, and he languishes with a painful wound from which he cannot die. "Fourth nature" is where a reintegration takes place. As Strang writes, "genuine sustainability relies upon beliefs, systems, and practices in which Nature is accepted as 'self' rather than repudiated as 'other'."[300]

The Green Wall

One of the dysfunctional behaviors as we move from Albrecht's second to third stages is the literal backgrounding of the living world as an environment. The word "*environment*' makes us think of a stable and reliable backdrop as in the theater, in front of which 'real' human life and history takes place." However, the neat distinction between foreground and background is illusory,[301] and the illusion is founded in hubristic habits of mind.

The ethnobotanist and herbalist Hayden Stebbins uses the term "green wall" to refer to a habit of perception in which people see plants and even the entire natural world as only a background to the real experience of the world they live in.[302] This is a symptom of what Glenn Albrecht would classify as the third stage of separation. However, it is possible to reverse this kind of green-blindness and begin to really see plants; then, the other non-human beings also start coming into focus.

In an interview, Stebbins recommended walking through any local green space that's available, finding a place where you can slow down and take a few moments to closely observe something growing there: perhaps a tree, a flower, a mushroom. But whatever it is, keep coming back to see it.

The interviewer followed up with: "It's an interesting concept, to come back to the same plant or a mushroom or a tree instead of, say, taking a long wander through nature. What's the psychology behind that?" And Stebbins replied:

---

[300] Strang, 52.

[301] Joseph Dodds (2020), 3. He also points out that this artificial distinction entirely collapses during a natural catastrophe, when it becomes evident that what was assumed to be a background is not fixed in the ways we imagined, and—even more terrifying—it has forms of agency that can burst forth in shows of overwhelming force.

[302] See Deitz.

> You start to see that plant over time. And when you do that, you see how it changes through the seasons. And I think that's one of the best ways to stop seeing plants as background—to see that they are individual organisms, and to see that they change. Just like visiting a friend. If you see a friend and you're just walking by and you say, "Hi," every morning, that's different than actually stopping and having a conversation with them.[303]

We cannot solve the problems caused by hubris by engaging in more of it. As paradoxical as it seems, sometimes the concept of "the environment" separates us from the forces of life. No one lives in "the environment" or experiences a particular location as "the environment." And yet, we ask it to supply us with resources, and even "environmental services"—such as cleaning the air—without limitations. Applying an insight similar to the Freudian critique of relating to the Earth as Mother, Brendan Myers writes:

> As a civilization we have assumed that the Earth can always bear the loss of what we take from it, and always carry the load of what we return to it. This assumption, which I shall call the illusion of infinite carrying capacity, was not seriously examined or doubted in the whole history of civilization until the rise of mathematical ecology in the mid-nineteenth century. Plenty of people today, perhaps yourself among them, understand that this assumption is false. But plenty more people still behave as if they believe it's true.[304]

Like the tales of heroes who discovered the answer to the riddle of what women want most, just having a theoretical answer is not enough. There has to be a thoroughgoing change in perception that puts it into action.

---

[303] Ibid.
[304] Myers; no page number available prior to forthcoming publication.

Sophrosyne and the Extended Mind

A quote spuriously attributed to Carl Jung goes: "People don't have ideas. Ideas have people" (his real quote related to "complexes" having people).[305] But I want to leave pathological or hubristic states of mind back in the last chapter: here, we'll begin examining how non-human input opens our minds up like raising the blinds and opening the window in a stuffy room. The poet e.e. cummings gifted us with a beautiful image: "your head is a living forest full of song birds." Let's now make a chiasmus out of his line: *the forest full of song birds is your head*. This is because your mind is partially constituted by other beings and elements—living things, and also the land, the weather, the time of day, and much more.

What effect will opening the mind more to a flow with the outside world have? For one, overweening ego, cultural neuroses, and the endless arguments among competing human points of view may be drowned out by a just little birdsong.

---

[305] Jung's exact words were:"Everyone knows nowadays that people 'have complexes.' What is not so well known, though far more important theoretically, is that complexes can have us." See Jung, paragraph 200.

The opposite of hubris is *sophrosyne* (σωφροσύνη), a Greek word which is sometimes said to have no true equivalents in other languages. It is derived from the roots σῶς (*sôs*, "safe, sound") and φρήν (*phrḗn*, "mind"), and is considered to be a virtue or ideal of excellence, as well as "soundness of mind" or moral sanity. The classical philologist and literary scholar Helen North has described sophrosyne as the union of self-knowledge with self-restraint, and that is where we will find a perspective that allows for readjustment.[306]

One who has sophrosyne should also display qualities such as temperance, moderation, prudence, purity, and self-control.[307] For the Stoic philosopher Zeno of Citium, sophrosyne was one of the four cardinal virtues, along with wisdom, courage, and justice. Heraclitus's Fragment 112 ranks it first among them: "Sophrosyne is the greatest virtue, and wisdom is speaking and acting the truth, paying heed to the nature of things." Choosing sophrosyne over hubris is choosing temperance over impatience, self-control over self-confidence, and calm over resentment.[308]

Greek literature, drama, and philosophy frequently contrasted behavior driven by hubris with behavior tempered by sophrosyne for edifying purposes. In "Hubris and the Green Wall" I discussed the vice of hubris, which is an excess of pride that leads people to arrogate capabilities, resources, or destinies to themselves beyond what ought to be provided for them. Here, we will look at the "nature of things" that shape our thoughts, and by the end we will arrive at perspectives that can dissolve hubris and reintegrate the human mind back into the world that gives rise to it.

Humans Are More Than Mind

The first matter that needs to be settled is that we are not just what's in our heads: cognition cannot be localized to our brains, nor is it a thing that can be directly observed or measured. Western thinking has treated the body as secondary to the mind, an object in a world of objects in a tradition

---

[306] See Le Cunff.

[307] Ibid. Also, let's recall the etymology of the Welsh name Pwyll discussed earlier: mind, wisdom, and intelligence, but also discretion, prudence, judgement, and sanity—all very sophrosynic qualities, and an example of similar ideals found outside of Greece.

[308] Ibid.

that reaches back (at least) to Plato. That unfortunate framework was then updated and extended by René Descartes, and promulgated widely during the Scientific Revolution.[309]

It has only been since the early 20th century that Western scholars even attempted to look for cognition in the body. The modern conception of embodied cognition has its intellectual roots in the work of John Dewey; it was further developed by the existentialist philosophers Martin Heidegger, John Dewey, Albert Camus, Jean-Paul Sartre, and Maurice Merleau-Ponty, and it has only been studied empirically (especially physiologically) in the past few decades.[310]

In recent years, medical researchers have also been exploring the symbiotic relationships between human bodies and microorganisms. One of their most important findings has been how the enteric nervous system and its microflora influence not just physical health, but also mental health, our behavior, and our moods. This is called the "gut-brain axis," and its implications for individual well-being, and our conceptual, social, and emotional worlds, are staggering.[311]

Maurice Merleau-Ponty's philosophical conception of the body/mind relationship arose from the simple idea that we "inhabit" our bodies rather than "having" them, which represents a shift in the earlier beliefs that of the that we are spiritual beings or pure intellect imprisoned within corruptible flesh. Such a false notion can be observed in certain religions, and is a primary tenet of the "transhumanist" movement I discussed in the last chapter. That's a movement which dreams of transcending the limitation of the flesh and the physical world for the benefit of a disembodied mind. When we hear someone speaking of inhabiting a "meat suit," or when they share memes with vaguely cosmic imagery, often accompanied by the Je-

---

[309] A kind of disenchantment also took place within ancient Israeli society. The Israelites "weren't scientists, but they gradually developed a sense that there are rules that govern what happens in the world, and violations of those rules, *miracles*, became more and more infrequent. *People still encountered God, but there was a definite movement from outside to inside; the soul gradually became what it had never been before, a kind of divine island in the midst of the human body.* Most of all, people's sense of self evolved; the divine no longer began where a person's fingertips ended, and people were no longer as open to an uncanny surprise just around the corner." However, this is as much as I want to engage with this line of evolution in the Abrahamic tradition (James Kugel, cited by Sigal Samuel, emphasis mine).

[310] See McNerney.

[311] Essentially, humans are holobionts—this means we are composite entities made up of a host that sponsors other species (such as viruses, bacteria, etc.) living in and around it rather than truly individual organisms. There is less DNA that is yours within you than there is DNA that belongs to other species. And we have this condition in common with all other animals as well as trees and other plants, whole forests, and coral reefs.

suit priest and theologian Pierre Teilhard de Chardin's[312] (usually unattributed) quote: "We are not physical beings having a spiritual experience, we are spiritual beings having a physical experience," we are seeing echoes of this traditional dualism. We also encounter it in New Age communities that emphasize ascension (or "ascended masters") or transcendence.

In order to create some distance from binary models of this ilk, Maurice Merleau-Ponty described an "objective" body that, like other physical objects, has particular physical properties (such as size, weight, and so on) which can be empirically measured or captured in a photograph. This "objective" body is far less important than the "lived body," the body through which we touch, feel, and move, which grounds us as "body-subjects" or as experiencing beings.[313]

Later, the cognitive linguist George Lakoff and the psychologist Rafael Núñez would explain that the human mind is an emergent phenomenon that arises out of "the nature of our brains, bodies, and bodily experiences. This is not just the innocuous and obvious claim that we need a body to reason; rather, it is the striking claim that the very structure of reason itself comes from the details of our embodiment."[314]

Merleau-Ponty wrote, in *Phenomenology of Perception*, that you'd never have to look for your right arm the way you look for an object on your desk, and you will never directly observe the back of your neck. We do not abstract ourselves the way others (such as scientists and philosophers) abstract us when we are actually engaged in the business of living. When we inquire into our everyday experiences, we always find that we are involved in some way with the world around us, and this world is shared with oth-

---

[312] Teilhard had other, shall we say, *interesting* conceptions that prioritized mind over matter. For example, he developed the "Omega Point" theory, which draws on physics and evolutionary theory to describe a progression from inanimate matter to a full "hominization" that suffuses the cosmos with a "noosphere" (cognitive dimension) that can be pushed toward an ultimate convergence called the Omega Point. This is a final evolutionary stage that takes total dominance over the biosphere and all matter and reaches a point of complete independence from physical factors and is, verily, God Himself. Talk about an Anthropocene—this is its extension from our planet and its immediate environs into all space and time and, using our "noosphere" (thoughts and prayers?), crushing the entire universe into a singularity that somehow matches the broad outlines of Near Eastern eschatology.
  The renegade priest was banished to China by the church authorities for his denial of the doctrine of Original Sin, for teaching that all people will be resurrected from the dead, and sundry other heresies. Yet his theories were, and still are, influential. Salvador Dali was one of those who drew upon his ideas, and some fifty years later, a physicist named Frank J. Tipler attempted to resurrect the Omega Point theory, with some concepts and equations in a book that was not very well received by the scientific community. As one critic dryly commented, Tipler wants us to know that "the Omega Point loves us" (see Johnson). Despite these mythical trappings and all the heat it's not such a different conception than what strictly materialist Enlightenment thinking offers, which is just the endless grinding of the gears of a giant and very complex machine until its eventual cold and meaningless death.

[313] See Dan Nixon's excellent essay on Merleau-Ponty and embodiment.

[314] These authors are cited by Samuel McNerney.

ers. "It's ultimately a bodily awareness of this 'intertwining' that fosters our sensitivity towards other people,"[315] or what philosopher Glen Mazis calls "embodiment's access to the heart."[316] In order to cultivate compassion, connection, and intimacy, we must be aware of others, and of their own sensitive, embodied, and vulnerable perceiving.[317]

Philosophers, theologians, and others working with reductive binary models had been looking for personhood in all the wrong places. Ari Freeman cites the philosopher Alva Noë, from the University of California, Berkeley, on how philosophers and scientists were missing the larger picture in their quest to isolate physical details. Trying to find consciousness within neurons is like

> trying to find the dancing in the musculature of the dancer. Or trying to find the value of money in the chemical composition of the dollar bill. It's the wrong kind of place to look. The idea that I've had in my work is that instead of thinking of consciousness as something that happens within us, in our brains or anywhere else, why don't we try and think of consciousness as something that we do, or enact, or perform in our dynamic involvement with the world around us.[318]

Félix Guattari was reaching toward a conceptualization of a subject that is an effect—rather than a cause—with his suggestion of "components" or "vectors" of subjectification (factors that create the thinking subject). His subject was not a starting point, but rather a certain outcome. However, this outcome is not a final one, because it becomes vector-like itself. Because it is both individuated and more capable of uniting with others, it is

---

[315] Certainly, contemporary humanities and social science disciplines have been moving beyond earlier ideas of atomistic individuals for quite some time already. The "network self" model began in the late 20th century, when philosophers began to take anthropological (ethnographic) views and narrative structuring that treats selfhood as an ongoing, dynamic process more seriously. Feminist scholars and communitarians have promoted relational models that foreground social embeddedness, relationships, and contexts (see Wallace.) I am not attempting here to win points against models that have by and large been abandoned by serious thinkers and left to rot with politicians and industry leaders. Atomistic individualism has been challenged for a long time in the arts, social sciences, and humanities, but it still remains entrenched in economics, law, politics, and even ethics (see Albrecht, 95), so it is necessary to focus energies on bringing the insights to those places. The point of the retrospective view is to take a look at ideas that were predominant and shaped institutions and behaviors that are still creating ill effects in the world today.

[316] Speaking of matters of the heart: medical science has known since the early 1990s that the heart contains some 40,000 neurons and has its own nervous system that does its own processing in a "little brain." The heart sends more signals to the brain than vice versa, and it is probably a key regulator of cognitive and emotional as well as physical pain signals—as poets have known for ages (see Alshami).

[317] See Nixon.

[318] See Freeman.

capable of engaging in more ecological modes of thinking and acting, and these modes resist the artificial closure of an excessively individualistic perspective.[319]

Nine years later, an influential paper titled "The Extended Mind," by Andy Clark and David Chalmers, both cognitive scientists and philosophers, provided a more functional description of some of the ways the objects in one's physical environment can serve as parts of the mind. They point out that the predominant model of the brain imagines it as a processing center, one that creates mental models of reality, calculating input, options, and likely outcomes. That processing center then gives us impulses we react upon, which is the moment when the mind-body barrier is breached. The problem, Sigal Samuel tells us, is that this proposed structure is a phantom.

> ... scientists cannot find anything physical in the brain that acts in such a way. The entity of "I myself" is a "mental construct" which is neither identical to our bodies or our brains, but is something emergent that evolved over millions of years. It's more like a function we use to explain to ourselves what's going on.

The problem is that certain kinds of cultural conditioning convince us that this is the "real me" that possesses the body and brain,[320] much in the same way as panentheism posits a Creator deity that both permeates and stands outside its creation.

Clark and Chalmers theorize that evolution has favored capacities ranging from "shortcuts afforded by bodily motion and locomotion to contingent facts about the structure of natural scenes in order to allow the local environment to reduce the burden on memory."[321] They were the first to introduce the term "extended mind" to Western scholarly literature. However, while they were explicitly discussing human beings, if their theory has biological, evolutionary justification, it should be applicable be applied to other species, as well.

---

[319] Guattari, 35-6; 68.
[320] See Clark and Chalmers; Samuel.
[321] See Clark and Chalmers.

"Everything Gardens"

As Bill Mollison said, "everything gardens." That is, every organism participates in the creation of its habitat—though some do it in ways that are more obvious. Trees exhale oxygen; animals exhale carbon dioxide; fungi help the trees grow; insects pollinate; bears excrete the remains of salmon and fertilize forest soil. Some of the more dramatic examples of animal "gardening" include arctic foxes (which create adorable little gardens around their dens) and beavers.

The ways these creatures interact with their environments suggest that they, too, have part of their mental processes involved in acts of intervention, as well as in the spaces they create. Octopodes have been known since 2009 to build cities for their kind. The first such sedentary colony was dubbed Octopolis, and then a colony of "gloomy octopus" (*Octopus tetricus*) was discovered 50 feet below the surface of the water in Jervis Bay, south of Sydney. This one, called Octlantis, is a kind of artificial reef constructed by the cephalopods, where they are safe from sharks, seals, and dolphins. The built environment even includes individual dens. Perhaps unsurprisingly, the life of urban octopodes is different than the life of their more solitary kin, as they engage in frequent squabbles over the dens, kicking others out when they intrude.[322]

One of the simplest forms of interaction between the world of material things, perception, and cultural ideas is found in *pareidolia*, the perception of a meaningful image in a random or ambiguous source material. It can happen spontaneously to anyone, and then the image, whether of eyes in the bark of a tree or Jesus in a piece of toast, can be communicated to others, who may also see the same image. Numerous experiments have proved that infants experience pareidolia with images that roughly resemble human faces. These tendencies go back very far indeed in our evolution: at least as far back as the Australopithecines, who found and cherished the Makapansgat pebble, a "river-worn stone whose naturally formed contours resemble crude eyes and a mouth ... they buried it with their dead at a site in South Africa, far away from its original source." Joanne Lee comments:

---

[322] See Hoare.

whilst it is impossible to know how this stone was viewed or interpreted at the time, and what were the perceptive and cognitive capabilities of such beings, thanks to its apparently purposeful relocations archaeologists have hypothesized that it may well have been recognized as a face, and that this seemed to have some significance for the hominids concerned.[323]

Beyond interaction with physical artifacts (which of course bear some form of culturally-mediated meaning), language appears to be a "central means by which cognitive processes are extended into the world." Clark and Chalmers write: "it may be that language evolved, in part, to enable such extensions of our cognitive resources."[324] Further aids we have developed to extend our minds from sensory inputs and current thoughts include anything used to record information, from notches on a stick or knots on a cord to paper and pencils to computers. All of these options for "offloading" cognition free up short-term memory, which is a huge advantage, since our short-term memory capacity is limited. By extension, if we can record and remember the physical world, then we can also change our depictions and ordering of it for the purpose of affecting changes within our minds or moods, which is one of the ideas behind the change of mood that can be effected by redecorating a room, and of course also by myths and magical rituals.

For at least the last 60,000 years (though it's probably much longer), humans have connected physical, mythical, and imaginary places through songlines (in Australia), *dindshenchas* (in Ireland), star maps, and the "method of loci" to aid memory and facilitate familiarity with landscapes.[325] These older methods of storing and sharing memories, and of participating in the ongoing process of creating the world, are parallel in some ways to the more recent practice of putting thoughts onto paper or into computers for accessing later.

Humans are not unique in doing such things. Brazilian biologist Hilton Japyassú observed spiders the using their webs as an extension of their sensory system and a supplement to their cognitive system.[326] This con-

---

[323] See Lee.
[324] See Clark and Chalmers.
[325] See Hamacher.
[326] See Sokol.

forms with theories that had hitherto only been applied to human beings. The use of such techniques by "simpler" creatures indicates just how widespread extended cognition may be across species, and this may be considered one of the aspects that defines living organisms.[327]

Human technology extends our connected minds through probes that have passed beyond the boundaries of our solar system or have been immersed into the deepest ocean trenches. We can communicate with any human being who has compatible technology and a communications signal at any other place on our planet. However, when we turn our gaze in the opposite direction—back towards ourselves—the view is much less impressive. As a hatha yoga teacher (one of my other jobs), the most common problems students ask me for help with are the many physical effects of spending hours hunched over their computer and telephone screens. Physically, we are starting to revert into the shape of fetuses or larvae, and we have aching backs and shallow breathing patterns. Humans are voluntarily participating in disembodiment for either part or most of every day, and the effects of this are painful when the trance wears off.

It's clear evolution required us to attune to our environments, or—as Brendan Myers put it—"human beings are 'already ecological' because our perceptual intelligence grants us the ability to gather deep knowledge of our surroundings." To head off any misconceptions, this doesn't mean that the ability to use this perceptual intelligence is automatic: it must be practiced and trained. He continues: "this knowledge is 'deep' in the sense that it requires years of patience and consistent attendance to gather, and requires the sentience of your whole body to process and to reason toward conclusions."

Myers connects the exercising of this faculty to the relationships we build with the landscapes around us:

> the more you get to know a landscape, the more the landscape rubs off on your mind, massaging it, working it over, planting seeds in it, pushing its footprints into it. Eventually the landscape becomes so much a feature of your mind that it also becomes a feature of your identity. It

---

[327] Taking things even farther, the theory of panpsychism advances a position that all matter, even down to simple particles like electrons, participates in consciousness to some extent. "Where there is mind, there is matter and where there is matter there is mind. They go together." I have sympathy for this view, and have in the past discussed the implications of particle behavior for Paganism, but any further discussion lies outside the purview of this present work. (See Hunt; Reidinger; in Giri.)

gets that far when a complete account of who you are must necessarily include a few statements about the places where you possess this kind of deep knowledge, the time you spent acquiring it, and the things you've done in your life because of it.[328]

But if the two-dimensional images on our screens become our landscapes of reference, we are going to forfeit a lot of well-being.

The Mind of Nature

Spending more time outdoors is crucial to restoring physical, mental, and spiritual health, not only to ourselves, but to all the other beings we interact with. These salutary effects were well known by the Transcendentalist authors of the 19th century.[329] For instance, Henry David Thoreau found restorative value in reverential, observant hauntings of places left to self-manage, such as Mt. Katahdin, and the environs of Walden Pond. In *Walden*, he writes:

> We can never have enough of nature. We must be refreshed by the sight of inexhaustible vigor, vast and Titanic features, the sea-coast with its wrecks, the wilderness with its living and its decaying trees, the thunder cloud, and the rain which lasts three weeks and produces freshets. We need to witness our own limits transgressed, and some life pasturing freely where we never wander.[330]

The Transcendentalists had a profound influence on John Muir, who not only appreciated wild landscapes, but also put a great deal of effort into preserving them from civilized "development." Muir believed that nature is good for everyone, and he is a premiere example of how a love for wild lands can lead to an ardent desire to protect them from destructive inter-

---

[328] See Myers.

[329] The Transcendentalists were voicing views that were fairly radical for their time; a time when tall tales of Paul Bunyan clearing massive tracts of forest were considered amusing and heroic. Alexis de Tocqueville, who described a journey in Michigan in 1831 (before the Transcendentalists were writing) was hoping to enjoy the kind of wilderness that had long ago disappeared from Europe. Hannah Lewis relates that when he and his guides asked for directions, they found themselves forced to introduce themselves as land prospectors in order to receive any help because it was incomprehensible to anyone that the wilderness itself was something that people might seek out and appreciate. When he reached his destination at Saginaw, he wrote:
"All that one feels in passing through these flowery wildernesses where everything, as in Milton's Paradise, is ready to receive man is a quiet admiration, a gentle melancholy sense, and a vague distaste for civilized life, a sort of primitive instinct that makes one think with sadness that soon this delightful solitude will have changed its looks. In fact, already the white race is advancing across the forest that surrounds it, and in but a few years the Europeans will have cut the trees that are now reflected in the limpid waters of the lake and forced the animals that live on its banks to retreat into new wildernesses."
This landscape would soon give way to a timber town, and then a manufacturing hub, and then it fell into the same postindustrial decline as other Rust Belt cities. See Lewis, 26-7.

[330] Thoreau, 238.

ventions. He wrote in one of his (originally unpublished) journals: "There is a love of wild nature in everybody, an ancient mother-love showing itself whether recognized or no, and however covered by cares and duties."[331] Getting out of our over-civilized spaces and habits revitalizes us:

> Thousands of tired, nerve-shaken, over-civilized people are beginning to find out that going to the mountains is going home; that wildness is a necessity; and that mountain parks and reservations are useful not only as fountains of timber and irrigating rivers, but as fountains of life. Awakening from the stupefying effects of the vice of over-industry and the deadly apathy of luxury, they are trying as best they can to mix and enrich their own little ongoings with those of Nature, and to get rid of rust and disease.[332]

When we have recognized mind's essential embeddedness in its surroundings, it is a short step from there to understanding that it would be *healthful*, *wise*, and *enjoyable* to cultivate the open exchange of information among sensing and receiving centers. As Tany Roniger puts it,

> The world is abuzz with animate forces, and we are among its many transmitters and receivers ... but then, if all bodies and things are always moving and changing, everything throbbing and pulsating with the animacy of the universe, this capriciousness should not be so surprising.[333]

Why does this visceral enthrallment feel so satisfying? The late Edward O. Wilson's biophilia hypothesis borrows the essential insight from Erich Fromm (who probably adapted it from Albert Schweitzer): humans have an innate psychological attraction to all that is alive and vital. Numerous studies document the reasons why we are *not* indulging in this more, which include overwork, online distractions, parenting styles that discourage children from unstructured outdoor play, and newer laws and guidelines for social workers penalizing parents who allow their children to explore their local habitats without adult supervision.

---

[331] Cited by Worster, 319.

[332] From Muir, *Our National Parks*, 1. See O'Donoghue (2021), 103, for the claim that people who spend a long time alone in the wilderness will have elevated serotonin levels that "lead to a greater attunement to the subtle sensory information coming in from the world around them and a greater ability to think in nonlinear ways."

[333] See Roniger.

Those of us who must spend much of the day confined indoors are clearly not experiencing optimal levels of immersion in our ecosystems. Many of us live in cities and other places where the ecosystems have been horrifically blighted. The (US) Environmental Protection Agency estimates that the average American spends 93% of their time indoors.[334] If they would like to make more connection with "nature"—even a park—conscious effort is required to do so.

If "biophilia" is an innate drive to seek pleasure in the natural world, our bodies and minds suffer when we are separated from participation in the animacy of our biomes. There is a growing literature that describes the baneful effects of "nature-deficit" disorder on adults and children, and on society as a whole,[335] as well as a "life-force deficit" or "ecological boredom"[336] that robs us of a certain spark or inspired sense of purpose.

When it is possible to spend time in outdoor settings, it's ideal to select somewhere large enough to stroll around. In recent years, there has been a fair amount of hype around a form of outdoor mindfulness or ecotherapy called *shinrin yoko*, "forest bathing." The practice was developed in Japan in the 1980s, with the intention of remedying burnout in tech-sector workers, and to inspire people towards connection to the country's forests so they would want to protect them.[337] Qing Li, the president of the Japanese Society of Forest Medicine and the author of several popular books and scientific articles on the benefits of forest bathing, writes:

> This is not exercise, or hiking, or jogging. It is simply being in nature, connecting with it through our senses of sight, hearing, taste, smell and touch. *Shinrin-yoku* is like a bridge. By opening our senses, it bridges the gap between us and the natural world.[338]

This brings very tangible benefits to overall health, including reduced stress, reduced blood pressure, lower blood sugar levels, better mood, improved ability to focus (even for children with ADHD),

---

[334] See Li.
[335] Richard Louv coined this term, and discusses it in *Last Child in the Woods: Saving Our Children From Nature-Deficit Disorder* (2005) and *The Nature Principle: Human Restoration and the End of Nature-Deficit Disorder*.
[336] See Mortali; MacFarland; Monbiot (2014).
[337] See Fitzgerald.
[338] See Li.

faster recovery from surgery or illness, increased energy level, improved sleep, and better immune system functioning.[339]

Got more time? Go on a longer hike. Rob Greenaway, one of the founders of ecopsychology, noted that "civilization is only four days deep." By this, he meant that the first three or four days hikers spend on a wilderness trek are marked by discomfort as they experience the loss of running water, phone signals, and other comforts. Once this passes, then they begin to feel "an increased sense of aliveness" and "feelings of expansion or reconnection." This "wilderness effect" has been observed by guides for decades.[340]

There are social benefits found in cultures that perceive nature as a spiritual force. The American eco-psychologist and activist Chellis Glendinning describes a connection between the minds of those who live in Indigenous cultures to what she calls the Primal Matrix:

> The state of a healthy, wholly functioning psyche in full-bodied participation with the healthy earth. Our Primal Matrix grew from the earth, is inherently part of the earth, and is built to thrive in intimacy with the earth.[341]

Indigenous scientists have also pursued lines of research that reconcile Indigenous perspectives with formal academic discourse. This work is not only theoretical, but also proposes practical solutions. While non-Indigenous peoples might consider land as a form of personal property they own, a commodity to trade, or an asset to make profits from, Indigenous populations have a deeper connection that doesn't partake of these views.

I do not want to make excuses for land theft from Native populations and the ongoing exploitation that are the background to some people's decisions to move to cities. However, the findings I cite, which discuss Native populations in urban environments, demonstrate that

> maintaining connections with and having a relationship to nature and the "land" is not dependent on access to a literal material place or physical location, but can often involve symbolic or sacred representations, and spiritual relationships with broader more universalizing notions of "Mother Earth."

---

[339] See Hatala et al.
[340] Cited by White, 233-34.
[341] Cited by O'Donoghue (2022), 72.

As Andrew Hatala and his coauthors point out, health is not conceived of in many Indigenous cultures as merely physical health, nor as merely the absence of disease, but it also comprises a balance of four elements—the physical, emotional, mental, and spiritual—integrally bound together. When people are able to draw on these four elements, they show more positive adaptation and resistance "in the face of colonization, historical traumas, or structural violence, as well as current stresses, challenges, and demands." This study emphasizes that nature (or Mother Earth, or the healing elements of place) need not be sought out in remote rural locations, but can also be accessed in an urban environment. The researchers conclude that natural environments should be conserved, expanded, and made culturally safe and meaningful.

One place where this is being implemented successfully is on the grounds of the Yakama National Correctional and Rehabilitation Facility, in Washington State. Volunteers created a small forest there, shaped like a traditional medicine wheel—a vehicle for health and well-being. This forest is used as an outdoor classroom, where tribal elders can teach traditional crafts and hunting, foraging and gardening skills. Clients also meet there with staff who try to help them with drug and alcohol addictions and other problems. The rehabilitation program also teaches clients to grow herbs and corn, and they cook wild game together and participate in sweat lodges. It's a promising start to efforts at healing the many intergenerational traumas this community has endured. Tribal Elder Marylee Jones commented: "Now they're aware of their own culture, their own curriculum, their own calendar. The forest will teach every one of those inmates ... The plants are coming up out of the ground. We're also coming up."[342]

Practicing Sophrosyne

Those not part of a traditional or contemporary Earth-based religion can regardless benefit from a spiritual connection. Forest bathing, with its cultivation of sensory awareness, is certainly a valuable practice, but there is another dimension beyond the basic five senses that can be activated by those who want to feel more connected to the landscapes they move in, to

---

[342] See Lewis, 97-101.

penetrate the "green wall" and involve themselves in the animacy of being. It's a dimension that is often connected with religious or spiritual experiences: *awe.*

An experiment was conducted by a team of researchers from San Francisco and Dublin. They divided the research subjects of healthy older adults into two groups, both of which took weekly fifteen-minute walks for a period of eight weeks. A control group was simply sent out on walks, but the "awe" group were given a description of the emotion by the researchers, and it was suggested that they try to experience it on their walks. In contrast with the control group, who mainly focused on their usual concerns while they were out walking, the "awe" group of participants reported "increased positive emotions and less distress" in their lives. They were also asked to take photos of themselves while out on their walks. Interestingly, as they continued the practice, the photos showed their portraits growing smaller over time, as their focus increasingly shifted to their surroundings. The size of their smiles also grew measurably as they continued. Control group participants didn't know what the aim of the research was. Many guessed it had something to do with exercise, so they tended to walk more often than the "awe" group (perhaps in hopes of impressing the researchers), and they did not achieve the same level of psychological benefits.[343]

Being a small element in a large landscape, filled with many more non-human creatures than humans, is the condition our Paleolithic ancestors experienced and depicted in their cave paintings. The hypothesis proposed by Henri Breuil, which states that cave artists were depicting creatures they would like to hunt and eat, has not been borne out by empirical evidence such as faunal remains. Scholars have never arrived at a definitive interpretation of these images, but essayist Barbara Ehrenreich cites the conspicuous fact commented on by paleoarchaeologist Jean Clottes, that "the essential role played by animals evidently explains the small number of representations of human beings. In the Paleolithic world, humans were not at the centre of the stage."

---

[343] See University of California, San Francisco in *Medical Express.*

It is hard for modern human beings, such as the ones who work at the Centers for Disease Control, to fathom a worldview in which we are only one of many beings that make up the world. The CDC "expresses puzzlement over the omission of naturalistic depictions of humans, attributing it to Paleolithic people's 'inexplicable fascination with wildlife' (not that there were any non-wild animals around at the time)."[344]

Many of Breuil's followers have suggested interpretations of this art as acts of sympathetic hunting magic, while some art historians saw the images as a "great spiritual symbol" of human triumph over other species. These views interpret the pictures filled with huge beasts as a time "when man had just emerged from a purely zoological existence, when instead of being dominated by animals he began to dominate them." But, as Ehrenreich points out, the few human figures that do appear seem puny and self-effacing, rather than self-aggrandizing. While it is a fact that humans eventually killed off many other species, Paleolithic art doesn't seem to celebrate this.[345] Ehrenreich argues that people in the Paleolithic age probably cared little about other people's opinions of them and their amazing hunting skills. Rather, they concerned themselves with the

> actions and intentions of the far more numerous megafauna around them. Would the herd of bison stop at a certain watering hole? Would lions show up to attack them? Would it be safe for humans to grab at whatever scraps of bison were left over from the lions' meal?

They knew that they occupied a middling position on the food chain, and she speculates that some of the goofier images indicate that they even had a sense of humor about it.

The great era of cave art came to an end with the Neolithic revolution. With the subsequent sedentary lifestyle and social stratification, human faces began to appear in art. First, there were the mother goddesses of the Neolithic Middle East, and then kings and heroes in the Bronze Age. No longer were humans only abstract figures in a landscape, they were individuals with ranks and attributes that befit these ranks, as well as personal traits and stories they wanted preserved for posterity. Eventually, even the

---

[344] See Ehrenreich.
[345] Ibid.

bourgeoisie were commissioning their own portraits and writing memoirs,[346] and now we can constantly create portraits of ourselves on smartphones and share our "brands"— which mainly consist of personalized attributes that show off one's status—with potentially unlimited audiences.

The first step in practicing sophrosyne—that is, determining how much is enough and refraining from overtaking—is putting things into their correct perspectives. When we acknowledge and feel grateful for our relationships to the living beings that provide for us, the blessings tend to spread. We can practice gratitude by taking a moment to see truly and to thank (as opposed to "being thankful for," as though it were given by someone or something else) a flower, a sip of cool water, a perfect falling leaf, a deer sighted at the other end of a clearing, for being there, for being part of you and of your reality in that moment.

Then, we can work on exercising the restraint that is the necessary second part of the virtue of sophrosyne, and finally, we will be moved to act generously. As Robin Wall Kimmerer, a member of the Potawatomi Nation and professor of environmental and forest biology writes,

> Gratitude is so much more than a polite thank you. It is the thread that connects us in a deep relationship, simultaneously physical and spiritual, as our bodies are fed and spirits nourished by the sense of belonging, which is the most vital of foods. Gratitude creates a sense of abundance, the knowing that you have what you need. In that climate of sufficiency, our hunger for more abates and we take only what we need, in respect for the generosity of the giver.
>
> If our first response is gratitude, then our second is reciprocity: to give a gift in return. What could I give these plants in return for their generosity? It could be a direct response, like weeding or water or a song of thanks that sends appreciation out on the wind. Or indirect, like donating to my local land trust so that more habitat for the gift givers will be saved, or making art that invites others into the web of reciprocity.

---

[346] Ibid.

Gratitude and reciprocity are the currency of a gift economy, and they have the remarkable property of multiplying with every exchange, their energy concentrating as they pass from hand to hand, a truly renewable resource. I accept the gift from the bush and then spread that gift with a dish of berries to my neighbor, who makes a pie to share with his friend, who feels so wealthy in food and friendship that he volunteers at the food pantry. You know how it goes ... [347]

---

[347] See Kimmerer.

At Last Setting Our Lands in Order

It can be dismaying to reflect on what kind of wasteland we now occupy, and how little is being done to reverse the process. Humanity's collective hubris has guided our species to the point where our actions have pushed the climate, the land, and many species of animals, plants, and aquatic organisms past their regenerative or restorative capacities. In some areas, we will see positive developments: species brought back from the brink of extinction; tracts of land preserved from extractive industries and development; here and there a ban on some harmful material or technology. But let's not delude ourselves: the human population is growing, and it is hungry for energy, technology, transport, medicine, meat, and cheap clothing and trinkets. These appetites have not been tamed by calls for voluntary reductions. Therefore, we will continue to witness objective deteriorations in the Earth's climate, biosphere, and species during our lifetimes.

Too many people still believe these realities pale in importance before an impending Biblical apocalypse. Others put forth secular arguments that say we cannot afford to slow down economic growth (increasing consumption) because it would lead to basic human needs not being met. Or, they claim, the opportunity costs of not logging, mining, transporting, and developing in a particular place now will result in a competitive disadvantage in relation to other nations later. This creates a perverse mandate to root up and grind whatever is wholesome, beautiful and unique into money—a currency that enables us to purchase things we don't really need, while destroying what we do.[348]

Suggestions that affluent consumers are going to meaningfully reverse these processes—by buying organic vegetables or globally distributed "green" products—are based in wishful thinking. It seems that everyone wants more of everything; this is supposed to be provided by "growth," a deceitful euphemism for the subtraction of trees, soil, minerals, and wild species. We are asked to believe growth is going to allow the poor to live like the rich, and the rich to live like royalty forever and ever. Yet, baselines shift with each generation, not only for how much loss is supposed to be considered normal, but also for how much consumption is standard or aspirational. As George Monbiot points out, thirty years ago it was absurd to buy water in bottles if tap water was available; by 2017, people were consuming a million plastic bottles every minute. Occasions for extravagance are becoming routinized while also scaling up. Shopping is considered a hobby and an informal form of "therapy" for bad moods in wealthy countries year-round. In the late autumn until the New Year, strings of twinkling lights, gaudy red and green decorations, and holiday songs create a "festive" atmosphere that pressures us to shop to the limits of our means—and even beyond them. We feel that we need to move resources (and then trash) around the planet to produce the impression that we, and all our friends, family, and even co-workers, are living the dream of ever-expanding affluence.

In recent decades, we have been able to observe some of the wealthier global citizens attempting to step back from this model and front a "minimalist" or "green" consumer lifestyle. However, all indications are that this serves more as virtue signaling, rather than a real reversal of trends, much like the occasional purchase of a free-range grass-fed steak does little to offset the effects of industrial beef production. Research indicates no significant difference between the ecological footprints of people who care

---

[348] This pithy and heartbreaking summary of the state of affairs is quoted from Charles Eisenstein by Robin Wall Kimmerer.

about their impacts and those who don't. The reason is that, while awareness of and access to "green" options are highest among the wealthy, their lifestyles are already outliers on the upper end of consumption and impacts. Recycled yoga mats, sustainably-grown teak patio furniture, and a fanatical devotion to recycling every bit of household trash cannot offset their air travel and second homes. Those who perceive themselves as green consumers mainly focus on behaviors that have relatively small benefits, while they neglect those that would make much more difference.[349] The rest, who believe they are participating in an economy of abundance and are only "temporarily embarrassed millionaires," as John Steinbeck put it, should sober up: the majority of them are only one or two missed paychecks away from poverty or homelessness.

Some economists have proposed that we should "decouple" economic growth from the use of materials. Despite modest success according to limited benchmarks, there is no country that has achieved "absolute decoupling" in the last 50 years. Growth increases faster than efficiencies, and it is on a wicked curve of 3% per year (i.e., doubling every 24 years). Expecting anything other than more disasters as an outcome is unrealistic.[350]

Knowing these facts but looking to someone else to solve the problem (scientists, renegade economists, politicians, international organizations, or even the Pope) is likewise based in delusional thinking. There are many proposals for climate goals, treaties, "Green" this or that, de-growth programs,[351] and other macro-level commitments that can (and should) be implemented at the national and international levels. Many of them are earnestly conceived and likely to do more good than harm, but even with

---

[349] See Monbiot (2017) "Everything Must Go."

[350] Decarbonization efforts, including electric cars, and wind, solar and other renewable sources of energies so far have only produced "more energy for growth." To clarify a little: if, for instance, 2% of the energy system has converted to renewable sources, but the global economy has also grown by 2% that year, the same amount of fossil fuel has still been used. See Hunziker.

[351] De-growth (degrowth) is a widely misunderstood concept that is promoted by certain Marxists and is reviled by mainstream economists and pundits and the elite they serve. The origin of this term is found in Romance languages, where "la décroissance" in French or "la decrescita" in Italian refer to a river going back to its normal flow after a disastrous flood. The common misunderstanding is that degrowth is something like a permanent, accelerating recession that would beggar everyone. It has also been inappropriately compared with austerity, but in fact they could not possibly have more opposite means and aims. As Matthias Schmeltzer and Aaron Vansintjan point out, austerity (cutting wages, benefits, and services while also reducing taxes for the rich) is always imposed for the sake of growth. Both the austerity programs and any further growth have the effect of creating more inequality. Degrowth, on the other hand, attempts to expand public services to create a stronger baseline of well-being, while reining in excessive growth in wealth and overconsumption. Recessions are unintentional, even though they are inevitable in any economy committed to growth. The crises are often exploited by elites, who use them as excuses to deregulate industries and allot themselves windfall profits by pumping inflation. When recessions appear they often motivates politicians to abandon policies that support sustainability and social welfare and bailing out polluting industries and corrupt banks. Also see: degrowth.org/degrowth.

these interventions we are going to experience an accelerating deterioration of conditions.

Sometimes it's more painful to contemplate what's happening close to home, and it may even seem easier to focus one's environmental distress on, for example, the plight of polar bears or rising sea levels (if you don't live in the Arctic or near a coast). Some become dispirited or depressed, or act out more hedonistic forms of denial, taking their short-lived pleasures from consumer society. At the same time, we see others suffering from hunger, malnutrition, obesity, and (particularly in the United States) a lack of access to health care. Addiction, overmedication, debt, neurotic hoarding, despair, self-harm, and suicide are endemic. People live paycheck to paycheck, worried that they will lose jobs they hate and be turned out on the streets. They run around

> doing trivial things to perpetuate ourselves in a culture that had us evading our own souls. We have been kept at attention with an endless series of wars, even—absurdly—"wars" against such things as poverty, drugs, and terrorism, which are symptoms of the continual splitting of self from other, and of more complex social pathologies.[352]

It is hardly surprising so many turn to distractions, self-medication with intoxicants, or to religious or political movements that promise a big, dramatic end to all the pain and misery. When people are suffering, their emotional hardship can override any considerations of thinking or acting differently. It can seem insensitive to suggest they could or should be doing anything other than just trying to survive, maintaining whatever semblance of normality they have created amidst these circumstances. Nevertheless, we must have public discourse about problems and solutions; any efforts that result in real improvements in the state of the world we live in will become our legacy—the only legacy that truly matters.

As Peter Grey expressed it:

> Rewilding is alas the final position of an ecological movement facing catastrophic losses. It is a beautiful thing to see a living system revivified in a cascade of life and more life. It has given those in the often

---

[352] See Rittenberry.

harrowing world of the ecological movement a glimpse of what can occur in a system that is enabled to right itself ... Although I believe that their project is doomed it does not mean that we should not commit to these principles. I am not suggesting quitting, far from it. These small victories will make a difference as we approach the choke point and particularly for those who, in spite of the facts, choose to have children.[353]

Bioregionalism

Not everyone is going to save vast tracts of forest from logging, nor discover enzymes that might dissolve the huge garbage patches in the ocean, but there are ways to find appropriate levels of engagement everywhere. Without burdening ourselves with too much attachment to final outcomes, we need only start somewhere, and we might as well begin where we are—an approach called bioregionalism.

There has long been a perception that environmentalism mainly focuses on preserving "virgin" wilderness areas and tightly controlling people's access to the preserved lands. At times, this perception has been correct. However, the bioregional approach is not misanthropic (it doesn't expect to exclude people from bioregions), and it has communitarian aspects. Peter Berg, who helped found the movement, explains that bioregionalism encourages proactive efforts at "carrying the concept of a life-place into the activities and goals of human society." Crucially, it is a philosophy of action that brings to life that which is wanted, instead of only struggling and protesting against what isn't.

Within a bioregion, there are different zones of human interface with natural systems: urban, suburban, rural, and wilderness, each of which calls for different appropriate reinhabitory approaches.[354] The key shift in perspective is recognizing that the earth that needs protecting is right where you are, and that the way we interact with it is part of our cosmology."[355] Bioregionalism proposes that the worlds we live in are best known and interacted with locally. A "just right" scale of action has been described

---

[353] See Grey.
[354] See Richard Evanoff's interview with Peter Berg.
[355] Ibid.

by Kirkpatrick Sale as one that is neither so small that comprehension and accomplishment are powerless and impoverished, nor so large as to be ponderous and impervious. It must be a "scale at which at last human potential can match ecological reality."[356]

Bioregional theories and actions promote sustainability, ecological rehabilitation, and a preference for local over imported resources, particularly foods. Some of my friends laugh at me for growing foods that I could acquire much cheaper at a store—but they also want to come over and eat these foods! I contend that time spent growing, preparing, and enjoying food with *terroir* is more joyful than time spent earning and then spending money on foods that lack it. A more general objection sometimes heard is "we can't go back to the old times" (whether the old time means their grandparents' childhood, or the time before industrial agriculture, or before agriculture altogether), or even "you don't want to live like a caveman, do you?"

Those who reject the idea of looking to our ancestors for inspiration may be missing valuable perspectives, as I have attempted to explain throughout this book. Of course, there is also the opposite problem: romantically fantasizing about a perfect primitive lifestyle or noble savages. This usually occurs when the outer trappings of the culture are appropriated in the absence of an understanding of the concepts and identities the symbols represent. It's necessary to find a realistic and joyful balance between old and new ways of living on, and working with, the land.

Animism and Reinhabitation

Sometimes, these romanticized notions are tied to the idea that the best ideas and cultural forms from a culture existed in the past, and that the people who represent that cultural lineage have been corrupted by exposure to global cultures. While it is lamentable that contact with colonizing regimes and evangelizing religions has robbed many peoples of some of their valuable cultural heritage, we should aspire to learn from them their adaptability, continuity, and resilience in the face of change. Some Indigenous wisdom is indeed ancient, and one of the most

---

[356] See Humphrey.

miraculous aspects is that it's responsive enough to have lasted, despite all the threats and challenges.

Australian Ngarinyin law man, land activist, and thinker David Banggal Mowaljarlai said that *this* is a gift that his people truly wanted to share. In a radio broadcast, he said:

> We are really sorry for you people. We cry for you because you haven't got meaning of culture in this country. We have a gift we want to give you. We keep getting blocked from giving you that gift. We get blocked by politics and politicians. We get blocked by media, by process of law. All we want to do is come out from under all of this and give you this gift. And it's the gift of pattern thinking. It's the culture which is the blood of this country, of Aboriginal groups, of the ecology, of the land itself.[357]

Anthropologist Veronica Strang agrees with this perspective, pointing out that the "place-based" forms of knowledge and environmental relationships found among hunter-gatherers and other Indigenous societies are more supportive of both environmental goals (e.g., sustainability) and cultural survival than those of industrialized societies. She offers the caveat that this must be approached with a flexible mindset, because the integrated concepts of sustainability that can be found in Indigenous cultures are

> deeply embedded in cultural concepts and forms of social identity that are not readily transferable to different economic modes, or to large-scale forms of social organisation. However, there remains some potential for western societies to make use of such examples to develop clearer and more integrated visions of sustainability, and to recognise that reconciliation and identification with Nature depends on the encouragement of more collective social forms and long-term relationships with place.[358]

Animism, a concept introduced by Western thinkers to describe the beliefs of cultures who never used that term, first signified that such cultures were "primitive," "childlike," and "underdeveloped." To this day, cultures

---

[357] White, 103; 106-7.
[358] Strang, 28, 52.

that did or do honor the life force in the natural world are sometimes lampooned as worshiping sticks, or other natural objects that seem risible.[359] Western Christian supremacism has seen (and still sees) those who spiritually focus on the "lower" orders of animals, plants, and even stones (harking back to the Medieval Chain of Being) as anachronistic, fated to die out after people were exposed to their "higher" truths. However, they were wrong in every way about these other cultures and their philosophies and theories of mind; there is now a powerful resurgence of (neo-)animist theory and practice in countries where monotheism once held sway. It's returning now as a primary way those of us living in cultures without open lines of communication with non-human beings can begin to re-enmesh themselves in a living world.

While animism has many academic and working definitions, a simple one is "the belief that the world is made up of persons, only some of whom are humans." These persons are constantly engaged in relations, and a responsible animist seeks to ensure and promote "right relations." When one has learned to give full attention to one's surroundings, this is when learning begins.[360]

---

[359] The same approach is also applied to Europe's pre-Christian past, and this model is still taught to children. For example, in the Christian children's animated *VeggieTales* episode on the life of St. Patrick, after mocking the future saint's original name (Maewyn Succat) and describing how the Christian lad was carried to Ireland from his homeland in England, the narrator explains how the culture over there was different: "The Druids also didn't know about God. They practiced a religion known as Paganism." After this is said, Maewyn Succat kicks over a tiny Stonehenge-type trilithon. "Paganism?" the future saint asks. The next frame shows a sketchy-looking Druid (who also happens to be Maewyn Succat's new master) standing on a hilltop, and the narration continues: "Instead of praying to God, Pagans prayed to things like—twigs!" The Druid whips out a branch with leaves on it and exclaims: "Oh, mighty twig, you are powerful and, and—twiglike!" Then he is shown next to a pond and the narrator adds pond scum to the list of things Druids worship. The Druid on screen obliges, by saying "Oh, mighty pond scum, you are powerful and—scummy!" The narrator finishes this characterization by saying "And they painted with all the colors of the rainbow," and the Druid throws the contents of a bucket full of multicolored paint against a tree and it splashes back on his face, giving him rainbow stripes. The Druid tries to proselytize to his slave, asking: "Would you like to pray to my twig?" and Maewyn declines. His master is then seen on a hilltop dancing and making chants with his twig in his hand in the background when Maewyn Succat decides to escape. The boy flees Ireland, only to return later and preach the new religion to people who are depicted as extremely stupid and literal minded about worshipping whatever Patrick (his new name) puts in front of them. He is seen teaching them what a metaphor is, because they didn't seem to know. But after he explains it, all the Irish dimwits threw their twigs away and "turned to God."

In addition to teaching religious bigotry, this show has also been criticized for using "white" accents for the good characters and ethnically-inflected accents for villains in other episodes. *VeggieTales* productions have achieved extraordinary outreach: according to Wikipedia, as of 2019, 75 million videos (various formats), 16 million books, 7 million music albums, and 235 million music streams have been sold.

[360] White, 12, 60, 193. Are you an animist? White suggests the following diagnostic check: is your pet a being or an object? What about a tree you see every day? If you saw your grandmother standing at the kitchen stove wearing an apron, would you say "Look, it is making soup. It has grey hair"? White cites Robin Wall Kimmerer, who discusses that in her native Anishinaabe language the words used to address all living beings are the same as those used to address family. Both White and Kimmerer are speaking about the way objectification vs personification is encoded in English grammar. In the latter's words, "In English, you are either a human or a thing." By contrast with English, in Slavic languages all words are assigned a gender, and some additionally have "animacy"—a grammatical category that distinguishes the living from the non-living (though only in masculine nouns, for some reason). Thus, in Czech, something that is alive and is grammatically male (a man, a dog, a ghost) is animate in a way that a castle or an idea is not. Honorable animacy is granted to things that people are fond of: bread, cheese, and joints (the kind that are smoked, not the kind where two bones are connected).

Because most of us are not living on land that our ancestors have inhabited over generations, and because we have lost their technologies and become separated from their cosmologies, the concept of "reinhabitation" can be useful. Reinhabitation is not the newest buzzword—its use, in the present form, dates to the 1970s, when it was introduced by the poet and ecologist Gary Snyder. He describes how people removed from their ancestral territories, those who moved to work in towns, or on pipelines, or who went to pan for gold, would look down on those who had stayed rooted:

> Actual inhabitants—peasants, paisanos, paysan, peoples of the land, have been dismissed, laughed at, and overtaxed for centuries by the urban-based ruling elites. People in all of the world's regions have developed subsistence patterns over the course of millennia through inspiration, trial, and error through which they gained knowledge of plants, waterways and boats, cooperation with animals.

Snyder mentions dogs, but of course people also cooperate with many other species, from French truffle hogs to Bengali fishermen's otters. He continues:

> From steep jungle slopes of Southwest China to coral atolls to barren arctic deserts—a spirit of what it was to be there evolved that spoke of a direct sense of relation to the "land"—which really means, the totality of the local bioregion system, from cirrus clouds to leaf mold. Inhabitory peoples sometimes say, "This piece of land is sacred"—or "all the land is sacred." This is an attitude that draws on awareness of the mystery of life and death, of taking life to live, of giving life back—not only to your own children but to the life of the whole land.[361]

One may hold the belief that "all land is sacred," but "this land is sacred" is a more actionable premise. Digging in your heels and learning from the land is an act of resistance to political and economic powers which benefit from people suffering from their loss of connection to the land. As Wendell Berry wrote in his essay "The Unsettling of America," any person or group of people who tries to stay in one place and do some one thing well, long enough to be able to say, "I really love and know this place," stands to be penalized economically (and perhaps in other ways as well.) Some of these

---

[361] Snyder, 44-5.

people have "always" been there, such as Indigenous people; some have been there for multiple generations, such as the descendants of settlers.

There is a third group: the small numbers of people who escape industrial societies in order to stay in one place and who fall in love with the land: these are the reinhabitors. Some are motivated by a rational realization of "interconnectedness and planetary limits. But the actual demands of a life committed to a place, and living somewhat by the sunshine green-plant energy that is concentrating in that spot, are so physically and intellectually intense that it is a moral and spiritual choice as well."[362] And there is also a fourth group: those who reclaim the wastelands.

The concept of reinhabitation may seem irrelevant to those who live in cities or suburbs, but it is not. A book by David Holmgren titled *Retrosuburbia* (2018) discusses how suburban homesteads can be transformed by homeowners (rather than by unsympathetic communities or governments) to be more resilient to shocks in energy and supply lines. They can be sites of productivity and joy, rather than excess consumption and despair. Even those in cities, and those who lack a connection to a traditional or contemporary Earth-based religion, may create deep connections to the land in city parks, municipal gardens, or nature preserves outside the city limits. They can also meaningfully support urban farm projects,[363] or other initiatives managed by a few for the benefit of many more.

One of the most beneficial project types of reinhabitation for city dwellers are urban gardens. As Rebecca Solnit writes,

> to garden is to make whole again that which has been shattered: the relationships in which you are both producer and consumer, in which you reap the bounty of the earth directly, in which you understand fully how something came into being.

The scale isn't as important as the dynamics and the realignment of one's way of being in the world.[364] Ownership and access schemes can vary from "guerrilla gardening" to squatting to cooperative ownership, or even in-

---

[362] Ibid, 47-8.

[363] Don't get me started on the well-meaning folly of planting fruit trees along sidewalks. Instead, see Stapleton for the top five reasons it's a bad idea. Public fruit trees along country roads? Definitely! It's a time-honored tradition in Central Europe and could be implemented elsewhere. Fruit trees in parks—absolutely. But not on city streets.

[364] Solnit, 73.

clude individual ownership of plots concentrated in a small area. These aren't just places to convert dirt and sweat into salad, but sites where more wholesome relationships can begin flourish. Erik Rittenberry shares a vision of what it looks like when people dig in and connect more with the land and their neighbors:

> Can you see it? Community gardens, neighbors helping neighbors, more candlelight and less blue light, a joyous rebellion, a refusal "to subscribe to the general demand" of eager consumption, a total reconstruction of our frivolous economy because our warped appetites will have waned, our lives decorated with poetry, music, and purposeful work instead of the degrading cog in the machine ways we've succumbed to.[365]

Church Forests and Sacred Groves

There have also been dramatically successful programs that preserve and restore rural lands that seem otherwise impossible to remediate. One of the worst examples of a human-created "wasteland" offering only meager support for human life is the northern Ethiopian highlands. This territory used to be densely forested, but it was stripped of 97% of its wooded cover by human activity, mostly during the past century. The region's typical intense rainstorms, falling on the steep slopes devastated by deforestation and devegetation, caused the hills to quickly lose their soil. Additionally, overworking new farmlands depleted the nutrients in what little soil was left. Even animal dung was not being returned to the soil, because people were burning it for fuel. But there were small preserves where the land was not plowed or grazed: in the area to the east of Lake Tana are some 35,000 "church forest" oases. These appear around the Orthodox Tewahedo churches, where the old growth was tended by priests. For over 1,500 years, they preserved these tiny, precious areas while the surrounding land was progressively degraded by farmers.

There are several theological reasons offered for why the ecclesiastics of this Orthodox sect preserved the wooded areas. One, the forests serve as miniature Gardens of Eden, and another is that they serve as meeting points for God's transcendent ("up there") aspect with his imminent

---

[365] See Rittenberry.

("down here") aspect. A simpler concept is that the grounds are "clothing" for the churches. By contrast with the arid fields and scrublands ravaged by cattle, church forests are blessed with beauty, fruits, and sweet fragrances, and they are inhabited by birds, monkeys, gazelles, wild pigs, and even caracals and civet cats.

They are also said to be a habitat for elusive hermits, called *menagn*, who rank just below angels in holiness and can only be seen by those with "eyes of faith." Yet even those whose faith inheres in things that can be counted and measured can observe that church forests raise the water tables, palpably cool the air, preserve soil, block harmful winds, and provide shelter to pollinators that help the crops. There are now international efforts to help church authorities build stone walls to keep ranging cattle out. Moving stones out of the fields and stacking them around the forests has improved the fields, and also provided paid employment and volunteer engagement for some people in the communities.

Many people today have a dysfunctional habit of perceiving plants (and everything else in the natural world) as only a background to their real experiences—the "green wall." One of the most inspiring aspects of the church forests is the way they allow for human spiritual and cultural needs to interweave with living organisms and habitat. Alexei Lidov's concept of "hierotopy," which is a complex and interdisciplinary approach to sacred space, was proposed as an interpretive approach for Ethiopian church forests by the documentary photographer Kieran Dodds. Hierotopy doesn't only encompass a piece of land or the space within the building, but provides an experiential framework for taking into account sacred artwork, dramaturgy of light and dark, liturgical gestures, fragrances, resounding words, and the recollection of miracle stories. Once more, I will return to Baudelaire's "Correspondences," but this time I want to draw attention to the final stanza:

> Nature is a temple, where the living
> Columns sometimes breathe confusing speech;
> Man walks within these groves of symbols each
> Of which regards him as a kindred thing.
>
> As the long echoes, shadowy, profound,

> Heard from afar, blend in a unity,
> Vast as the night, as sunlight's clarity,
> So perfumes, colours, sounds may correspond.
>
> Odours there are, fresh as a baby's skin,
> Mellow as oboes, green as meadow grass,
> —Others corrupted, rich, triumphant, full,
>
> Having dimensions infinitely vast,
> Frankincense, musk, ambergris, benjamin,[366]
> Singing the senses' rapture and the soul's.

When land, loved and tended by humans, participates in such rich sensory experiences (as well as the mythic dimensions and hints of subtle intelligences), the "green wall" has been dissolved. As Fred Bahnman writes in his article analyzing the sacred, human, and ecological aspects of the forests, they are:

> ... but one of many voices now asking us to consider what indigenous cultures like the Orthodox Christian people of Ethiopia have long known is true, that trees are not a green backdrop against which all our vaunted human dramas play out, but actors in their own right ... Thanks to several decades of research on the fungal networks of mycorrhizae, we know that trees enact a surprising degree of agency. They respond to threats; nurture their young; share nutrients, even with unlike species. Most intriguing of all, through the mediums of leaf chemicals and underground strands of mycelium, trees communicate.

Each new church that the faithful describe as being "planted" also means more trees planted around it. As they grow, those trees provide ever-richer enchantment of the senses, mythical immersion in a world of spirit, and obvious material benefits to those seeking refreshment. This is a tangible bit of hope flourishing in a severely degraded land.[367]

In Japan, the botanist and ecologist Akira Miyawaki noticed something similar: trees in the sacred groves maintained around temples, shrines, and cemeteries were survivals from the islands' primary forests that had been reduced to only 0.06% of their former extent. The *Chinju no Mori* are

---

[366] Another name for the incense known as benzoin.
[367] See Bahnson, and also Kieran Dodds' photo essay.

forests that surround old Shinto shrines; their size varies, but typically they enclose the approach to the temple and the place of prayer on the site. The forests are home to Kannabi, a *kami* (god or spirit) of the ancient Shinto (Koshinto) religion predating the arrival of Confucianism and Buddhism. *Chinju no Mori* is written with a character that means "a god's forest," distinguishing them from other types of forests. The layout of these sites suggests that the sacred groves are an element older than the shrines themselves, and they were the first sites of worship.[368] Like the Ethiopian church forests, they are rich in species of animals, plants, insects, and microorganisms.

Miyawaki advocated for the protection of native forests worldwide, and argued that the forests planted to replace them were not as resilient or as suited for resisting climate change. If a forest should be replaced, it should be done using species determined to be "potential natural vegetation," which means vegetation that would be expected there, given natural constraints in the absence of human intervention or natural disasters. Over the course of several decades, he developed, refined, and applied a multistep method for restoring native forests which has accomplished remarkable results, even in places that have suffered a great deal of damage to their vegetation and soil quality.

When a site has been selected for a Miyawaki forest, the surrounding area must be very rigorously surveyed for potential native vegetation. Next, seeds are collected from living plants and germinated in nurseries under conditions mimicking their natural environment (for example, some seeds have to pass through an animal's digestive tract, or they need symbiotic fungi to be present). The soil on the proposed site must also prepared. Then, when the sapling trees and plants are transplanted, they're set into patterns that mimic natural distributions. This sets up sequences that greatly accelerate the successions of pioneer and secondary species. As Miyawaki wrote,

---

[368] See Japanese Wiki Corpus.

> Each new group of species arrives because the environmental conditions, especially the soil, have been improved; each new species becomes established because it is more shade-tolerant than the previous species and can grow up under their existing foliage ... The plant community and the physical environment continue to interact, until the final community most appropriate for the environment comes into being, one that cannot be replaced by other plant types. In regions with sufficient precipitation and soil, the final community is a forest.[369]

Restoring forests using the Miyawaki method is not only done in places that have ancient ties to spiritual traditions, as is the case with Ethiopian church forests or the holy forests around Shinto shrines. Sites that have been badly degraded by human activities, or which have been bare of trees and other significant vegetation for centuries, can be restored to a condition that is whole and holy within a single generation. That means that babies born this year can experience the wonder of hierotopy of the forests being planted now when they reach adulthood. Astoundingly, sanctuaries hosting more than 500 species and drawing down about 250 kg/550 lbs of carbon out of the air each year, can even be created in "mini forest" patches—as small as half an acre in diameter.

Miyawaki projects have been carried out in Japan, China, India, Indiana, Sri Lanka, Thailand, the Netherlands, Pakistan, Lebanon, Iran, and Jordan, among many other locations. The city of Paris, which has witnessed such dry and devastating heat waves in recent summers, is one of Europe's least green cities. But even the leaders of the "City of Light" have recognized that forests are the only thing that can save them from the heat that accumulates in their buildings and paved avenues. City planners intend that no one should be farther than a seven-minute walk from the nearest "cooling island" of green space open to the public, such as a park, cemetery, churchyard, or swimming area.[370]

Remarkably, these newly-planted forests become fully self-sufficient after three years. After that, they will no longer require any watering, mulching, weeding, or pruning. They do, of course, require protection

---

[369] Akira Miyawaki, cited by Lewis, 13.
[370] Lewis, 127, 53.

from "development," pollution, and other potential harms. As long as this is provided, and commitments are made to keep the forests intact into the future, they will continue to offer an interactive and sacred lifeworld to humans and many other species in a healthful, virtuous, and growing cycle. This method can be applied nearly anywhere, even on lots that have been paved over, if the asphalt is removed and the soil is prepared properly.[371]

Rewilding and Permaculture

Turning blighted and wasteland areas into forest is crucial for many reasons, but we still need to establish a more flexible system for provisioning ourselves with food. Clearly, no one is going "back" to Paleolithic lifestyles if they are living in the modern world. But it's equally clear that mistreatment of our ecosystems is going to kill us, and will make us very miserable before we finally die. For the sake of an inspiring synthesis of these two ideas, I want to offer a quick look into permaculture practices developed in the Mesolithic Age in Europe, because they suggest horticultural styles applicable to people in Northern temperate regions, even in non-rural areas.

Farming systems ("agrilogistics" in Timothy Morton's term) which emerged in the Neolithic Age are still widely practiced today. These systems put all their focus into a few staple crops which sometimes prove to be very fickle and often end in disaster. On the other hand, another model from ancient times has quietly coexisted alongside extractive practices: "forest gardens" managed by peasants in marginal areas. In Europe, when the last glaciers retreated in the Mesolithic Age, people seized on hazel as a Tree of Life, leading some scholars to refer to this period as the "Nut Age." Hazelnuts have a very healthy nutritional profile. They contain

> about 60% fat and 20% carbohydrates, and contain a wide range of proteins, vitamins, and minerals—a few handfuls can cover most of a person's daily energy needs. Its branches, tall and flexible but slender enough to cut with a flint axe, were used for tools and firewood. Mesolithic thatched huts were often made with hazelwood beams.

---

[371] Those interested in learning more should read Akira Miyawaki and Elgene O. Box's pioneering *The Healing Power of Forests* (2007), and Hannah Lewis's 2022 *Mini-Forest Revolution*, which provides up to date information on projects completed and resources for those who would like to plant Miyawaki forests where they live.

> From cradle to grave, the people of Mesolithic Europe relied on hazel more than any other single plant. Excavations of habitation sites from this period can turn up hundreds of thousands of roasted hazelnut shells. For over five thousand years, this single plant was a major source of sustenance for nearly all of Europe's people.[372]

But that wasn't all: Mesolithic Europeans used as many as 450 other edible plants species. As Max Paschall points out, many of the species they focused on are those that treated as weeds today, because they're adaptive, resilient (aggressive, even), and can be encouraged to grow with minimal effort.

The Mesolithic diet was nutritionally diverse and provided more than adequately for people's needs. Those living a hunting and gathering lifestyle worked far few hours than farmers or modern people. Mesolithic Europeans enjoyed a rich, diverse, and wholesome diet, and they took it with them everywhere they went, bringing their favorite plants and seeds along and establishing new forest gardens. Europe was not a pristine wilderness, but "a continent of handcrafted nut orchards and semi-wild forest gardens carefully managed for thousands of years," managed using hand tools and fire. Controlled burning created open habitats that could lead to a tenfold increase in game animal populations, including red deer, boar, and aurochs. Sometimes, they created ivy patches to lure deer. There, the deer could be hunted or possibly even semi-domesticated. Wood production was sustainably managed with coppicing, a sustainable practice of harvesting branches rather than cutting down entire trees. When grains were introduced, they were not originally grown in monocultures, but alongside legumes: a field might have a mix of emmer, einkorn, and barley with peas and lentils. Hemp, flax, and poppies were also grown in these fields.[373]

One example of a Mesolithic-style permaculture is the Iberian *dehesa* silvopastural system. These are oak savannahs in Spain and Portugal, where traditional landraces of livestock forage under holm oak and cork oak. Wild game and other foods such as truffles, mushrooms, honey, and cork abound. The system also supports endangered species, such as the Iberian lynx, imperial eagle, and black vulture, and it "challenge[s] the very notion

---

[372] See Paschall.
[373] Ibid.

of farming, and show[s] us what agriculture can be when people create is as a fully-fledged ecosystem, rather than simply a way to mine nutrients from the soil."374

The case is similar with the chestnut culture in Corsica—which has variously existed as intensively managed orchards, as mixed gardens of the Mesolithic type, or semi-wild or semi-domesticated *castagnetu*—in a fluidity that has enabled successful resilience in the face of varying climatic and political conditions, while also preserving the soil and water.375 Chestnuts have also been significant for the Haudenosaunee (Iroquois) Nation, as well as in parts of Italy, where, as late as WWII, chestnut trees meant the difference between life and death in areas pillaged by Nazis.376

Creating more diverse productive landscapes is one area of activity that will make a difference in local resiliency and, ultimately, survival. The process goes two ways: alongside people's actions in shaping the land, there is also the way the land affects people, which is where the concept of "rewilding" comes in. The word rewilding debuted in dictionaries in 2011,377 and has been popularized in recent years in several forms. These have been contested among various factions, with some using the concept in a strict sense, such as in description of attempts at restoring Ice Age wildlife to an ecosystem. Others advocate a "passive" approach, in which humans should simply refrain from further interventions. Still others have applied the concept to everything from people's lifestyles in general and women's lives in particular (as a twist on eco-feminism), to specific large or small bioregions, to gardening with native species, or beekeeping with native bees.378

I will not wade through these discussions or particularistic applications, nor will I try to exclude certain conceptions, because I believe the diversity of usage reflects broad interest in some of the central ideas behind this

---

374 Ibid.

375 See Michon.

376 Bhagwandin, 12-13.

377 Monbiot (2014), 8. It had been present in academic discourse before this, but the original definitions were highly technical and not understood by a wider public.

378 This last one is me: see Reidinger on rewilding bees and beekeeping, tips for responsible honey consumers, and the little-known legacy of Nazi beekeeping in Central Europe.

movement. This is how George Monbiot explained his own idea of rewilding in *Feral* (2014):

> The rewilding of natural ecosystems that fascinates me is not an attempt to restore them to any prior state, but to permit ecological processes to resume ... Rewilding recognizes that nature consists not just of a collection of species but also of their ever-shifting relationships with each other and with the physical environment ... Rewilding, to me, is about resisting the urge to control nature and allowing it to find its own way ... The ecosystems that result are best described not as wilderness, but as self-willed.[379]

Rewilding, in essence, grants the land and the organisms that live on it much more power in self-determination, and it does not attempt to impose an end state. It is interactive animism in practice, taking responsibility for the restoration needed after the land has been damaged. It's participating in the creation of a new story—one that emerges from the land's own sovereignty—rather than repeating the tired story of "the land was raped" as a final verdict.

Akira Miywaki understood the imminence of regenerative processes: just when a community of plants appears to be reaching its fullest potential, the seeds of the succeeding community are already germinating in the shade.[380] Sometimes, the seeds can wait for hundreds of years for the right conditions to arise. For example, a bare hilltop called Bye Wood in Exmoor National Park, Somerset, has been lacking the trees that gave it its name for several hundred years. The clearance to prepare the land for 12 acres of new planting also disturbed ancient bulbs, now no longer dormant.[381]

The concept of a "finished product" is an offshoot of hubristic materialist thinking, rather than from the kind of thinking which ascribes intelligence and agency to non-human beings. We'll need to overshoot a little, and even allow some of the projects to fail in order to increase the chance of some form of equilibrium developing. There isn't a fixed assemblage of organisms or a fixed landscape that must be preserved or achieved. Animals, plants, fungi, the land, the rivers, and all else must find their own dynamic

---

[379] Monbiot (2014), 8-10.
[380] Paraphrased by Lewis, 13.
[381] See BBC Somerset.

balances as they adapt and respond to one another, to us, and to the changing climate. Making space for as many different species to participate as possible provides for more potential resilience.[382]

Rewilding shares life-renewing sovereignty with the Earth and non-human life forms, and it is part of way we will recover from ennui, solastalgia and other maladies of our age. Rewilding can slow down the ongoing wave of extinctions, and can help species that have been locally extirpated return to their original biomes. This, too, will have benefits for the people who will live to see the fruits of these policies. Glenn Albrecht writes:

> I have always argued that solastalgia (like nostalgia) is not irreversible, in the sense that it may take only the repair and satisfactory restoration of a place to return solace and comfort to those who seek it. When the mining stops and rehabilitation commences, solastalgia begins to fade, just as it does when rain ends a prolonged drought. There can be a time in the future when people [whose home was affected by drastic mining projects] are once again in love with their home as a place that gives them heart's ease, even though it may be a restored or rehabilitated landscape. [383]

Even miracles can happen that remind us that sometimes an "end state" is no end at all. Sioux elder Vine Deloria Jr. told members of the Society for Ecological Restoration:

> traditional Indian knowledge says that beings never become extinct. They go away, but they have the power to come back. I predicted that, in their restorations, if they were preparing the area right, plants they thought were extinct would begin coming back unaided after four or five years. Plants would come back first, and then animals, and then birds.

Then, during the conference break, participants who had been working on these projects for longer told him this is exactly what they saw happen:

---

[382] See Sahn's interview with Monbiot. I have paraphrased some of his ideas here.
[383] Albrecht, 60.

the plants returned, followed by birds presumed extinct. Deloria confirmed these observations were in conformity with Traditional Knowledge understood and believed by the elders of his nation.[384]

"The land and the king are one" was an insight that made sense when the king was the party most responsible for decisions on how land would be used, as we saw in the old tales. Now that political sovereignty and decisions on land use are more diffused, the responsibility for wise stewardship falls upon more people. This means that more people need to see what they stand to gain, and what they could lose as a consequence of their ecological choices.

Inspiring them to action requires good storytelling (which is most enjoyable around a fire, but probably really means lots of PR and online influence-building today). As Aldo Leopold wrote in *A Sand County Almanac*, ethics are based on what is immediate and tangible: "we can only be ethical in relation to something we can see, understand, feel, love, or otherwise have faith in."[385] A land ethic that "changes the role of *Homo sapiens* from conqueror of the land-community to plain member and citizen of it" is profoundly egalitarian. It "enlarges the boundaries of the community to include soils, waters, plants, and animals, or collectively: the land."[386] It's

---

[384] Cited in White, 207. Seán Pádraig O'Donoghue shares a story from an herbalist who told of a place in New England "that had been deforested for over 200 years—cleared first for timber, then for farmland. But left alone, the fields began growing back into a forest. Before long, even before its food source appeared, Ghost Pipe [*Monotropa* spp.] re-emerged. Ghost Pipe, an eerie white saprophytic plant, is notoriously hard to cultivate. The scientists watching the forest's return were baffled: where did the plant come from? Were there seeds in the soil just waiting to return? Or were the roots themselves dormant all that time, stirred back to life by the flow of nutrients between the trees taking root around them?" (2022), 68. Ghost pipe is a particularly interesting species: it burrows its roots into the nodes where tree root rhizomes connect with myceliae, and it draws information and nourishment from both networks.

[385] Leopold, 214. At this point, I want to also mention the grandest eco-optimistic utopian movement: Solarpunk. These visualizations are of well-ordered societies that live in harmony with the land. They anticipate advanced renewable, non-polluting energy technologies, more rational agriculture and horticulture, and the remedying of old damages to the land. The new economy will be fully circular, which means that all wastes are recycled into resources. Scarcity and poverty will be abolished, as will social inequality. There are small-scale Solarpunk visions that only aim at creating self-sufficient villages or small settlements, and there are also anarchist approaches that count on more spontaneous and "organic" social developments—and this is all well and good. However, Solarpunk cities planned out in perfect symmetrical detail can create a very chilling and totalitarian impression. If you're not sure what I mean, see Jacques Fresco's Venus Project, which is often cited as an inspirational model. The absolute centralization of decision-making and the necessity of everyone's strict obedience to the plan required to organize a large-scale civilization of this type runs counter to the biological and sociological principles of diversity and plurality. Aesthetically, it has much more in common with a factory than a garden.

Aldous Huxley wrote in *Brave New World*: "However hard they try, men cannot create a social organism, they can only create an organization. In the process of trying to create an organism they will merely create a totalitarian despotism," and I think he was right. Social "organisms" have to arise out of local conditions rather than abstractions. But even if its proponents assure us that this is not the intention, many of these centralized Solarpunk utopias seem to anticipate very different political and economic institutions than the ones we live with today.

[386] Ibid, 204.

like in the Yakama creation myth told to Hannah Lewis by an Indigenous storyteller:

> In the beginning, the Creator made plants and animals. Then the Creator made people, who were naked and vulnerable and unable to survive on their own. "What am I going to do with you?" groaned the Creator. The plants and animals, who had been listening, responded by offering themselves to feed, clothe, and heal people when they became sick. In return, we promised to take care of them and preserve their habitat—the water, soil, and air.[387]

When we wield sovereignty with a sense of responsibility for the beings and systems that are intertwined with our minds and bodies, we must generously give and receive. We link to the past and the future, knowing we have just as much of a right to be here as those before and after. The worthiest legacy we can create serves the purposes of life spreading and diversifying, both in the human and other-than-human populations.

---

[387] Cited by Lewis, 98.

Songs of Sovereignty

As I have discussed in the chapters on hubris and on sophrosyne, a smooth connection between the living world and the human mind is essential for optimal health and a full and satisfying existence. It facilitates caring about landscapes, and it inspires action to protect lands and the beings that live on them. The most important scale of action is almost always local. However, some people feel daunted: are they really a part of the world around them? Is this all a simulation? Where and how should they start if they want to take action? A sense of overwhelm can block the best intentions from finding expression, so I'm suggesting seven techniques that I believe can help one become unstuck from the mind's interior spaces and the worries that can overwhelm intentions.

Connecting With the Five Senses

The first exercise is a simple grounding practice, which many find useful when they experience anxiety or feelings of disconnection from their surroundings. When I teach yoga outdoors, I often use it either before we begin with our regular exercises, or after we have ended the final relaxation phase. It helps students focus on themselves and the place they are in, and it helps them feel a flow between themselves and their surroundings.

First, make sure you are safe and you can pay full attention to what's in your environment. Then reach out with your senses and bring into your awareness:
- 5 things you can see
- 4 things you can hear
- 3 things you can touch
- 2 things you can smell
- 1 thing you can taste

This simple exercise applies a powerful yank on the plug connecting us to technologically mediated worlds and the endless chatter loops in our minds. It returns us to the warm breathing animal life in us and to our innate curiosity about what's around. We become subjects again, instead of merely objects alienated from everything, including ourselves. You can do this as often as you want—the more, the better. After you have tasted the last thing, keep your senses sharp while also maintaining awareness of your breathing.

I feel obligated to add: please don't touch, smell, or taste anything that you cannot identify, in case it might be toxic. If you are unsure, try something familiar, even if it's only the taste or scent of your own skin. Later, you can look up new discoveries (plants, fungi, minerals, etc.) in a field guide and find out how safe they might be to sniff or ingest before sampling them.

Breathing More Expansively and Consciously

First, do the five senses exercise I described above. After you have checked in with the sensory information from your environment, feel into the sensations in your body. Do not linger on pleasure, pain, or any other particular sensation. Simply scan your entire body, from your toes to the crown of your head, and notice what is there without attaching meanings or letting your thoughts run away. Breathe into places where you perceive resistance, with awareness to soften its boundaries.

After you have breathed into those places, without lingering too long on any of them, look ahead of you. Now, breathe and send your awareness forward, taking in whatever can be seen, heard or otherwise sensed. Next, breathe, while sending your awareness to the left of you—but don't turn your head. Take in whatever is available to your peripheral vision and senses. Now do the same thing, extending your awareness to the right. What's behind you? Don't look: breathe, try to recall what you saw before you sat down, and extend your sensory awareness and a little of your imagination behind you.

Take another breath, and check in again with your body. You should experience a feeling that is more calm and expansive than before. As you continue consciously breathing, feel your chest rise and fall. This is the scale of your individual breathing, but it is not the entire scale of breathing. You are sharing air and chemical messages with living creatures. That, also, is not the entire scale of breathing, because animals cannot survive without plants.

In their photosynthetic process, the green ones exhale what we need and take in what we give. Photosynthesis is the capture of a photon, its energy then used to turn air into sugars, and then sugars into wood, leaves, and roots. Redwoods and giant sequoias? They're made of light and air. At the planetary level, the ocean breathes into the sky. The scale of breathing is this immense, is this interconnected. You are always a part of these processes, and *you are never alone.*[388] You do not have to bear unbearable burdens alone, because all the life which sustains us is interconnected.

If this exercise seems to be getting us too far away from the place where we are sitting or walking, we should look back to the much more intimate relations we have with plants. As we all know, they heal us as food and medicine, but even their close proximity helps immensely. When the suffering of the Earth and other people, and other forms of collective grief weigh heavy, Séan Pádraig O'Donoghue reminds us that we can ease it and begin heal by connecting with "our wild kin, the plants." The aromatic compounds and light molecules they exhale mediate the connection between the brain and the heart, and they help our heart return to its naturally flexible rhythms. He continues:

---

[388] I took inspiration for this meditation from Alexis Gumbs, 1, and from Rebecca Solnit, 59.

In times of grief, I am drawn most to the evergreens. I spend time among Spruce and Pine, eat Spruce tips, brew teas with Pine needles, gather and burn Spruce resin and Pine resin. They help me move the grief I hold in my lungs. The goal is not to suppress the grief or separate from it, but to allow it to move through. And to find the support in connection to be able to respond to loss and destruction with presence and creativity.

When we take the time to feel how we are part of a vast and ancient web of life forms which are all continually shaping our consciousness and the state of our minds and bodies it offers opportunities for deep healing.

Cultivating Dirty Thoughts

Have you seen too many memes that remind you that you're "star stuff?" The thing is, everyone and everything is "star stuff"—so what's the point of thinking or saying something so banal?

At a distant level of resolution, we can spend a moment lingering over the thought in slack-jawed awe. However, this small vacation from the things that vex us (decisions to make, difficult relationships, stupid politicians, etc.) takes us away not only from mundane hassles, but also from what *matters* in the most literal way. Matter at the "stardust" level doesn't really interest most of us for more than a perspective-adjusting second or so. It's only when the subatomic bits level up into atoms, molecules, chemicals, tissues, organisms, species, communities, and ecosystems that it's possible to really connect and engage with it.

For example, you might meditate on dirt. It has a specific color, a specific feel in your hand, and even a specific smell and taste. If you want to, you can determine what it's made from (that is, which minerals, as well as which bodies of dead plants and animals, and perhaps mycelial tissue) and what life forms it supports. Rub it between your fingers, smell it—and taste it, if you dare.[389]

These are vanished traces of organisms you may connect with, or even mourn. Perdita Finn tells us that the dirt in her backyard comes from

---

[389] If common sense or knowledge of something unsavory in your local environment (pollution, agriculture or highway runoff, mold, manure, etc.) make tasting your local dirt seem like a bad idea, or if you trust institutional science more than authors you've never met who have admitted to having sketchy personal habits, don't do it. For a brief take on why people engage in geophagia—eating dirt—along with some of the purported risks and benefits, see Maypole's article at Healthline. Then go ask your doctor whether Eating Dirt is right for you.

the bodies of vanished hemlock forests, felled by the tanners come to skin the hides from the vanished bodies of beavers, wildcats, wolves, and mink. It comes from the vanished bodies of the great chestnut trees nourished by the vanished flocks of passenger pigeons. The dirt in my backyard is the ground down stones compressed by oceans and still filled with the fossilized bodies of brachiopods and too many lives to count.[390]

This dead matter is also the matrix (mother, womb) of specific life forms we can interact with here. Thus, it participates in the life and death mysteries revered by our distant ancestors, without any mythological overlays. At any level of resolution, things are breaking down into smaller and smaller pieces which are no less complex if you look closely. Then, they build right back up again, and the shapes rhyme, repeat, connect, and communicate along interfacing networks of roots, mycelia, and neural pathways.

In his short essay, titled "Joy is Such a Human Madness: The Duff Between Us," Ross Gay tries to articulate what, exactly, joy might be:

> it has occurred to me that among other things—the trees and the mushrooms have shown me this—joy is the mostly invisible, the underground union between us, you and me, which is, among other things, the great fact of our life and the lives of everyone and thing we love going away ... We might call it sorrow, but we might call it a union, one that, once we notice it, once we bring it into the light, might become flower and food. Might be joy.[391]

It's definitely a form of euphoria. Hard-nosed science types may attribute this to the effect of *Mycobacterium vaccae*, a microorganism present in soil that increases the biosynthesis of serotonin (the "happy molecule") in the brain.[392] Biophilia types say it's our birthright to feel this happy.

---

[390] Perdita Finn teaches workshops on Getting to Know the Dead. Find out more at https://wayoftherose.org/

[391] This selection from Gay's book was published by the ecologist and feminist Ambika Kamath in a blog post.

[392] After this discovery was made, gardening and parenting blogs enthused over the wholesomeness of children and adults benefiting from "natural antidepressants" as they play or work with the soil. Meanwhile, medical science of course has more profitable and patentable ideas in mind: the bacterium may eventually be administered in pills, injections, or in inhalant form to soldiers before deployment or emergency room workers "to buffer the physical and behavioral side-effects that can result from high stress." This would make it easier and cheaper to put them through hell and still keep them maximally productive. See University of Colorado Boulder.

Visiting a Sit Spot

There is a quote credited to W.B. Yeats which states: "the world is full of magic things, patiently waiting for our senses to grow sharper." Regardless of its incorrect attribution[393] and its habitual misinterpretation, in my experience it is absolutely true.

The practice of regularly visiting a "sit spot" to connect with the life of a specific place is the best way you can sharpen your senses. You also find more magical things around you, in both the mundane and esoteric senses. With no exaggeration, this is the most powerful "magical" practice I have ever experienced, and it can break your senses wide open to the processes and even the moods of the land. It will also reveal deeper layers of myths and stories told by perceptive observers of the places where they lived, because you will start to see the same kinds of things.

You cannot expect big benefits with only minimal practice. It is ideal to commit to visiting your sit spot for at least a full lunar cycle, starting at the phase that feels most propitious. You can, of course, keep going indefinitely, or revisit the practice later if you give it up for a while. I tend to return to this exercise when my life feels chaotic, and it always does me a world of good.

Your spot should be outdoors, ideally where there is even the tiniest patch of native flora. You don't want it to be too far away from where you live, work, or otherwise move around, because the distance or difficulty will become an obstacle to regular practice. A back yard is great, or a city park is perfect if you feel safe (and won't have to interact with other people).

Choose your site well before you begin the practice, and try to visit it at the same time of day or night each time, dressed appropriately for the weather. If your life is a constant circus and you're the ringmaster, either get up before everyone else in the household, or do it after they've all gone to bed. Sitting on the ground is ideal, but if this isn't possible for you, find

---

[393] Yeats didn't write this, and it's been more reliably attributed to the English author Eden Philpotts, who moreover wrote "wits" instead of senses, and by "wits" he was not referring to our mental faculties but enhancements to our perceptive abilities such as magnifying glasses. According to Quote Investigator, "the phrase 'wits to grow sharper' referred to the development of sufficient knowledge by mankind to create and use a magnifying lens to reveal the splendor of the buckbean. Phillpotts was suggesting that there are many other 'magical things' that will be revealed in the future as our knowledge and capabilities grow. See Quote Investigator: "The Universe is Full of Magical Things ..."

something else you might sit on. I use a small waterproof mat to prevent my clothes from getting wet or muddy. Remain rooted to your spot for fifteen to twenty minutes, not looking at your phone. If you must have it with you, put it on airplane mode, set a vibrating alarm, and make sure it stays in a bag or your pocket.

Connect your senses to the "5, 4, 3, 2, 1 things around you," as described in the first exercise. Then, try to empty your mind of thoughts, and just give yourself over to quiet observation. We are not trying to be "mindful" here; we are trying to mesh our senses with sensation. When thoughts, ideas, memories, or items on a "to do" list creep up on you, take a moment to honor their presence, silently comment to yourself, "thinking," and let them pass. Don't allow the worry that you are already doing the exercise wrong to creep in: even separating thoughts from direct sensory experience for a little while is beneficial. Exhale and let the thoughts move out though your mind, like clouds passing through the sky on a warm summer day. Breathe slowly and deeply, and sink into full presence in your sit spot.

After each session comes to an end, address a simple "thank you" to the site itself and to all the beings that kept company with you. Tell them you'll be back. A lunar month seems like a long time to commit to a practice that may seem dull on these pages, but I guarantee you will begin to "see things" very early in this practice. For example, you may gain insight into the vegetative cycle of the shrub that you've been communing with. You may begin to hear the distinctive voice of the wind through the trees and hear how that changes when its buds grow into full leaves, and then when they fall off in the autumn. You may notice that certain kinds of birds or insects have arrived or departed. If the tree is cut down, as happened to the largest poplar in my village, the silencing of its voice will be heartbreaking—but your heart will attach to other trees and other sounds.

You may see animals you usually just pass by without noticing. It is also likely you'll gain even more subtle perceptions and begin making new connections that will enrich your knowledge of the life of the land. Some of these may be very mystical, and the longer you engage with the practice over time, the more available they will be to you.[394]

Testing your knowledge

You can test your knowledge of your bioregion, and if you find your awareness of the place where you live isn't very good, decide to remedy it—ideally, by going on nature walks with knowledgeable local people.

Some questions to think about include:

- Where does the water that runs from your tap come from? I don't mean just a reservoir or a well—how did it get there, and where was it before that?

- What phase of the moon's cycle are you in right now? When and where does it rise and set? This will change, so look for it every day. Is there a name given to the moon by local cultures?[395]

- What kind of soil is under your feet when you're outside? What plants thrive in it, and which ones cannot survive unless it's amended?

- What kinds of rocks are found in your area? How did they develop, and how have they been used?

- Are fires endemic in your region? When was the last time there was a wildfire?

- What were the dietary staples and primary subsistence techniques of cultures that lived in your area in the past?

- How many edible native plants can you identify, and when should they be harvested? Which plants in your area are toxic if ingested or touched?

- Where do your wastewater and household garbage go?

---

[394] For more outdoor sensitivity-training exercises, I highly recommend Micah Mortali's *Rewilding: Meditations, Practices, and Skills for Awakening in Nature*. Mortali is the founder and director of the School of Mindful Outdoor Leadership at the renowned Kripalu Center for Yoga and Health, which offers certification programs for those who are interested in helping others safely and deeply connect with the land.

[395] Publications like farmer's almanacs love to tell us that it's the strawberry moon, or the salmon moon, or whatever. However, their readership spans vast regions where these are not necessarily relevant markers of the seasons, and sometimes these designations are based in errors and mistranslations. The Farmer's Almanac page recently came clean about one of these issues, when they admitted that the name of "Worm Moon" that has sometimes been assigned to the full moon in March was not—as they previously supposed—a reference to the appearance of earthworms when the soil warms up. The real source was from the observations of Captain Jonathan Carver, who had been visiting the Naudowessie (Dakota) and other Native peoples and described that "Worm Moon" refers to a different creature: beetle larvae, which begin emerging from the thawing bark of trees and other places at this time. The page also tells us that other names Indigenous people have used for this moon include Eagle Moon, Goose Moon, Crow Comes Back Moon, Sugar Moon (for maple syrup), Wind Strong Moon, and Sore Eyes Moon (because of the blinding effect of strong sunlight reflected from snow. For many Christians, the last full moon before the Spring Equinox is the Lenten Moon. See The Old Farmer's Almanac. If you can find out what names local cultures have given to the full moons, ask yourself why they saw this phenomenon as so important that it characterized an entire 28-day cycle. Or perhaps consider what is emerging, or what's happening around you each lunar month that you believe encapsulates the feeling of that time and create your own name for it. Just don't pass it off as "traditional."

- Which species have become extinct where you live?
- When do the wild animals rut or mate in your region, and when are their young born?
- Are there any invasive species of plants or animals in the area? What are their impacts?
- What geological processes influenced the land form where you live?
- Can you easily find the cardinal directions: North, South, East, and West?

Naturally, this list is only a starting point.[396] There is much more you can learn in order to understand the place where you live. If your knowledge of your bioregion is good, be generous and share it with your neighbors.

Re-enchanting yourself and the land

The concept of enchantment has its origins in the following complex of ideas:

> Enchantment: late 13c., from Old French *encantement*, from *enchanter* "bewitch, charm," from Latin *incantare*, literally "enchant, cast a (magic) spell upon," from *in–* "upon, into" (see in- (2)) + *cantare* "to sing" (see chant (v.)). Figurative sense of "alluring" is from the 1670s. Cf. Old English *galdor* "song," also "spell, enchantment," from *galan* "to sing," source of the second element in nightingale.[397]

Sharon Blackie reminds us what we so often forget: we live on an animate earth, but we find ourselves lonely and alienated, because we no longer know how to belong. Too many find meaning only within themselves and distracting gadgetry, and they discover that they inhabit a wasteland, which can be exited through re-enchantment. She says:

> To enchant, then, is literally to *sing into*. To be enchanted? It's to be sung into being by the world—and then to *sing back* and weave you into the place. Enchantment is about becoming, living these stories of the land which it sings into us. Once we remember that, once we reclaim our enchantment, everything changes. Because enchantment is as gritty as it gets. Enchantment grounds us, roots us right back in the dark, fe-

---

[396] This list was inspired by the bioregional awareness test developed by Leonard Charles, Jim Dodge, Lynn Milliman, and Victoria Stockley, which is easily found online.
[397] Online Etymology Dictionary, cited by Sharon Blackie.

cund earth where we belong—where we have always belonged, only we learned a long time ago to forget it.

This is the same magic as the chiasmus made with e. e. cummings' line about bird song—"your head is a living forest full of song birds." *The forest full of song birds is your head*: this is re-enchanting our senses and sensibilities. The rhythms and sounds made by animals, plants, landforms, and other aspects of the land and its life have been understood by peoples—present and past—as expressions of language and song. Their movements, gestures, or interactions, such as the wind moving through trees or waves on a shore, are assumed to be communicative. In animist oral cultures, these are conversations that people assume they can participate in. For example, Jack Hunter cites the example of "throat singers" from Tuva, who originally developed their unique vocal art as a means to communicate with their environment—not as art or entertainment. They know where to find geographical factors which maximize the reverberations. At one such location, a singer called Kaigal-ool sang to the cliff and surrounding features, which sang back to him in what the singer called "a kind of meditation—a conversation that I have with nature."[398]

Maybe you don't quite have this level of vocal skill, and you don't think there is a suitable natural echo chamber nearby. Look for whoever is nearby, showing you something about their lives and their world.

> Well, what do you say to Magpie? What do you say to Rattlesnake when you meet him? What do we learn from Wren, and Hummingbird, and Pine Pollen, and how? Learn what? Specifics: how to spend a life facing the current; or what it is perpetually to die young; or how to be huge and calm and eat anything (Bear). But also, that we are many selves looking at each other, through the same eye.[399]

Maybe you aren't sure what they're telling you—get a little closer and ask. The poet and ecofeminist Sophie Strand suggests:

> Go to the oak tree and ask for its story. Go to the river and ask for its story. Go to the goldenrod and ask without saying anything. Ask with your nose, your belly, your eyes. The answer won't always be words.

---

[398] Levin and Suzukei, 2006, quoted by Hunter, xv.
[399] Snyder, 46.

Won't always be sound. Sometimes it will be a feeling in your body. Sometimes it will be a smell. Stories don't belong to human beings. But human beings belong to stories. Let's enter back into the complex, tangled work of letting go of authorship and letting ourselves be told.[400]

Still not sure what to say? "Thank you" is always appropriate. John Beckett suggests:

> ... Pray. Don't worry about who you're praying to and whether or not he or she can hear you. Stand in the Face of the Sun and the Eye of Light and speak your gratitude. There is much we enjoy we did not earn, much we owe to those who keep things moving. It did not have to be this way, but it is—give thanks. Speak your devotion—express your love for those who are precious to you and for that which is greater than us all, however you see it.[401]

When we give thanks, we give it to a being we are grateful to. If we offer thanks to the Earth herself, we are bringing awareness to the complexity of the miracle we participate in every moment in our lives. Giving our full attention makes the moment, the gesture, the place sacred for as long as we can hold it. If giving thanks to the Earth isn't possible for you, give thanks to whatever you have been holding in your attention and seeking a connection with: a bird, a leaf, the wind.

Believing What You Experience Is Real

These are foundational practices and knowledge that will help you to become a sensitive observer ready to "reinhabit" the land where you live. They will also lead to knowing that there is more to the life of the land than meets the eye. In the excellent work *Standing and Not Falling*, Lee Morgan discusses "belief-belief" as a deep acknowledgement that what we experience which falls outside the commonplace is, indeed, real. It is real, despite the "assault against our magical senses, which begins when we are children and never lets up," and which often—perversely—leads people to a sense of shame about what they believe and what they have experienced. It

---

[400] From her essay "MYCO ECO MYTHO Storytelling." This essay, as well as other meditations on storytelling and ecological processes can be found in The Flowering Wand (2022).
[401] See Beckett.

is not a "one-off achievement," but something that must be cultivated and lived as a reality throughout one's life.

Morgan suggests students start a diary, with accounts of "the most potent supernatural or magical experiences/successes" they have in as much vivid detail as possible. Then, keep returning to it, re-read the entries and keep adding to it as more details return. Eventually, it is good to share these experiences with like-minded others and affirm with them: "These are things that happen." Belief-belief is not a matter of dogmatic faith, but instead taking such things seriously and trying to learn from them. A person's actions are always a better indicator of what they truly believe than their words. The action that counts here is recognizing extraordinary experiences. This provides for the likelihood they will recur and bring benefit to oneself and others.[402]

As Morgan points out, one of the most important questions when puzzling through the meaning of an extraordinary experience should always be: what effect on a person's life does this belief have? An experience shared by Mark Fitzpatrick provides a very good illustration. He encountered several extraordinary visions in the summer of 2020, when he, his wife, and their children were sheltering in the isolated, very beautiful domain in the southwest of France belonging to his extended family.

Mark was consciously working through the lessons in Lee Morgan's *Standing and Not Falling*, making personal commitments to love and serve the land there. He was dedicating himself to finding belief-belief, and expanding both regular sensory perception and the subtle senses: faculties such as seeing things out of the corner of an eye or through a hole in a hagstone,[403] and trusting that sensations like pricking on the back of his neck were not just a "chill." Over the course of several hazy, moonlit summer nights; he did sensitizing exercises outdoors to open himself to, and invite in, subtle presences. In his words, it was "very much part of an ongoing work of encounter with this land, this particular place, this particular geography."

---

[402] See the first chapter of Morgan's book, which is titled "Belief-belief."

[403] A "hagstone" or holey stone is simply any stone that has a natural hole in it. Folklore in various parts of Europe says that one can see fairies or other enchanted visions by looking through it, or that it brings luck or magical protection to one who wears it around their neck.

A vision of a white stag was the second in a series of three uncanny experiences which brought him closer to a soul-deep belief that the land saw and knew him, and that it accepted his stewardship:

> I was sitting, looking at that area that I'd been in. And I saw—for the first time as an adult—just remarkably, unmistakably something moving. And it seemed to shift shape, slightly, as it moved. And I kept checking in with myself and saying: "Are you seeing this? Is this real? Is this real? Is this real?" And I'm just kind of saying to myself: "Allow this to be, if this is it." And it looked like it was the form of a large, white stag. The form was slightly indistinct, and it was a moonlit night—but kind of misty. And all of these things added to a ghostliness about it—it wasn't very sharply defined. But I could see it moving, and walking across the way behind the willow tree, and back out. And it seemed to look at me. And I just stood there, maybe 30-40 feet away from it, and it seemed like we were just looking at each other. Like there was this recognition. And it went away after quite a while. Obviously, a white stag is particularly significant and personal and it's particularly significant to me personally. And I just felt this great humbling sense of gratitude, and I felt like I had been given that thing to believe that I needed somehow. And I sort of formulated a prayer of thanksgiving ...[404]

One of the first reactions after the initial buzz of wonder fades away is a second-guessing what you have just seen. Was it a trick of the light? Of auto-suggestion? Alcohol, medications, or other substances? Psychiatric symptoms? No doubt, all of these can participate in some people's eerie experiences. Yet, what's important after the moment has fled is what we're left with in the aftermath. I suppose that most people will feel grateful, perhaps humbled, and more deeply connected—and committed—to the place where the vision happened. It may also weaken our identification as incomplete consuming entities, entities who endlessly measure ourselves against others. If these help you better align with your values, the vision has been true.

It may happen that these encounters will change you:

> Sometimes, when a bird calls,
> or a wind moves through the brush,

---

[404] Spirit Box interview with Mark Fitzpatrick, 15:50 – 17:58.

or a dog barks in a distant farmyard,
I must listen a long time, and hush.

My soul flies back to where,
before a thousand forgotten years begin,
the bird and the waving wind
were like me, and were my kin.

My soul becomes a tree, an animal,
a cloud woven across the sky.

Changed and unfamiliar it turns back
and questions me. How shall I reply?[405]

At the very end, we don't find closure: the loop, the *wyrd*, remains open. When we can put aside our over-civilized cares, and choose to perceive what the land and the other beings we share it with are communicating, we will discover what is needed to serve the pulse of life within and around us.

Go now, it's time. Go to work.

As I told you at the outset of this journey, *de te fabula narratur*: the story is told about you. You've been to strange places and kept *wyrd* company. You have been witness to devastating losses, and you've found friends and allies where you least expected them. It's time now to recognize where you have been heading the entire time.

Cailleach Bhéara[406]

I have been too long questing; my horse died under me.
You stopped the blood.
My lance held high, tilting at everything that passed,
A whiff of Odyssey, the shadow of a sail.
Your forebears carried bags, you said.
Forbearance is a mother's love.
Lay down your weapons at the shrine
And go to where the waters meet.
The rushing glen, the sylvan glade.

---

[405] "Sometimes" by Hermann Hesse, translated from the original German and published online by Anne E. G. Nydam.
[406] "Cailleach Bhéara" is from Mark Fitzpatrick's forthcoming collection titled *The Adorations*.

> There is a place for you, if you know how to look.
> Half-close one eye and tilt your head:
> The overgrown meadow is a labyrinth,
> The stone a face;
> Remember, when you were a child,
> How far away the bottom of the garden,
> How endless Summer afternoon?
> You must learn to see that way again.
> Pour your libation, pour it on the ground,
> 'Til not a drop is left.
> The thirsty Earth will ask for more.
> Yield, bend, never break, supple as the reeds.
> Don't ever shape it in your own image;
> Only see what's there.
> Give everything,
> Point your ship towards home.
> Go now, it's time.
> Go to work.

I have drawn a very broad circle, with the white deer standing in the middle, a fateful reminder of our mortality, and of the old wisdom that reminds us of our place in the world. This book is alive, just as you, your surroundings, and everything else you interact with is alive.

It is entangled with all of these things, and it seeks to help you realign with symbols and ideas that will help you do the needful work. That's the work of keeping company with the living, guarding the threatened, learning skillful and thrifty ways, respecting the dead, and cultivating new life.

We need to remain open to messages arriving from a field of life vaster than our senses and imagination, a field always trying to reach in to remind us that we are part of all of it.

We can integrate our minds more closely, and we can play better roles.
De te fabula narratur.
The story is told about you.
It is time now to find the place to begin, and to renew, the work.

Works Cited

A Clerk of Oxford. "St. Mildred and the Foundation of Minster-in-Thanet." In A Clerk of Oxford (blog). 13 July 2012. https://aclerkofoxford.blogspot.com/2012/07/st-mildred-of-thanet.html

A Clerk of Oxford. "St. Wihtburh and the Miracle on Holkham Beach." In A Clerk of Oxford (blog). 8 July 2014. https://aclerkofoxford.blogspot.com/2014/07/a-miracle-on-holkham-beach.html

Abano, Imelda and Chavez, Leilani. "Wildlife Trafficking, Like Everything Else, Has Gone Online During Covid-19". In *Mongabay*. 1 June 2021. Available at: https://news.mongabay.com/2021/06/wildlife-trafficking-like-everything-else-has-gone-online-during-covid-19/

Albrecht, Glenn A. *Earth Emotions: New Words for a New World*. Ithaca: Cornell University Press, 2019.

Alekseev, Konstantin P., et al. "Bovine-Like Coronaviruses Isolated from Four Species of Captive Wild Ruminants Are Homologous to Bovine Coronaviruses, Based on Complete Genomic Sequences". In *Journal of Virology*. Vol. 84, No. 24. 22 December 2020. Available at: https://journals.asm.org/doi/full/10.1128/JVI.01586-08

Alshami, Ali M. "Pain: Is it All in the Brain or the Heart?" In *Current Pain and Headache Reports*. Vol. 23. No. 12. 14 November 2019. Available at: https://pubmed.ncbi.nlm.nih.gov/31728781/

Alwan, Wes. "Love and Metamorphosis in Fairy Tales and Philosophy". In *The Partially Examined Life* (blog). 17 July, 2012. Available at: https://partiallyexaminedlife.com/2012/07/17/love-and-metamorphosis-in-fairy-tales-and-philosophy/

Andrews, Evan. "When Did the White Flag Become Associated With Surrender?" Originally published 4 November 2015; updated 22 August 2018. In *History.com*. Available at: https://www.history.com/news/when-did-the-white-flag-become-associated-with-surrender

Ansari, Maira. "Birds Dying in Indiana and Kentucky Remains a 6 Mystery". WVLT, Wave 3 News. 26 June 2021. Available at: https://www.wave3.com/2021/06/26/birds-dying-indiana-kentucky-remains-mystery/

Arnold, Carrie. "Horseshoe Crab Blood is Key to Making a Covid-19 Vaccine But The Ecosystem May Suffer." In *National Geographic*. 2 July 2020. https://www.nationalgeographic.com/animals/article/covid-vaccine-needs-horseshoe-crab-blood

Artisson, Robin. *An Carow Gwyn: Sorcery and the Ancient Fayerie Faith*. Bangor: Black Malkin Press, 2018.

Artisson, Robin. *The House of the Giantess: Material, Relationship, History, and Primal Harmony*. Hancock Co., Maine: Black Malkin Press, 2021.

Bahnman, Fred. "The Church Forests of Ethiopia." In *Emergence Magazine*. 11 January 2020. Available at: https://emergencemagazine.org/feature/the-church-forests-of-ethiopia/

Baichwal, Jennifer (director) and Burtynsky, Edward. *Manufactured Landscapes* (film). New York: Zeitgeist Films, 2006.

Barnea, A, and F Nottebohm. "Seasonal recruitment of hippocampal neurons in adult free-ranging black-capped chickadees." In *Proceedings of the National Academy of Sciences of the United States of America* vol. 91,23 (1994): 11217-21. Available at: doi:10.1073/pnas.91.23.11217

Bar-On, Yinon M., Rob Phillips, and Ron Milo. "The Biomass Distribution on Earth." In Proceedings of the National Academy of Sciences of the United States of America. 115 (25) 6506-6511. 19 June 2018. Available at: https://www.pnas.org/content/115/25/6506

Bateson Gregory. *Mind and Nature: A Necessary Unity*. New York: E.P. Dutton, 1979.

Baudelaire, Charles. *The Flowers of Evil*. Trans. James N. McGowan. Oxford: Oxford University Press, 2008.

BBC. "Gower Carve Reindeer Carving is Britain's Oldest Rock Art." In *BBC*. 29 June 2012. https://www.bbc.com/news/uk-wales-south-west-wales-18648683

BBC. "Exmoor: 'Stunning' bluebells hint at a wooded past." In *BBC* | England |Somerset. 25 May 2022. Available at: https://www.bbc.com/news/uk-england-somerset-61583521

Beckett, John. "Reclaiming Your Sovereignty" In *Under the Ancient Oaks* (blog). *Patheos Pagan*. 17 March 2013. Available at: https://www.patheos.com/blogs/johnbeckett/2013/03/reclaiming-your-sovereignty.html

Bek-Pedersen, Karen. *Norns in Old Norse Mythology*. Edinbirth: Dundein Academic Press, 2011.

Berry, Wendell. *Sex, Economy, Freedom & Community*. New York: Pantheon Books, 1992.

Bhagwandin, Annie. *The Chestnut Cook Book: Recipes, Folklore, and Practical Information*. Tucson: Hats Off Books, 2003.

Blackie, Sharon. "Why Enchantment Matters." Author's blog. 22 March 2016. https://sharonblackie.net/why-enchantment-matters/

Botero, Carlos A. et al. "The Ecology of Religious Beliefs". In *Proceedings of the National Academy of Sciences*. 25 November 2014. 111 (47). Available at: https://www.pnas.org/content/111/47/16784

Bower, Bruce. "Neandertals Were the First Hominids to Turn Forest into Grassland 125,000 Years Ago." In *Science News*. 15 December 2021. https://www.sciencenews.org/article/neandertals-first-hominid-modify-environment-forest-grassland

Brooks, Michael. "Is the Universe Conscious? It Seems Impossible Until You Do The Maths". In *New Scientist*. 29 April, 2020. Available at: https://www.newscientist.com/article/mg24632800-900-is-the-universe-conscious-it-seems-impossible-until-you-do-the-maths/

Bryce, Emma. "What's the First Species Humans Drove to extinction?" In *LiveScience*. 10 October 2020. Available at: https://www.livescience.com/first-human-caused-animal-extinction.html

Bugge, John. "Fertility Myth and Female Sovereignty in The Weddynge of Sir Gawen and Dame Ragnell." In *The Chaucer Review*. Vol. 39, No. 2. 2004, pp. 198-218. Available at: https://www.jstor.org/stable/25094283

Carrington, Damian. "Plummeting Insect Numbers 'Threaten Collapse of Nature'". In *The Guardian*. 10 February 2019. Available at: https://www.theguardian.com/environment/2019/feb/10/plummeting-insect-numbers-threaten-collapse-of-nature

Chainey, Dee Dee. *A Treasury of British Folklore: Maypoles, Mandrakes & Mistletoe*. London: National Trust Books, 2018.

Chakrabarty, Dipesh. "The Climate of History: Four Theses." In *Critical Inquiry*. Vol. 35, No. 2, pp. 197-222. Winter 2009. Available at: https://www.jstor.org/stable/10.1086/596640

Charles, Leonard et al. "Where You At? A Bioregional Quiz." In *Coevolution Quarterly* 32. Winter, 1981, p. 1. Available at: https://dces.wisc.edu/wp-content/uploads/sites/128/2013/08/Where-You-At-Quiz.pdf

Christensen, Villy, et al. "Fish Biomass in the World Ocean: A Century of Decline." In *Marine Ecology Progress Series*. Working Paper #2011-06. January 2011. Available at: https://www.researchgate.net/publication/266684781_A_century_of_fish_biomass_decline_in_the_ocean

Clark, Andy, and David Chalmers. "The Extended Mind." In *Analysis* 58:1. 1998. Available at: http://consc.net/papers/extended.html

Clark, John. "The Temple of Diana." In *Interpreting Roman London: Papers in Memory of Hugh Chapman*. Oxford: Oxbow Books, 1996. Available at: https://www.academia.edu/5937963/The_Temple_of_Diana

Classen, Albrecht (ed). *Meeting the Foreign in the Middle Ages*. Routledge: New York, 2002.

Cohen, Nick. "Surely, the Link Between Abusing Animals and the World's Health is Now Clear". In *The Guardian*. 11 April 2020. https://www.theguardian.com/commentisfree/2020/apr/11/surely-the-link-between-abusing-animals-and-the-worlds-health-is-now-clear

Collins Dictionary. "Hybris". Available at: https://www.collinsdictionary.com/dictionary/english/hybris

Coomaraswamy, Ananda. "On the Loathly Bride". In *Speculum: A Journal of Medieval Studies*. Vol. 20, No. 4. October 1945. Available at: https://www.jstor.org/stable/2856723

cummings, e. e. *Complete Poems 1904-1962*. George J. Firmage, ed. New York: Liveright Publishing Corporation, 1973/1991.

Curzon, Catherine. "Franz Ferdinand Killed Almost Everything on his 1893 World Tour". In *History Answers*. 10 July 2017. https://www.historyanswers.co.uk/kings-queens/franz-ferdinand-killed-almost-everything-on-his-1893-world-tour/

Darimont, Chris T. et al. "The Unique Ecology of Human Predators". In *Science*. 21 August 2015. Available at: https://www.science.org/doi/10.1126/science.aac4249

Dash, Mike. "Curses! Archduke Franz Ferdinand And His Astounding Death Car." In *Smithsonian*. 22 April 2013. http://www.smithsonianmag.com/history/curses-archduke-franz-ferdinand-and-his-astounding-death-car-27381052/

David, Bruno, et al. *Muséum Manifesto: Facing the Limits*. Trans. Letitia Farris-Toussaint. Paris: Éditions du Muséum National d'Histoire Naturelle Publications, 2020.

David, Bruno, et al. *Muséum Manifesto: Humans and Other Animals*. Trans. Letitia Farris-Toussaint. Paris: Éditions du Muséum National d'Histoire Naturelle Publications, 2019.

Davidson, Helen. "Hong Kong to Kill Thousands of Hamsters After Covid Found in 11". In *The Guardian*. 18 January 2022. Available at: https://www.theguardian.com/world/2022/jan/18/hong-kong-cull-thousands-hamsters-covid-pet-shop-virus-animals

Definition of Degrowth. Degrowth.org. Available at: www.degrowth.org/definition

Deitz, Bibi. "The Phenomenon of the Green Wall: An Interview with Ethnobotanist Hayden Stebbins." In *Medium*. 23 October, 2017. Available at: https://medium.com/the-assemblage-journal/the-phenomenon-of-the-green-wall-an-interview-with-ethnobotanist-hayden-stebbins-d44d0288aef9

De Voraigne, Jacobus. *The Golden Legend*. Wyatt North, ed. Wyatt North Publishing: Boston, 2020.

Dodds, Joseph. "Animal Totems and Taboos: An Ecopsychoanalytic Perspective." In *PSYART: A Hyperlink Journal for the Psychological Study of the Arts*. 26 November, 2012. Available at: https://www.researchgate.net/publication/340653246_Animal_Totems_and_Taboos_An_Ecopsychoanalytic_Perspective

Dodds, Joseph. "Elemental Catastrophe: Ecopsychoanalysis and the Viral Uncanny of Covid-19." In *Stillpoint*. Undated. Available at: https://stillpointmag.org/articles/elemental-catastrophe-ecopsychoanalysis-and-the-viral-uncanny-of-covid-19/

Dodds, Joseph. "The Ecology of Phantasy: Ecopsychoanalysis and the Three Ecologies." In *Vital Signs: Psychological Responses to Ecological Crisis*. Oxfordshire: Routledge, 2012. Available at: https://www.researchgate.net/publication/340967212_The_ecology_of_phantasy_ecopsychoanalysis_and_the_three_ecologies

Dodds, Kieran. "Hierotopia." Online photography exhibition with commentary. Available at the author's website: https://www.kierandodds.com/work/hierotopia/

Dolnick, Edward. "Why it Took Scientists So Long To Figure Out Where Babies Come From." In *Atlas Obscura*. 11 July 2017. https://www.atlasobscura.com/articles/discovery-where-babies-come-from

Doucleff, Michaeleen. "How SARS-CoV-2 in American deer could alter the course of the global pandemic." In *NPR*. 10 November 2021. Available at: https://www.npr.org/sections/goatsandsoda/2021/11/10/1054224204/how-sars-cov-2-in-american-deer-could-alter-the-course-of-the-global-pandemic

Dressler, Mason and Jake Maynard. "The History of Unicorns." In *Sutori.com* Available at: https://www.sutori.com/story/the-history-of-unicorns--8ggbWQeM5qTiqpDj6N3h6fUA

Dryden, John. "The Hind and the Panther a poem in three parts." Printed for Iacob Tonson at at the Iudges Head in Chancery Lane near Fleet Street: London 1687. https://quod.lib.umich.edu/e/eebo/A36627.0001.001?view=toc

Dubow, Ari. "Ornithologists, bird watchers uncover staggering magnitude of bird population decline." In *The Cornell Daily Sun*. 26 September 2019. Available at: https://cornellsun.com/2019/09/26/ornithologists-birdwatchers-uncover-staggering-magnitude-of-bird-population-decline/

Dunk, Marcus. "How the Magical White Hart Inspires Legends (As Well As The Name of A Thousand Pubs)." In *Daily Mail*. 14 February 2008. http://www.dailymail.co.uk/news/article-514249/How-magical-white-hart-inspires-legends-thousand-pubs.html#ixzz56Z3qCcgd

Dwyer-Hemmings, Louis. "'A Wicked Operation'? Tonsillectomy in Twentieth-Century Britain." In *Medical History* 62 (2) April 2018. Available at: https://pubmed.ncbi.nlm.nih.gov/29553012/

Eco, Umberto (ed). *History of Beauty*. New York: Rizzoli International Publications, 2004.

Ehrenreich, Barbara. "'Humans were not centre stage': how ancient cave art puts us in our place." In *The Guardian*. 12 December 2019. Available at: https://www.theguardian.com/artanddesign/2019/dec/12/humans-were-not-centre-stage-ancient-cave-art-painting-lascaux-chauvet-altamira

Eisenstein, Charles. "The Coronation" (essay). March, 2020. Author's blog: https://charleseisenstein.org/essays/the-coronation/

Eisenstein, Charles. *The Coronation: Essays from the Covid Moment.* White River Junction: Chelsea Green Press. 2022.

El Organillero. "Alectryon, the Ancient Greek model for our cucklod's horns?" In *El Organillero* (blog). 16 April 2010. Available at: https://elorganillero.com/blog/2010/04/16/alectryon-the-ancient-greek-model-for-our-cuckolds-horns/

Encyclopaedia Britannica. "Hubris." Available at: https://www.britannica.com/topic/hubris

Etymology Geek. "Pwyll." Available at: https://etymologeek.com/cym/pwyll/62340740

Etymology Online. "Hubris." Available at: https://www.etymonline.com/word/hubris

Etymology Online. "Lord." Available at: https://www.etymonline.com/word/lord

Etymology Online. "Quaint." Available at: https://www.etymonline.com/word/quaint

Evanoff, Richard. "Bioregionalism Comes to Japan: An Interview with Peter Berg" In *Sustainable City* (blog). June 1998. Available at: http://sustainablecity.org/intervws/berg.htm

Evans, Zteve T. "British Legend: The Outlaws of Inglewood and the Feminine Influence." In *Folklore Thursday* (blog). 26 September 2019. https://folklorethursday.com/legends/british-legends-the-outlaws-of-inglewood-and-the-feminine-influence/

Evans, Zteve T. "Legend of the Church of the White Stag". In *Folkrealm Studies* (blog). https://folkrealmstudies.weebly.com/the-legend-of-the-church-of-the-white-stag.html

Faulkner, Travis. "Should Hunters Shoot Albino Deer?" In *Outdoor Life*. 12 September 2011. https://www.outdoorlife.com/blogs/big-buck-zone/2011/09/should-hunters-shoot-albino-deer/

Ferreira, Becky. "Five Million People Die Every Year Now Due to Abnormal Temperatures, Study Reports." In *Vice*. 8 July 2021. Available at: https://www.vice.com/en/article/v7eyn8/five-million-people-die-every-year-now-due-to-abnormal-temperatures-study-reports

Filthy Staff (collective). "Unicorns as Phallic Symbols." 2016. Available at: https://vocal.media/filthy/unicorns-as-phallic-symbols

Fitzgerald, Sunny. "The secret to mindful travel: a walk in the woods." In *National Geographic*. 18 October 2019. Available at: https://www.nationalgeographic.com/travel/article/forest-bathing-nature-walk-health

Ford, Paul F. *Companion to Narnia, Revised Edition: A Complete Guide to the Magical World of C. S. Lewis's Chronicles of Narnia*. New York: HarperCollins, 2005.

Forste-Grupp, Sheryl L. "A Woman Circumvents the Laws of Primogeniture in *The Weddynge of Sir Gawen and Dame Ragnell*." In *Studies in Philology*. Vol. 99, No. 2. Spring 2002. Available at: https://www.jstor.org/stable/4174373

Fox-Davies, Arthur Chares. *A Complete Guide to Heraldry*. (Project Gutenberg e-book #41617). Available at: https://www.gutenberg.org/files/41617/41617-h/41617-h.htm#page191

Freeman, Ari. "Why you aren't just your brain." In *Practical Magical Thinking* (blog). 11 January 2021. https://pragmaticmagicalthinking.blogspot.com/2021/01/10.html

Freud, Sigmund. "The Uncanny" in *The Standard Edition of the Complete Psychological Works of Sigmund Freud* Volume XVII. Trans. and ed. James Strachey and Anna Freud. 1919/1925. London: The Hogarth Press and the Institute of Psycho-Analysis. PDF available at: https://uncanny.la.utexas.edu/wp-content/uploads/2016/04/freud-uncanny_001.pdf

Gardner, Charlie. "Nature's Comeback? No, the Coronavirus Threatens the World's Wildlife." In *The Conversation*. 14 April 2020. Available at: https://theconversation.com/natures-comeback-no-the-coronavirus-pandemic-threatens-the-worlds-wildlife-136209

Gay, Ross. *Book of Delights*. Chapel Hill/New York: Algonquin Books, 2019. The excerpt I cited can be found online on Ambika Kamath's blog: https://ambikamath.com/2020/08/08/love-letter-ross-gay/

Geddes, Linda. "Oldest cooked leftovers ever found suggest Neanderthals were foodies." In *The Guardian*. 23 November 2022. Available at: https://www.theguardian.com/science/2022/nov/23/oldest-cooked-leftovers-ever-found-suggest-neanderthals-were-foodies

Ghose, Tia. "New Theory on Why Stonehenge Was Built." In *Live Science*. 23 April 2013. Available at: https://www.livescience.com/28881-stonehenge-hunting-ground-discovered.html

Giordano, Chiara. "Cats and dogs may need Covid vaccine to curb infections, scientists say." In *The Independent*. 25 January 2021. Available at: https://www.independent.co.uk/news/science/coronavirus-vaccine-cats-dogs-covid-b1792178.html

Glaser, Rabbi Samuel Z. "The Evolution of Civilization: The Biblical Story." In *TheTorah.com* (blog). Available at: https://www.thetorah.com/article/the-evolution-of-civilization-the-biblical-story

Godfrey, Neil. "Thighs: Pythagorean, Biblical and Other." In *Vridar "Musings on Biblical Studies, Politics, Religion Ethics, Human Nature, Tidbits from Science* (blog). 30 April 2020. Available at: https://vridar.org/2020/04/30/thighs-pythagorean-biblical-and-other/

Gorman, Richard. "Atlantic Horseshoe Crabs and Endotoxin Testing: Perspectives on Alternatives, Sustainable Methods, and the 3Rs (Replacement, Reduction, and Refinement)." In *Frontiers in Marine Science*. 30 September 2020. https://www.frontiersin.org/articles/10.3389/fmars.2020.582132/full

Gradige, Sarah, et al. "A Structured Literature Review of the Meat Paradox." In *Social Psychological Bulletin*. Vol 16 (3) Article e5953. 23 September 2021. Available at: https://www.researchgate.net/publication/353804709

Graeber, David and David Wengrow. *The Dawn of Everything: A New History of Humanity*. London: Allen Lane, 2021.

Graham-Rowe, Duncan. "Biodiversity: endangered and in demand." In *Nature*. 480, S101—S103 (2011). 21 December 2011. Available at: https://www.nature.com/articles/480S101a

Grant, Richard. "Biggest. Antlers. Ever. Meet the Irish Elk." In *Smithsonian*. June 2021. Available at: https://www.smithsonianmag.com/smithsonian-institution/irish-elk-biggest-antlers-ever-180977706/

Graves, Robert. *The White Goddess: A Historical Grammar of Poetic Myth*. New York: The Noonday Press, 1948/1992.

Green, Anna. "The Screaming Skulls of England." In *Mental Floss*. 29 October 2015. Available at: https://www.mentalfloss.com/article/70464/screaming-skulls-england

Green, Miranda. *Animals in Celtic Life and Myth*. New York: Routledge, 1998.

Greenfield, Patrick. "Global coral cover has fallen by half since 1950s, analysis finds." In *The Guardian*. 17 September 2021. Available at: https://www.theguardian.com/environment/2021/sep/17/global-coral-cover-halves-since-1950s-analysis-finds-aoe

Grey, Peter. "Rewilding Witchcraft." Lecture for the Pagan Federation, delivered 7 June 2013. Available at: https://scarletimprint.com/journal/rewilding-witchcraft

Grigsby, John. *Warriors of the Wasteland*. London: Watkins Publishing, 2003.

Grigsby, John. *Skyskapes, Landscapes, and the drama of proto-Indo European myth*. Doctoral thesis. University of Bournemouth, 2018.

Grimm Brothers (Jacob and Wilhelm). "The White Snake" (based on translations from the Grimms' *Kinder und Hausmärchen* by Edgar Taylor and Edgar Taylor and Marian Edwardes). Available in the public domain at: http://www.authorama.com/grimms-fairy-tales-36.html

Grover, Natalie. "Deadly Pig Disease Could Have Led to Covid Spillover to Humans, Analysis Suggests." In *The Guardian*. 10 March 2021. Available at: https://www.theguardian.com/environment/2021/mar/10/deadly-pig-disease-could-have-led-to-covid-spillover-to-humans-analysis-suggests

Guattari, Félix. *The Three Ecologies*. Trans. Ian Pindar and Paul Sutton. Brunswick, NJ: Athlone Press, 1989/2000.

Guest, Charlotte Elizabeth (trans.). "Peredur the Son of Evrawc from: *The Mabinogion from the Llyfr Coch o Hergest, and Other Ancient Welsh Manuscripts, with an English Translation and Notes*, 1838. Available in the public domain at: https://d.lib.rochester.edu/camelot/text/guest-peredur

Gumbs, Alexis. *Undrowned: Black Feminist Lessons from Marine Mammals*. Chico: AK Press. 2020.

Hahn, Thomas (ed.) "The Wedding of Sir Gawain and Dame Ragnell" in *Sir Gawain: Eleven Romances and Tales*. Kalamazoo: Medieval Institute Publications, 1995. Available in the public domain at: https://d.lib.rochester.edu/teams/text/hahn-sir-gawain-wedding-of-sir-gawain-and-dame-ragnelle

Hamacher, Duane. "The Memory Code: How Oral Cultures Memorise So Much Information." In *SBS*. 5 October 2016. Available at: https://www.sbs.com.au/topics/science/fundamentals/article/2016/09/28/memory-code-how-oral-cultures-memorise-so-much-information

Harris, Carissa M. "Rape and Justice in *The Wife of Bath's Tale*." In *The Open Access Companion to the Canterbury Tales*. 2017. Available at: https://opencanterburytales.dsl.lsu.edu/wobt1/

Hatala, Andrew et al. "Land and nature as sources of health and resilience among Indigenous youth in an urban Canadian context: a photovoice exploration." In *BMC Public Health* 20. Article number 538 (2020). 20 April 2020. Available at: https://bmcpublichealth.biomedcentral.com/articles/10.1186/s12889-020-08647-z

Heidegger, Martin, *The Fundamental Concepts of Metaphysics: World, Finitude, Solitude*. Trans. William McNeill and Nicholas Walker. Bloomington and Indianapolis: Indiana University Press, 1995.

Heiniger, Abigail. "'The Supreme Question:' Gratifying the Loathly Lady in James Joyce's 'Ulysses'". In *James Joyce Quarterly*, Vol. 49, No. 2. Winter, 2012. pp. 315-334. Available at: https://www.jstor.org/stable/24598823

Hennessy, Mark. "From the Archives: Shooting of Archduke Franz Ferdinand, June 1914." In *Irish Times*. 30 June 2014. Available at: https://www.irishtimes.com/news/world/europe/from-the-archives-shooting-of-archduke-franz-ferdinand-june-1914-1.1849584

Herbermann, Charles George. *The Catholic Encyclopedia: An International Work of Reference on the Constitution, Doctrine, and History of the Catholic Church*. New York: The Encyclopedia Press, Inc., 1913.

Hess, Richard S. *Studies in the Personal Names of Genesis 1-11*. College Park, PA: Penn State University Press, 2009.

Hetherington, David. "A Short History of Scotland's Lost Species 4: The Reindeer." 2 September 2019. Available at: https://www.linkedin.com/pulse/short-history-scotlands-lost-species-4-reindeer-david-hetherington

Hmori, Fred. "The Origin of the Legend of the White Stag." Adapted 10 June 2004. In *whitestag.org* (blog). Available at: https://www.whitestag.org/program_spirit/legend/ethnic_stories_of_the_white_stag.html

Hoare, Philip. "Octlantis: the underwater city built by octopuses." In *The Guardian*. 18 September 2017. Available at: https://www.theguardian.com/environment/shortcuts/2017/sep/18/octlantis-the-underwater-city-built-by-octopuses

Holden, Emily. "US and Canada Have Lost 3 Billion Birds Since 1970." In *The Guardian*. 20 September 2019. Available at: https://www.theguardian.com/environment/blog/2019/sep/19/us-canada-bird-population-losses

Holmgren, David. *RetroSuburbia: The Downshifter's Guide to a Resilient Future*. Seymour, Australia: Melliodora, 2018.

Hubbell, Diana. "The Once Extinct Auroch May Roam Europe Again." In *Atlas Obscura*. 26 January 2022. Available at: https://www.atlasobscura.com/articles/aurochs-rewilding

Hui, Yuk. "On the Persistence of the Non-Modern." In *Afterall Journal*. No. 51. Undated. Available at: https://www.afterall.org/article/on-the-persistence-of-the-non-modern

Humphreys, Olivia. "Why Do We Commemorate Wars but Not Pandemics?" In *CBC Radio*. 21 November 2021. Available at: https://www.cbc.ca/radio/ideas/why-do-we-commemorate-wars-but-not-pandemics-1.6246133

Hunt, Tam. "Electrons May Well Be Conscious." In *Nautilus*. 3 August 2021. Available at: https://nautil.us/electrons-may-very-well-be-conscious-3-9890/

Hunter, Jack (ed.). *Greening the Paranormal: Exploring the Ecology of Extraordinary Experience*. Milton Keynes: August Night Press, 2019.

Hunziker, Robert. "The Truth About IPCC Reports." In *Counterpunch*. 25 March 2022. Available at: https://www.counterpunch.org/2022/03/25/the-truth-about-ipcc-reports/

Ingold, Tim. *Lines: A Brief History*. Oxon: Routledge, 2016.

Ingram, John. *The Haunted Homes and Family Traditions of Great Britain*. London: Gibbings & Company, Ltd., 1901. Available at: https://archive.org/details/hauntedhomesand01ingrgoog/page/n10/mode/2up

INPE Earth Observation. "Monitoring of the Deforestation of the Brazilian Amazon Forest by Satellite." Available (in Portuguese) at: http://www.obt.inpe.br/OBT/assuntos/programas/amazonia/prodes

International Union for the Conservation of Nature Red List: "Species Extinction – The Facts." Available at: https://www.iucn.org/sites/dev/files/import/downloads/species_extinction_05_2007.pdf

Japanese Wiki Corpus (trans.) "Chinju no Mori: Sacred Shrine Forest." Available at: https://www.japanese-wiki-corpus.org/Shinto/Chinju%20no%20Mori%20(Sacred%20Shrine%20Forest).html

Jarvis, Brooke. "The Insect Apocalypse Is Here: What Does It Mean For The Rest of Life on Earth?" In *The New York Times*. 27 November 2018. Available at: https://www.nytimes.com/2018/11/27/magazine/insect-apocalypse.html

Jiang, Mimi. "Diary in Shanghai." In *London Review of Books* (blog). Vol. 44 No. 9. 12 May 2022. Available at: https://www.lrb.co.uk/the-paper/v44/n09/mimi-jiang/diary

Johnson, Greg. "The Odds on God" (book review). In *The New York Times*. 9 October 1994. Available at: https://www.nytimes.com/1994/10/09/books/the-odds-on-god.html

Jung, Carl. Gerhard Adler and R.F.C. Hull (trans). *Collected Works of C.G. Jung*, Volume 8: Structure & Dynamics of the Psyche. Princeton: Princeton University Press, 1970.

Keren, Robert. "The Language of Gendered Violence." 15 March 2012. In *Middlebury Magazine*. The article is longer accessible on the original web page, but can be found on featured speaker Jackson Katz's personal page: http://www.jacksonkatz.com/news/language-gender-violence/

Kimbrough, Liz. "As animals vanish, the plants they spread can't keep pace with climate change." In *Mongabay*. 19 January 2022. Available at: https://news.mongabay.com/2022/01/as-animals-vanish-the-plants-they-spread-cant-keep-pace-with-climate-change/

Kimmerer, Robin Wall. "The serviceberry: an economy of abundance." In *Emergence Magazine*. 10 December 2020. Available at: https://emergencemagazine.org/essay/the-serviceberry/

Kindy, David. "Why Early Humans Built Fires in the Center of Lazaret Cave." In *Smithsonian Magazine*. 22 February 2022. Available at: https://www.smithsonianmag.com/smart-news/why-early-humans-built-fire-in-center-of-cave-180979549/

Koehl, Robert B. "The Chieftain Cup and a Minoan rite of passage." In *The Journal of Hellenic Studies*. Vol. 106. 1986. Available at: https://www.jstor.org/stable/629645

Kuperus, Gerald. "Attunement, Deprivation, and Drive: Heidegger and Animality." In *Philosophy*. Paper 37. Available at: http://repository.usfca.edu/phil/37/

Lang, Andrew. *The Orange Fairy Book*. Originally published in London by Longmans, Green & Co., 1906. Available in the public domain at: https://onemorelibrary.com/index.php/en/?option=com_djclassifieds&format=raw&view=download&task=download&fid=12066

Laskow, Sarah. "The Decapitated Saints Who Still Managed to Hold Their Heads Up." In *Atlas Obscura*. 30 October 2015. Available at: https://www.atlasobscura.com/articles/the-decapitated-saints-who-still-managed-to-hold-their-heads-up

Lecouteaux, Claude. *The Tradition of Household Spirits: Ancestral Lore and Practices*. Trans. Jon E. Graham. Rochester, Vermont: Inner Traditions, 2000.

Lecouteaux, Claude. *Encyclopedia of Norse and Germanic Folklore, Mythology, and Magic*. Trans. Jon E. Graham. Rochester, Vermont: Inner Traditions, 2016.

Le Cunff, Anne-Laure. "Sophrosyne: The Art of Mindful Moderation." In *Ness Labs* (blog). Undated. Available at: https://nesslabs.com/sophrosyne

Lee, Joanne. "I see faces: popular pareidolia and the proliferation of meaning." In: Malinowska, Ania and Lebek, Karolina, (eds.) *Materiality and popular culture: the popular life of things*. Routledge Research in Cultural and Media Studies. Abingdon, Oxon, Routledge, 2016. Available at: https://core.ac.uk/reader/42542150

Lenin, Vladimir Ilyich. *Materialism and Empirio-Criticism*, in *Collected Works*, Vol. 14. Trans. Abraham Fineberg, Clemens Dutt (ed), 1962. Available in the public domain at: https://www.marxists.org/archive/lenin/works/cw/pdf/lenin-cw-vol-14.pdf

Levi-Strauss, Claude. *The Structural Study of Myth*. In *The Journal of American Folklore*, Vol. 268, No. 270. Myth: A Symposium. pp. 428-444. Available at: http://users.uoa.gr/~cdokou/MythLitMA/levi-strauss.pdf

Lewis, Hannah. *Mini-Forest Revolution: Using the Miyawaki Method to Rapidly Rewild the World*. White River Junction: Chelsea Green Press, 2022.

Li, Qing. "'Forest bathing' is great for your health. Here's how to do it." In *Time*. 1 May 2018. Available at: https://time.com/5259602/japanese-forest-bathing/

Lovgren, Stefan. "Many freshwater fish species have declined by 76 percent in less than 50 years." 27 July 2020. In *National Geographic*. Available at: https://www.nationalgeographic.com/animals/article/migratory-freshwater-fish-decline-globally

Mabinogion: Owain ap Urien. Trans. Will Parker. Available in the public domain at: https://www.mabinogion.info/owain.htm

MacFarlane, Robert. "Surprised by Joy: Robert MacFarlane interviews George Monbiot." In *The Guardian*. 29 May 2013. Available at: https://www.monbiot.com/2013/05/29/surprised-by-joy/

MacFarlane, Robert and Jackie Morris. *The Lost Words*. London: Hamish Hamilton, 2017.

Madl, Pierre. "Raping Mother Earth: The Rise and Fall of Western Dominance." Discussion Paper (Adam Lecture) presented in Salzburg on 16 January 2002. Available at: https://biophysics.sbg.ac.at/transcript/rape.pdf

Malory, Thomas. William Caxton, ed. *Le Mort d'Arthur: King Arthur and his Noble Knights of the Round Table*. Available in the public domain from Project Gutenberg: https://www.gutenberg.org/files/1251/1251-h/1251-h.htm#chap51

Mambrol, Nasrullah. "Analysis of John Dryden's The Hind and the Panther." in *Literariness: Literary Theory and Criticism*. 8 July 2020. https://literariness.org/2020/07/08/analysis-of-john-drydens-the-hind-and-the-panther/a

Marshall, Will. "'Climate Change' is Missing the Point. We Have an *Ecosystem Emergency*." In *Medium*. 19 October 2019. Available at: https://medium.com/@will12000/climate-is-missing-the-point-we-have-an-ecosystem-emergency-211b1a348fd

Martin, George R. R. *A Game of Thrones*. New York: Bantam Books, 1996/2011.

Martin, George R. R. *A Clash of Kings*. New York: Bantam Books, 1999/2011.

Marx, Karl. *The Eighteenth Brumaire of Louis Bonaparte*, 1852. Available in the public domain at: https://www.marxists.org/archive/marx/works/1852/18th-brumaire/

Masterson, Andrew. "Origin of drinking horns a hit and myth affair." In *Cosmos Magazine*. 27 November 2018. Available at: https://cosmosmagazine.com/people/origin-of-viking-drinking-horns-a-hit-and-myth-affair/

Matthews, Caitlín. *Arthur and the Sovereignty of Britain: King and Goddess in the Mabinogion*. London: Arkana, 1989.

Matthews, John and Caitlín. *The Complete King Arthur: Many Faces, One Hero*. Rochester, VT: Inner Traditions, 2017.

McEachern, Claire. "Why Do Cuckolds Have Horns?" In *Huntington Library Quarterly*. Vol 71, No. 4 (December 2008). Pp. 607-631. Available at: https://www.jstor.org/stable/10.1525/hlq.2008.71.4.607#metadata_info_tab_contents

McKay, J. G. "The Deer-Cult and Deer-Goddess Cult of the Ancient Caledonians." In *Folklore*. Vol. 43, No. 2. 30 June 1932. Available at: https://www.jstor.org/stable/1256503

McKie, Robin. "Battle to Save Frogs From Global Killer Disease." In *The Guardian*. 20 April 2019. Available at: https://www.theguardian.com/environment/2019/apr/20/battle-to-save-frogs-from-global-killer-disease-amphibians-pathogens

McNerney, Samuel. "A Brief Guide to Embodied Cognition: Why You Are Not Your Brain." In *Guest Blog* (blog). *Scientific American*. 4 November 2011. Available at: https://blogs.scientificamerican.com/guest-blog/a-brief-guide-to-embodied-cognition-why-you-are-not-your-brain/

Mentzer, A.P. "The Role of a Consumer in an Ecosystem." In *Sciencing*. 29 May 2019. Available at: https://sciencing.com/role-consumer-ecosystem-5770576.html

Merchant, Carolyn. "The Violence of Impediments: Francis Bacon and the Origins of Experimentation." In *Isis*. Vol. 99 No. 4. December 2008. Available at: https://www.jstor.org/stable/10.1086/597767

Merriam-Webster. "Hubris." Available at: https://www.merriam-webster.com/dictionary/hubris

Michon, Genevieve. "Revisiting the Resilience of Chestnut Forests in Corsica: from Social-Ecological Systems Theory to Political Ecology." In *Ecology and Society*. Vol 16. No. 2. 2011. Available at: https://www.ecologyandsociety.org/vol16/iss2/art5/

Middle English Compendium (online etymological dictionary). "Grōm." Available at: https://quod.lib.umich.edu/m/middle-english-dictionary/dictionary/MED19560

Monbiot, George (2014). *Feral*. New York: Penguin, 2014.

Monbiot, George (2017). "Everything Must Go." In *The Guardian*. 24 November 2017. Available at: https://www.monbiot.com/2017/11/24/everything-must-go/

Monbiot, George (2017). "George Monbiot: how do we get out of this mess?" In *The Guardian*. 9 September 2017. Available at: https://www.theguardian.com/books/2017/sep/09/george-monbiot-how-de-we-get-out-of-this-mess

Morgan, Lee. *Standing and Not Falling: A Sorcerous Primer in Thirteen Moons*. Winchester: Moon Books, 2019.

Mortali, Micah. *Rewilding: Meditations, Practices, and Skills for Awakening in Nature*. Boulder: Sounds True, 2019.

Morton, Timothy. *Dark Ecology: For a Logic of Future Coexistence*. New York: Columbia University Press, 2016.

Mrozek, Carl. "Nature Up Close: White Deer." In *CBS News*. 19 January 2020. Available at: https://www.cbsnews.com/news/nature-up-close-white-deer-carl-mrozek/

Muir, John. *Our National Parks*. Kaysville, Utah: Gibbs Smith, 1901/2018.

Muir, Tom, and Martin MacIntyre. *Scotland's Storybook: A Magical Collection of Scotland's Tales, Folk and Fairy Stories for all of Scotland's Children, Young People, and Big Folk*. Edinburgh: Scottish Storytelling Center, 2010. Available at: https://tracscotland.org/wp-content/uploads/2019/05/Scotlands-Storybook-2.pdf

Myths, Oddities & Legends of Northeast Wales. "The White Stag of Llangar." In *Curious Clwyd: The Beauty, The History, the Folklore of North East Wales* (blog). Available at: https://www.mythslegendsoddities-north-east-wales.co.uk/white-stag-of-llangar

National Deer Alliance. "For the Few Who Have Albino Deer Superstitions, They're No Joke." 19 February 2020. Available at: https://nationaldeeralliance.com/editorial/for-the-few-who-have-albino-deer-superstitions-theyre-no-joke

Newman, Mike. "Decoded: Jägermeister." In *Cool Material*. https://coolmaterial.com/feature/decoded-jagermeister/

Newton, I. "Weather-related mass-mortality events in migrants." In *Ibis: International Journal of Avian Science*, Vol. 7 149, Issue 3. May 2007. pp. 453-467. Available at: https://onlinelibrary.wiley.com/doi/full/10.1111/j.1474-919X.2007.00704.x

Nixon, Dan. "The Body as Mediator" In *Aeon*. 7 December 2020. Available at: https://aeon.co/essays/the-phenomenology-of-merleau-ponty-and-embodiment-in-the-world

Nordseth, Anna. "Hantavirus study shows restoring forests can reduce zoonotic transition risk." In *Mongabay*. 11 May 2021. Available at: https://news.mongabay.com/2021/05/hantavirus-study-shows-restoring-forests-can-reduce-zoonotic-disease-risk/

Nydam, Anne E. G. (trans.) "Sometimes" by Hermann Hesse. In *Black and White Words and Pictures: A Blog About Block Prints and Juvenile Fantasy (Mostly)* (blog). 8 April 2014. Available at: https://nydamprintsblackandwhite.blogspot.com/2014/04/sometimes.html

O'Donoghue, Seán Padraig. *The Forest Reminds Us Who We Are: Connecting to the Living Medicine of Wild Plants*. Berkeley: North Atlantic Books, 2021.

O'Donoghue, Seán Padraig. *Courting the Wild Queen*. Rodenbourg: Ritona, 2022.

Oswald, Alice (ed.) *A Ted Hughes Bestiary*. London: Faber & Faber Ltd., 2014.

Our World in Data. "Meat consumption vs GDP per capita, 2017." Available at: https://ourworldindata.org/grapher/meat-consumption-vs-gdp-per-capita

Oxford Reference. "Charlton Horn Fair." In *A Dictionary of English Folklore*.

Palmer, Parker. "Their Slow Way" (poem) is found in the article "A Wilderness Pilgrimage: Where We Go When We Die." In *On Being* (blog). 2 September 2015. Available at: https://onbeing.org/blog/a-wilderness-pilgrimage-where-we-go-when-we-die/

Papp, Sandor. Entry on the Târîh-i Üngürûs (Hungarian chronicle compiled and translated by Tercüman Mahmud). Available at: https://islamansiklopedisi.org.tr/tarih-i-ungurus

Parker, Clifton. "Hallucinatory 'voices' shaped by local culture, Stanford anthropologist says." In *Stanford Report*. 16 July 2014. Available at: https://news.stanford.edu/news/2014/july/voices-culture-luhrmann-071614.html

Parker, Will. *The Four Branches of the Mabinogi: Celtic Myth and Medieval Reality*. Oregon House: Bardic Press, 2007.

Paschall, Max. "The Lost Forest Gardens of Europe." In *Shelterwood Forest Farm Blog*. 22 July 2020. Available at: https://www.shelterwoodforestfarm.com/blog/the-lost-forest-gardens-of-europe

Perez, Chrystal. "The Little-Known Tale of the Medieval Unicorn." Art Stories, Series: *Book of Beasts* (blog). Getty.edu. 12 May 2018. Available at: https://blogs.getty.edu/iris/the-little-known-tale-of-the-medieval-unicorn/

Pesic, Peter. "Wrestling with Proteus: Francis Bacon and the 'Torture' of Nature." In *Isis*. Vol. 90 No. 1. March 1999. Available at: https://www.jstor.org/stable/237475

Phippen, J. Weston. "Kill Every Buffalo You Can! Every Buffalo Dead is an Indian Gone!" In *The Atlantic*. 13 May 2016. Available at: https://www.theatlantic.com/national/archive/2016/05/the-buffalo-killers/482349/

Pliny the Elder. *Natural History*, Volume III, Books 8-11 (Loeb Classical Library No. 353). Trans. H. Rackham. Cambridge: Harvard University Press, 1940.

Plutarch, "Life of Sertorius" in *Lives*: Volume VIII: Sertorius and Eumenes. Phocion and Cato the Younger. (Loeb Classical Library No. 100). Trans. Bernadotte Perrin. Cambridge: Harvard University Press, 1919. Available in the public domain at: https://penelope.uchicago.edu/Thayer/e/roman/texts/plutarch/lives/sertorius*.html

Pseudo-Aristotle. *De mirabilibus auscultationibus* (On Marvellous Things Heard), in Minor Works. (Loeb Classical Library No. 307). Trans. W.S. Hett. Cambridge: Harvard University Press, 1936. Available in the public domain at https://penelope.uchicago.edu/Thayer/E/Roman/Texts/Aristotle/de_Mirabilibus*.html

Pursell, Allen, Troy Weldy, and Mark White. "Too Many Deer: A Bigger Threat to Eastern Forests Than Climate Change?" In *Cool Green Science* (blog). Nature.org. 22 August 2013. Available at: https://blog.nature.org/science/2013/08/22/too-many-deer/

Quote Investigator. "The World is Full of Magical Things Patiently Waiting for Our Wits to Grow Sharper." 7 July 2012. Available at: https://quoteinvestigator.com/2012/07/07/magical-things-waiting/

Quote Investigator. "What You Get by Reaching Your Goals is Not Nearly So Important As What You Become By Reaching Them." 12 June 2016. Available at: https://quoteinvestigator.com/2016/12/06/reach-goal/

Ratner, Paul. "Franz Ferdinand 'Radiated an Aura of Strangeness,' Killed Almost 300,000 Animals." 30 April 2018. In *Big Think*. Available at: https://bigthink.com/paul-ratner/the-crazy-story-of-how-archduke-franz-ferdinand-personally-killed-almost-300000-animals

Raypole, Crystal. "Is it Harmful to Eat Dirt, and Why Do Some People Do It?." In *Healthline*. 20 August 2019. Available at: https://www.healthline.com/health/mental-health/eating-dirt

Reidinger, Melinda "Paganism as Practical Spirituality" in Giri, Ananta Kumar (ed.) *Practical Spirituality and Human Development: Transformations in Religions and Societies*. London: Palgrave Macmillan. 2018.

Reidinger, Melinda. "ReWilding Bees: Steps Toward Bioregional Beekeeping." In *Plant Healer Magazine* Volume 5 No. 3. Summer 2015. Available at: https://www.academia.edu/19892140/ReWilding_Bees_Steps_Toward_Bioregional_Beekeeping

Rincon, Paul. "Ancient Britons 'replaced' by newcomers." In *BBC*. 21 February 2018. Available at: https://www.bbc.com/news/science-environment-43115485

Ritchie, Hannah. "The Largest Mammals Have Always Been at the Greatest Risk of Extinction – This Is Still the Case Today." In *Our World in Data*. 9 May 2022. Available at: https://ourworldindata.org/large-mammals-extinction

Rittenberry, Erik. "Rising from the Bones of a Dying World." In *Medium*. 12 April 2020. https://medium.com/@erikrittenberry/rising-from-the-bones-of-a-dying-world-9fba4b5d8fe8

Rogers, Paul. "Mystery of 'Ghosts of the Forest' May Be Solved." In *The Mercury News*. 11 September 2016. Available at: https://www.mercurynews.com/2016/09/11/albino-redwoods-mystery-of-ghosts-of-the-forest-may-be-solved/

Rokhlin, Sophie. "Social Distancing Turns the World Inside Out. That's Why Shamans Do It." In *Kaphi Magazine*. 17 April 2020. Available at: https://kahpi.net/intentional-social-isolation-amazon-shamanic-practices/

Roniger, Taney. "Thingly Affinities: On the Strange Power of Visual Form." In *Battery Journal*. 22 December 2019. Available at: https://www.batteryjournal.org/artculture/2019/12/22/thingly-affinities-on-the-strange-power-of-visual-form-by-taney-roniger

Ros, Karen. "The Late Classical Period of Ancient Greece." Lecture, Ancient Greek Art and Archaeology UIC, Chicago, Nov 2017.

Rowlands, Mark J. *The New Science of the Mind: From Extended Mind to Embodied Phenomenology*. MIT Press (Bradford), 2017.

Ruddiman, William F. "The Early Anthropogenic Hypothesis: Challenges and Responses." In *Review of Geophysics*, 45, Issue 4. December 2007. Available at: https://agupubs.onlinelibrary.wiley.com/doi/full/10.1029/2006RG000207

Russell, Deborah. "'Legend' of the White Deer: Lenape Legend." In *Authors' Den*. Available at: http://www.authorsden.com/categories/story_top.asp?catid=71&id=18862

Rutkoski, Marie. "The Nature of Cinderella." In *LA Review of Books*. 9 July 2012. Available at: https://lareviewofbooks.org/article/the-nature-of-cinderella/

Sahlins, Marshall. "The Original Affluent Society." In *Culture in Practice: Selected Essays*. New York: Zone Books, 2000.

Sahn, Jennifer and George Monbiot. "The Great Rewilding: A Conversation with George Monbiot." In *Orion Magazine*. 2014. Available at: https://orionmagazine.org/article/the-great-rewilding/

St. Osyth Priory. "A History of St. Osyth Priory: Legends and Legacy." Available at: https://www.st-osythpriory.co.uk/history

Salter, G. Connor. "Bible Story of Jacob and Esau." In *Bible Study Tools*. 20 September 2017. https://www.biblestudytools.com/bible-stories/jacob-and-esau-bible-story.html

Samuel, Sigal. "Reading the Bible Through Neuroscience." In *The Atlantic*. 19 September 2017. Available at: https://www.theatlantic.com/international/archive/2017/09/reading-the-bible-through-neuroscience/539871/

Samurović, Katarina. "Study finds Staggering Decline in Marine Fishery Biomass." In *Geography Realm*. 2 November 2020. Available at: https://www.geographyrealm.com/study-finds-staggering-decline-in-marine-fishery-biomass/

Sánchez-Bayo, Francisco, and Kris A. G. Wyckhuys. "Worldwide Decline of the Entomofauna: A review of its drivers." In *Biological Conservation*. Vol 232. April 2019. Pp. 8-27. Available at: https://www.sciencedirect.com/science/article/abs/pii/S0006320718313636 https://doi.org/10.1016/j.biocon.2019.01.020

Sargent, William. "This Animal is Central to Our Fight Against COVID. Now It Needs Our Help." In *WBUR Cognoscenti*. 29 September 2021. Available at: https://www.wbur.org/cognoscenti/2021/09/29/covid-19-horseshoe-crabs-lal-william-sargent

Schmelzer, Matthias and Aaron Vansintjan. "Degrowth is not austerity – it is actually just the opposite." In *Al Jazeera* Opinions | Climate Crisis. 19 September 2022. Available at: https://www.aljazeera.com/opinions/2022/9/19/degrowth-is-not-austerity-it-is-actually-just-the-opposite

Schulz, Kathryn. "Bambi is Even Bleaker than you Thought." In *The New Yorker*. 17 January 2022. Available at: https://www.newyorker.com/magazine/2022/01/24/bambi-is-even-bleaker-than-you-thought

Shakespeare, William. *Julius Caesar*. In *The Riverside Shakespeare*. Boston: Houghton Mifflin Company, 1974.

Shannon, Graeme, Amy Gresham, and Owain Barton. "White-tailed deer found to be huge reservoir of coronavirus infection." In *The Conversation*. 8 November 2021. Available at: https://theconversation.com/white-tailed-deer-found-to-be-huge-reservoir-of-coronavirus-infection-171268

Shiva, Vandana. "A Virus, Humanity, and the Earth." In *Deccan Herald*. 5 April, 2020. www.deccanherald.com/specials/sunday-spotlight/a-virus-humanity-and-the-earth-821527.html

Simon, Zoltan Andrew. "Revised Chronology of the Hungarians." Available at: http://www.correctingworldhistory.com/138796582

Smithers, Lorna. "Those are But Devils." In *From Peneverdant* (blog). 5 April 2019. Available at: https://lornasmithers.wordpress.com/2019/04/05/those-are-but-devils/

Snyder, Gary. "Reinhabitation." In *Manoa*, Vol. 25, Issue 1. Honolulu: University of Hawaii Press. Available via Project Muse at Tufts University at: https://sites.tufts.edu/mythritualsymbol2017/files/2017/08/snyder-reinhabitation.pdf

Sokol, Joshua. "The Thoughts of a Spiderweb." In *Quanta Magazine*. 23 May 2017. Available at: https://www.quantamagazine.org/the-thoughts-of-a-spiderweb-20170523/

Solnit, Rebecca. *Orwell's Roses*. London: Granta, 2021.

Sommer, et. al. "Range Dynamics of the Reindeer in Europe During the Last 25,000 Years." In *Journal of Bioecology*. 41:298-306. February 2014. Available at: https://www.researchgate.net/publication/259176049_Range_dynamics_of_the_reindeer_in_Europe_during_the_last_25000_years

Specht, Liz. "Modernizing Meat Production Will Help us Avoid Pandemics." In *Wired*. 13 March 2020. https://www.wired.com/story/opinion-modernizing-meat-production-will-help-us-avoid-pandemics/

Spirit Box. "Dr. Mark Fitzpatrick on belief, place, and dual observance." Podcast. No. 82, 21 January 2022. Available at: https://www.youtube.com/watch?v=QqmR_f1K4bA

Sports Illustrated Staff. "The Game Hog of Dallowgill: In A Lifetime of Warfare Against the Winged Kingdom Lord Ripon Downed More than 500,000 Birds." In *Sports Illustrated*. 22 May 1972. Available at: https://vault.si.com/vault/1972/05/22/the-game-hog-of-dallowgill

Stapleton, Taylor. "5 Reasons Why Planting Fruit Trees Along Sidewalks is a Terrible Idea." In *Land8* (blog). Landscape Architects' Network. 21 December 2015. Available at: https://land8.com/5-reasons-why-planting-fruit-trees-along-sidewalks-is-a-terrible-idea/

Stephens, Lucas, Earle Ellis, and Dorian Fuller. "The Deep Anthropocene." In *Aeon*. 1 October 2020. Available at: https://aeon.co/essays/revolutionary-archaeology-reveals-the-deepest-possible-anthropocene

Strand, Sophie. *The Flowering Wand: Rewilding the Sacred Masculine*. Rochester, VT: Inner Traditions, 2022.

Strang, Veronica. "Knowing Me Knowing You: Aboriginal and European Concepts of Nature as Self and Other." In *Worldviews*, Vol. 9 No. 1. 2005. Available at: https://www.jstor.org/stable/43809287

Swift, Deborah. "A History of the Cuckold's Horns. In *English Historical Fiction Authors* (blog). 15 February 2017. https://englishhistoryauthors.blogspot.com/2017/02/a-history-of-cuckolds-horns.html

The Old Farmer's Almanac. "Full Moon for March 2022." 16 March, 2022. Available at: https://www.almanac.com/content/full-moon-march

Thoreau, Henry David. *Walden; or, a Life in the Woods*, 1854. Various publishers. Available at: http://www.literaturepage.com/read/walden.html

Torres, Phil. "Against Longtermism." In *Aeon*. 19 October 2021. Available at: https://aeon.co/essays/why-longtermism-is-the-worlds-most-dangerous-secular-credo

Tomory, Zsuzsa (Susan). *Magyar Creation*. 2009. Available at: https://hungarians.weebly.com/uploads/2/0/0/3/20035969/tomory_zsuzsa_-_magyar_creation_01.pdf

Trillo, Sara. "Cursus Cerve." Author's blog. Undated. Available at: https://www.saratrillo.co.uk/cursus-cerve

Turner, Lauren. "Covid: Vaccines for all every four to six months not needed, says expert." In *BBC*. 4 January 2021. Available at: https://www.bbc.com/news/uk-59865108

Universal Leonardo. "Young Woman Seated in a Landscape with a Unicorn." Pages maintained by University of the Arts, London. http://www.universalleonardo.org/work.php?id=438

University of California, San Francisco. "'Awe walks' boost emotional well-being." In *Medical Express*. 21 September 2020. Available at: https://medicalxpress.com/news/2020-09-awe-boost-emotional-well-being.html

University of Colorado, Boulder. "Study linking beneficial bacteria to mental health makes top 10 list for brain research." In *CU Boulder Today*. 5 January 2017. Available at: https://www.colorado.edu/today/2017/01/05/study-linking-beneficial-bacteria-mental-health-makes-top-10-list-brain-research

Wallace, Kathleen. "The self is not singular but a fluid network of identities." In *Aeon*. 18 May 2021. Available at: https://aeon.co/essays/the-self-is-not-singular-but-a-fluid-network-of-identities

Walsh, Fergus. "Pfizer Boss: Annual Covid Jabs for Years to Come." In *BBC*. 2 December 2021. Available at: https://www.bbc.com/news/health-59488848

Warner, Marina. *Fantastic Metamorphoses, Other Worlds: Ways of Telling the Self*. Oxford: Oxford University Press, 2002.

Warner, Marina. *Six Myths of our Time: Little Angels, Little Monsters, Beautiful Beasts, and More*. New York: Vintage Books, 1994.

Warner, Marina. *Wonder Tales*. Oxford: Oxford University Press, 1994.

Wee, Sui-Lee. "Future Vaccines Depend on Test Subjects in Short Supply: Monkeys." In *The New York Times*. 23 February, 2021. Available at: https://www.nytimes.com/2021/02/23/business/covid-vaccine-monkeys.html

Weston, Phoebe. "Birds 'falling out of the sky' in mass die-off in southwestern US." In *The Guardian*. 16 September 2020. Available at: https://www.theguardian.com/environment/2020/sep/16/birds-falling-out-of-the-sky-in-mass-die-off-in-south-western-us-aoe

White, Gordon. *Ani.Mystic: Encounters With A Living Cosmos*. London: Scarlet Imprint, 2022.

Wikipedia. "Extended Mind Thesis," last modified 17 January, 2020. Available at: https://en.wikipedia.org/wiki/Extended_mind_thesis

Wiktionary. "Fey" Available at: https://en.wiktionary.org/wiki/fey

Wiktionary. "$h_1$el". Available at: https://en.wiktionary.org/wiki/Reconstruction:Proto-Indo-European/h%E2%82%81el-

Windling, Terri. "The Animals Returning." In *Myth & Moor* (blog). 7 June 2020. Available at: https://www.terriwindling.com/blog/2020/06/mueller-and-roux.html

Wise, Caroline (ed.). *Finding Elen: The Quest for Elen of the Ways*. London: Eala Press, 2015.

Worster, Donald. *A Passion for Nature: The Life of John Muir*. Oxford: Oxford University Press, 2008.

Wrangham, Richard. *Catching Fire: How Cooking Made Us Human*. New York: Basic Books, 2009.

Yong, Ed. "How Animals Perceive the World." In *The Atlantic*. July/August 2022. Available at: https://www.theatlantic.com/magazine/archive/2022/07/light-noise-pollution-animal-sensory-impact/638446/

Zhang, Sarah. "The Last Days of the Blue-Blood Harvest." In *The Atlantic*. 19 May 2018. Available at: https://www.theatlantic.com/science/archive/2018/05/blood-in-the-water/559229/

Zhao, Qi, et. al. "Global, regional, and national burden of mortality associated with non-optimal ambient temperatures from 2000 to 2019: a three-stage modeling study". In *The Lancet Planetary Health*. 1 July 2021. Available at: https://www.thelancet.com/journals/lanplh/article/PIIS2542-5196(21)00081-4/fulltext

Zhu, Dan, Galbraith, E.D., Reyes-García, V. et al. "Global Hunter-Gatherer Population Densities Constrained by Influence of Seasonality on Diet Composition." In *Nature, Ecology & Evolution* 5, 1536–1545 (2021).

Index

A

A Clerk of Oxford: 76-77
Abraham: 122
Absolutism, Age of: 188
Achaeans: 59
Actaeon: 61, 176
Adam and Eve:
Adam Bell, Clym of the Cloughe, and Wyllyam of Cloudslee: 176,
addiction: 208, 216
ADHD: 206
Adventures of the Sons of Eochaid Mugmedón: 153
afforestation (see Miyawaki method)
African swine fever: 102
afterlife: 166, 188
Agathocles: 60
agriculture (general): 105, 119, 166, 218, 229, 233, 238
agriculture, animal (livestock): 100-101
agriculture, slash-and-burn: 102
agrilogistics: 123, 228
Ajax: 185
Alaca Höyük: 58
Albrecht, Glenn: 11, 125,130, 190-193, 232
alcohol: 67, 208, 248
Alexander the Great: 61
Alfred, Lord Tennyson: 154
alicorn: 83
Alisoun (the Wife of Bath): 159-160
allodial title, allodium: 162-163
Altamira (cave): 54
Alwan, Wes: 141-142
Amangon: 159
amphibians: 126-129
An Carow Gwyn: 14, 46, 171
Anahita: 56
Anatolia: 54, 58
Anderson, Inger: 105
angels: 20-21, 46, 224
animacy: 205-206, 209, 220
animal, experiments on: 22, 28
animalcules: 47
animism: 218-222, 231
Ankisa: 54
Annwfn (see Annwn)
Annwn: 64-71, 173
antelope: 171
Anthropocene, the: 114
antlers: 44-45, 55-63, 69, 78-80, 170; 176-177, 182-183
apocalypse, Biblical 125, 213
Aquitaine: 78
Arawn: 63-65
Arca the Black: 175
ArchaeoGLOBE: 118
Arianrhod: 157-159, 173
art, Paleolithic: 45, 54, 209-210
Artemis (see also Diana): 69-63, 73
Artisson, Robin: 11, 46, 50, 75, 166-171, 181, 192
Athens: 61, 185
aurochs: 15, 45-46, 81
Avalon: 178
awe: 209

axial precession: 166-167

B

Baba Yaga: 74
Bacon, Francis 21-22
Bacon, Roger: 74
Baden-Powell, Robert Stephenson Smyth: 91-92
Bahnman, Fred: 225
Bardugo, Leigh: 25
Barfield, Owen: 140
barrow: 165
Barthes, Roland: 19
baseline: 114, 123-131, 214-216
Bateson, Gregory: 132, 186
Baubo: 167
Baudelaire, Charles: 42, 135, 224
Beardsley, Aubrey: 83
Beauty and the Beast: 27
beavers: 201, 239
Beckett, John: 181, 245
bees: 22, 28, 230
beheading: 73, 156, 164
Bek-Pedersen, Karen: 42
belief-belief: 245-246
Bell Beaker culture: 168
Berg, Peter: 217
Berry, Wendell: 221
bestiary: 21, 82-85
biodiversity: 102, 132, 138
biophilia hypothesis: 142, 204-205, 239
bioregionalism: 217-218
bison: 98, 132, 210
black maiden: 66, 81, 178
Blackie, Sharon: 243
Blanchemal: 154
Blodeuwedd: 173-175
Bloom, Molly: 154
bluebells: 191, 231
boar: 32, 93, 229
bog burial: 181
Book of Ballymote: 153
Book of Revelations: 48
Bors: 28
Botero, Carlos: 123, 186
brachet: 70, 71
Brân the Blessed: 69, 74
Brave New World: 233
breathing exercise: 236-237
Breuil, Henri: 209-210
Brittany: 69, 170
Bronze Age: 46, 58, 74, 167-168, 187, 210
Brutus (Brute the Trojan): 62
Bugge, John: 47, 161, 163, 175, 181
Bulars (Bulgarians): 57
burial mounds: 58, 158, 165, 169
bushmeat: 101

C

Caesar, Julius: 43, 45, 70, 84-85, 151
Cain and Abel: 120-121
Calan Mai (May Day): 173
camel: 102
Camus, Albert: 197
Candlemas: 62
Canterbury Tales: 153, 160-161
capitalism: 114, 183
Capitalocene, the: 114
Caradoc of Llancarfan: 172

Carmina Gaedelica: 54
Carpathian basin: 54
Cassiopeia: 165
castagnetu: 230
Castle of Wonders: 66
castration: 28
Cathol cave: 54
cattle: 43-46, 75, 100, 150, 224
Caucasus: 57-58
Caxton, William: 70
Centers for Disease Control (CDC): 108, 210
Celts: 45, 75
cephalophore: 15, 74
Cernunnos: 45
Cerneyian Hind: 59
Chainey, Dee Dee: 43
Chakrabarty, Dipesh: 114-115
Chalcolithic Age (Copper Age): 58
Chalmers, David: 200-202
Chappaquiddick Affair: 110:
chasse à courre: 80
Chaucer, Geoffrey: 153, 159-160, 165,
chestnut culture (see *castagnetu*)
Chieftain Cup: 166
Child Ballads: 176
Chinju no Mori: 225-226
Christmas: 55
Christy, Henry: 53
Chronicle of the Hungarians: 56
church forest: 223-227,
Church of All Saints Parish (Church of the White Stag): 75
civet, Himalayan palm: 102, 106, 224
Clark, Andy: 200
Clark, John: 62-63
climate change: 114-116, 124-130, 192, 226
Clytemnestra: 27, 55
CO_2 anomaly: 55
coffin: 48
cognition: 196-197, 202-203, 248
Coir Anman: 153
collar, golden: 60-61,67, 72, 149, 151
Collins, Andrew: 55-59, 185
colonialism: 21, 130
Comes, Natale (Natalis Contis): 83
Communism, Chinese: 23, 183
Communism, environmental policy of: 23_24
Conchobar mac Nessa: 175
Confucianism: 24, 226
consciousness: 182-183, 199, 203, 238
consumerism: 190, 214, 215-217
cooking: 113
Coomaraswamy, Ananda: 168
cooperative behavior: 186
coral reefs: 128, 197
Corbet, Richard bishop of Norwich: 62
cork (wood): 229
coronavirus: 102-103, 108, 110, 149-150

Corsica: 230
cosmology: 189-190, 221
Council of Trent: 84
Covid, in deer: 149-150
Covid, vaccine policy: 108-112
crab, horseshoe: 15, 107-109, 126-127, 132
Creator deity: 200
Creiddylad: 172-173, 179
Crimea: 57
crossroads: 178
crucifix: 78
Crux (constellation): 165-168
Csodaszarvas: 54-55, 91, 179
Cú Roí: 175
cults, stellar: 165-168
culture, Indigenous: 149, 207-208, 218-219, 225, 233, 242
culture, Vedic: 58
Cumhaill: 175
cummings, e.e.: 51-52, 195, 244
cunning man: 75
cup-bearer: 166
curse (see also *geas*): 30-37, 75, 87-88, 97, 120-121, 134, 158, 183, 186,
Cursus cerve: 77
Cŵn Annwn: 64
Cygnus (constellation): 55

D

da Vinci, Leonardo: 82
Dali, Salvador: 194
Daoism: 24
Dark Ecology: 42, 138
Dash, Mike: 96
David I, king of Scotland: 180
Davies, Owen: 48
DDT: 22
de Chardin, Pierre Teilhard: 198
de Fournival, Richard: 82
de France, Marie: 67
De heretico comburendo: 164
De te fabula narratur: 15, 24, 249-250
de Tocqueville, Alexis: 204
de Troyes, Chrétien: 66, 159
de Voraigne, Jacobus: 77-78
Dedalus, Stephen: 154
deer cult, Scotland: 54, 76, 177
deer priestesses: 154, 177
deer, Judas: 146
deer, leucistic: 145-147
deer, piebald: 75, 145-146
deer, red: 44, 51, 53, 58-59, 229
deer, roe: 53, 59; 134
deer, sacrifice of: 75
deer, white:
deforestation: 99-100, 105; 116-117, 223
degrowth: 215
Delmarva Peninsula: 148
Deloria, Vine Jr.: 232-233
Demeter: 167
Dereham: 76
Descartes, René: 22, 187-188, 197
Dewey, John: 197
Diana (goddess): 60-63, 73, 176, 178
Diana (Lady Diana Spencer): 63

dindshenchas: 202
Diomedes: 59-60
Dionysus: 28, 176
Diva triformis: 178
divine kingship: 40, 181
Dodds, Joseph: 24, 42-43, 105, 133, 138-139, 180, 193,
Dodds, Kieran: 224-225
doe, horned: 55, 57, 69
Domnena: 76-77
Donne, John: 64
druids: 81, 156, 220
Dryden, John: 84-86
dualism: 8, 187-188, 198
Dula: 57
dullahan: 74
Dylan ail Don: 158

E
eagle: 8, 75, 229
early anthropogenic hypothesis: 116
Easterlin paradox: 190
Ecgberht (Egbert): 76
Edenic Fall, Fall of Man: 21, 119-121
Edern ap Nudd: 172
Ehrenreich, Barbara: 209-210
einkorn: 229
Eisenstein, Charles: 111-112, 131, 147, 18, 214
Elaine of Astolat: 154
Elaphios: 59
Elen: 58, 154
elephant: 45, 58, 117
elk: 44, 45, 58
Elucidation: 159
Elysian oracle: 139
emmer wheat: 229
Enech: 56
Enéh: 56, 59
Enlightenment: 21, 187-188, 198
environment, as concept: 17, 25, 137, 193-194
Environmental Protection Agency: 206
Eurystheus: 59
Evans, Zteve T.: 177-178
exsanguination: 107
extended mind hypothesis: 200-203
extinction: 23, 46, 80-81, 98-99, 106, 117-118, 126-131, 191-192, 213, 232, 243

F
Fates: 41-42
Fear Doirich: 156-157
Feast of the Conversion of St. Paul: 62
Feast of the Holy Rood (Holy Cross): 80
Ferdinand, Franz (Archduke): 93-98
fey: 40, 80, 86, 148
Fianna: 156-157, 171
Fibonacci sequence: 58
Finn, Perdita: 238-239
Fionn mac Cumhail: 156-157, 171, 175
fire, used to transform landscapes: 113-118
Fisher King 27, 39, 66, 80, 93, 170, 193
Fitzpatrick, Mark: 11, 246, 248, 249-250
Flower Bride: 154, 172, 175, 178, 180
flu, Hong Kong 110
flu, Russian: 110
Flu, Spanish: 109-110
foot maiden: 15, 158, 173
forest bathing (see *shinrin yoko*)

Four Branches of the Mabinogi: 8, 63-65, 81, 155, 172, 183
fox: 114, 201
Freeman, Ari: 189, 199
Fresco, Jacques: 233
Freud, Sigmund: 24, 134-137, 140-141
Fromm, Erich: 188, 205
fungi: 142-143, 201, 226, 231

G
Gaheris: 71
Galahad: 26
Ganymede: 166
garden, forest: 228-229
garden, urban: 222
Gardener, Charlie: 102-103
Gawain: 11, 14, 17, 27-29, 71-74, 154-159, 161, 163, 169, 186
geas: 40, 147, 173
geophagia: 238
Gesta Hungarorum: 56-57
ghost: 15, 48, 49, 51, 136, 220
Ghost Pipe: 142-143, 233
Gilfaethwy: 158
Glendinning, Chellis: 207
Glover, Natalie: 102
God (Israeli): 119-124
god, solar: 164-187
goddess, triple: 178
Godfrey, Neil: 28, 69
gods, moralizing high: 123-124, 187
Goewin: 157-158
Good Friday: 78
gorilla: 102
Graeae: 178
Graeber, David: 98, 119
Graham-Rowe, Duncan: 103
Grail: 28, 66, 154, 159
Graves, Robert: 59, 81, 139, 149; 178
Great Chain of Being: 20-21, 130, 187
Green Wall: 193-194, 209, 224-225
Green, Miranda: 44-45, 75
Greenaway, Rob: 207
Grey, Peter: 216
Grigsby, John: 11, 74, 77, 159, 165-167, 176
Grimm, Brothers: 49, 136
Gronw Pebr: 175
groves, temple 225
Guattari, Félix: 138, 199-200
Guest, Charlotte: 66, 81, 172
Guide to Legendary London: 63
Guinevere: 70; 92, 155-156, 164, 169-179
Gumbs, Alexis: 237
gut-brain axis: 197
Gwenhwyfar (see Guinevere)
gwyddbwyll: 66
Gwydion: 258, 175
Gwyn ap Nudd: 169-172
Gwythr: 172-173

H
Hadrian's wall: 74
Haeckel, Ernst: 25, 137
hagiography: 73-78
hagstone: 246
hamartia: 185
Handler, Richard: 11, 21
Haraway, Donna: 114
hart: 7-9, 44, 51, 57, 59, 64-85, 92-93, 139, 153, 156, 161, 183
Hatala, Andrew: 207-208
Hathor: 167
Hattians: 58
Haudenosaunee: 230
hazelnuts: 228-229
head, oracular: 74, 159
head, stag's: 79, 81, 135-136, 155-156,
head, oracular: 74, 159
Heidegger, Martin: 22-23, 197

heimlich: 133-139
Hekate: 178
Helen (of Troy): 27, 61-62,
Hemingway, Ernest: 64, 99
Hepatitis E: 102
Hera: 178
Heracles: 59
Heraclitus: 196
heraldic emblem: 80-81
Hesse, Hermann: 249
hierotopy: 224-227
Hilderbrand, John: 125-126
hind: 44, 57-61, 76, 85-86, 177
Hinduism: 49, 83
hircocervus: 81
Hmori, Fred: 55-57
Hobbes, Thomas: 22
Holmgren, David: 222
holobiont: 197
Holocene: 53, 116-117
Holyrood Abbey: 80
Homer: 27-59
hominins: 113-118, 186, 198, 202
horse: 43-44, 48-49, 51-53, 64-72, 75, 80-81, 161, 172, 278-179, 249
hound: 8, 69-71, 85, 92, 156-157, 172
House of the Giantess: 167
How Culhwch Won Olwen: 172
hubris: 114, 185-186, 193-196, 213, 231
Hughes, Ted: 134-139
Hui, Yuk: 23
Humphreys, Olivia: 11, 218
Hungária (chronicle): 56
Hunor: 56-58
hunters and gatherers: 118-120; 219
Huxley, Aldous: 233
Hyperborea: 59, 81

I
Iguvine Tablets: 75
Iliad: 59
Illuminated Chronicle: 56
Ilona: 55-56, 58, 62
immortality: 81, 85, 189
inbreeding, in deer: 146
Industrial Revolution: 114-115, 131
infertility: 27-28, 93, 170
influenza, see flu
Iron Age: 44, 75
Iroquois (see Haudenosaunee)
Isaac: 122
Isidore of Seville: 82
Israelites: 197

J
Jägermeister: 79
Jandree: 179
Japyassú, Hilton: 202
Joel, Billy: 113
Jones, Marylee: 208
Jordan: 227
Joyce, James: 154
Julius Caesar (play): 84-84
Jung, Carl: 195

K
Kali Ma: 180
Katz, Jackson: 18
Kent: 76
Képes Krónika: 56
Kimmerer, Robin Wall: 211-214, 220
King Arthur: 21-40, 70-74, 92, 155-164, 170-183
King Henry IV: 164
King Richard II: 80
kingship, sacred: 40, 171-172, 181-184,
kurgan: 58

L

L'âge du renne (see Age of Reindeer)
La Tavola Ritonda: 170
Lady of Shalott: 154
Lais of Marie de France: 67
Lake Baikal: 45
Lakoff, George: 198
Lambert: 79
Lancelot: 170
Land of Nod: 121
landscape, harsh: 187
Lang, Andrew: 90
Lartet, Édouard: 53
Lascaux (cave): 54
Last Child in the Woods: 206
Latour, Bruno: 114
Lay of Guigemar: 69-70, 90
Le Morte d'Arthur: 92
Lecouteaux, Claude
Lee, Joanne: 201-202
Legenda Aurea (see The Golden Legend)
Lenape: 148, 183
Lenin, Vladimir: 23
Leopold, Aldo: 132, 233
Lévi-Strauss, Claude: 132-133
Lewis, C.S.: 90-93
Lewis, Hannah: 99, 106, 204, 208, 227-228, 231, 233-234
Li, Qing: 206
Libeaus Desconus: 154
libido: 140-141
Lidov, Alexei: 224
Life of Sertorius: 60
liminality: 66, 72, 90, 134
Limulus Amoebocyte Lysate (LAL): 107
lion: 53, 81-82, 90-91
Llangar: 75
Lleu Llaw Gyffes: 158, 173-175
lockdown: 105-106
Locke, John: 98
loins: 28
Lollards: 164
Long Island: 126-127
longtermism: 192
Lord of the Dead: 64-65
Louv, Richard: 206
Lugh: 173
Luna: 172, 178
lynx: 229

M
Mabinogion (see *Four Branches of the Mabinogi*)
macacque, rhesus
Macfarlane, Robert: 191
Madeglans of Oriande: #79
Madl, Pierre: 21-23, 99, 137
Magdalenian epoch: 53
Magor: 55-59
Magyars: 54, 56, 58
Maidens of the Wells: 157-159
Maikop (Maykop): 58
Makapansgat pebble: 210
Malory, Thomas: 70, 72, 164
mammoth: 53
Manufactured Landscapes: 13-17
Mark of Kált: 56
Marx, Karl: 15, 23-24, 114
Maslin, Mark: 116
Math fab Mathonwy: 158, 173
Matres: 178
Matronae: 178
Matter of Britain: 170
Mazis, Glen: 199
McKay, J. G.: 177
mechanistic worldview: 21-23, 188
Medicine, Traditional Chinese: 103, 106
Melwas: 172
menagn: 224
Menroth: 56
mental illness: 188
Merchant, Carolyn: 21-22, 138

Merleau-Ponty, Maurice: 197-198
Merlin: 30, 70
MERS (virus): 102
Mesolithic Age: 228-229
metallurgy: 121
midsummer: see solstice
migration: 46, 51, 56; of birds 126, 129
milk, of deer: 54, 76
Milky Way: 47, 55, 165-169
Mímir: 74
Minoan culture: 166
Miracle Stag: 54-55
Miyawaki method: 225-228
Miyawaki, Akira: 225-228
Moel Lladdfa: 76
Moirai: 41, 178
Molanus, Johannes: 85
Mollison, Bill: 201
moose: 45, 58
Mordred: 170-171
Morgan, Lee: 245-246
Morris, Jackie: 191
Mortali, Micah: 206
Morton, Timothy: 23-24, 42, 114, 123, 137-138, 228
Mother Goose: 153
Mowaljarlai, David Banggal: 219
Mueller, Lisel: 50-51, 60, 183
Muir, John: 80, 204-205
Muséum Manifesto: Humans and Other Animals: 21, 101, 186, 190
mushrooms (see fungi)
Myers, Brendan: 11, 129, 131, 194, 203-204
Mythologies: 19

N
Narnia: 90-91
nature, as healing: 208
nature, as mother: 179-180
nature, as raped woman: 21-22
Neanderthals: 113-114
near-death experience: 47
necrophilia: 188-191
Nietzsche, Friedrich: 140-141
Nimrod: 55-56
nipah (virus): 102
noble savage: 218
Noë, Alva: 198-199
Norfolk: 76
Normans: 40, 163
Norns: 41-42, 178
North, Ilelen: 196
Novum Organum: 21-22
nun: 73, 80, 170
nymph: 27, 61

O
oak: 175, 182, 229, 244
Object-oriented ontology: 138
octopodes: 128, 201
Oedipus: 185
oikos: 25, 137, 182
Oisín: 156-157
Oláh, Miklós (Nicholas): 56
Omega Point Theory: 198
orchard: 30, 156, 229-203
Orion: 55, 165, 167
Orpheus: 74
Orthodox church: 223-225
Otherworld: 8, 64-65, 70, 163
otters: 192
Otto, Rudolf: 154
overpopulation, deer: 16-150
Ovid: 67
Owain ap Urien: 83
owl: 175
ox: 75, 81

P
palfrey: 70
pallor mortis: 47
pandemic: 105-117, 138
panpsychism: 203
paradoxography: 60
Parcae: 41
pareidolia: 201
Paschall, Max: 166, 221
pastoralism: 119
pathogens: 101, 106-109, 111, 128, 149
peat bog: 45
pederasty: 166
Pella: 61
Perceval, the Story of the Grail: 66
Percival: 28, 66, 170, 178
Peredur: 66, 67, 81, 146, 159, 169
Peredur son of Efrawg: 66
Perlesvaus: 178
permaculture: 168, 228-229
pesticides: 129
Petrarch: 72
Pfizer: 108, 113
Phenomenology of Perception: 198
photography, spirit: 48
photosynthesis: 236
Physiologus: 102
pietà: 180
pigeon: 239
pigs: 75, 100, 224
Placidus: 77-79
Plato: 81, 197
Pleistocene: 53
Pliny the Elder: 60-61
Pliny the Younger: 81
Plutarch: 60-61
Pole Star: 55
poppy: 229
Pound, Ezra: 92
precession of the equinoxes (see axial precession)
predators: 47, 100, 105, 128, 145, 150-151
Primal Matrix: 207
primogeniture: 40
Princip, Gavrilo: 95, 97
Proserpine: 180
Pseudo-Aristotle: 59-60
psychology, Freudian: 42, 132, 194
psychopomp: 49
punt gun: 90
Pwyll: 8, 63-65, 196
Pwyll Pendefig Dyfed: 63

Q
Q fever: 102, 149
quartz: 165-167
Quaternary period: 117

R
Rabelais, François: 82
racism: 21, 66, 192
Ragnelle, Ragnell: 11, 14, 27-39, 74, 133, 154, 158-164, 175, 186
Ramayana: 119
rape: 17-21, 27-28, 37, 55, 61, 70, 73-74, 100, 157-159, 176, 186, 231
re-enchantment: 243, 244
rebirth: 171, 181
recombinant Factor C: 107-109
Reidinger, Melinda: 203, 230
reindeer: 43-44, 53-54, 59, 69, 76, 90, 177
Reindeer, Age of: 53-54
reinhabitation: 217-222, 245
relics: 62, 67
Remedia Amoris: 67
Renaissance: 60, 67, 72-73, 82, 84
Retrosuburbia: 222
rewilding: 216, 218, 228, 230-232, 242

rhinocerous: 53, 103
Rittenberry, Erik: 216, 223
Robinson, Frederick Oliver (Lord Ripon): 98
Roman empire: 190
Roniger, Tany: 205
Ruddiman, William: 116-117
Russell, Deborah: 148-149, 183

S
sacrifice, human: 87
Sadhbh: 156-157
Sahlins, Marshall: 119
Sale, Kirkpatrick: 217
Salk, Jonas: 111
Samuel, Sigal: 197, 200
Sánchez-Bayo, Francisco: 127
SARS (virus): 102, 106
SARS-CoV-2 virus, see Covid
Sartre, Jean-Paul: 187
Saussy, Briana: 11, 28, 140, 159-161, 186
Scientific Revolution: 137, 197
scouting (movement): 91
Scythians: 57-58
Second Treatise of Government: 98
semen: 28, 47, 83
Seneca Munitions Depot: 146
Shakespeare, William: 84-85
sheet, winding for corpse: 48
Shi, Hu: 23-24
Shiva, Vandana: 105-106
shifting baseline syndrome: 114, 124-132
shinrin yoko (forest bathing): 206-207
Sir Gawain and Lady Ragnelle: 11, 14, 27, 28-29, 35, 37, 154, 159, 163
Sir Gromer Somer Joure: 161-164
sit spot: 240-241
Six Myths of our Time: 20
skulls, screaming: 15, 74
Smith, Felisa: 117
Smithers, Lorna: 172-173
snake: 7, 50, 56, 168, 244
Snyder, Gary: 190, 221, 244
Solarpunk: 233
solastalgia: 125, 232
Solnit, Rebecca: 23; 131; 222; 237
songlines: 202
Sophie, Duchess of Hohenburg: 95-97
sophrosyne: 181, 185, 195, 208-211, 235
Southern Cross (see Crux)
sovereignty: 33, 37, 40, 85, 154-166, 170-172, 178-183, 231-235
Sovranty Hag: 153
speir-bhean: 154
St. Eustace (see Placidus)
St. Helena: 55, 62
St. Hubert (Hubertus): 77-79, 92, 98, 148
St. Mildred: 77
St. Osyth (Osgyth): 73
St. Patrick: 220
St. Paul: 62-63
St. Wihtburh (Withburga): 76
St. Winifred: 73, 77, 156, 159
Stag Hunt Mosaic: 61
stag, white: 28-39, 60, 69; 72-75, 80-81, 90-93, 97, 139, 248
Stalin, Joseph: 23, 155
stallion (see horse)
Standing and Not Falling: 245-246; 248
Stebbins, Hayden: 193
Steinbeck, John: 215
Stonehenge: 46, 165-169; 220
Strand, Sophie: 142, 244

Strang, Veronica: 190-193, 219
suburbs: 222
Suibhne (Sweeney, Mad Sweeney): 182-183
swan: 55

T
taboo, relating to death: 45-46
taboo, sexual: 28
Tarih-i Üngürüs: 56
taxonomy: 21, 45
teleology: 21, 23
temple (of Diana): 60, 62
Tercüman, Mahmud: 56-57
terroir: 218
terrorism: 112, 216
testicles: 28
The Adorations: 249
The Circle of Life is Broken: 129
The Dawn of Everything: 119
The Flowering Wand: 143, 245
The Fundamental Concepts of Metaphysics: 23
The Golden Legend: 77-78
The Healing Power of Forests: 228
The Lost Words: 191
The Odyssey: 27
The Old Farmer's Almanac: 242
The Orange Fairy Book: 90
The Persian Wars: 185
The Structural Study of Myth: 185
The Sun Also Rises: 99
The White Doe (fairy tale): 86-89
Thomas, Chris D.: 130
Thoreau, Henry David: 142, 204
Three Gorges Dam: 14
Thunor: 76-77
Thuróczy, János (John, Johannes): 56
time, cyclica: 55, 86l
time, linear: 85
Tipler, Frank J.: 198
Titans, Titanesses: 178
Tóállás (lake): 56
Tomory, Zsuzsa: 49, 54-56
tonsillectomy: 111
Tower of London: 74
Transcendentalism: 204
transhumanism: 188-191, 197
Treatise on Sacred Images: 84
Troy, siege of: 59-62
Tuatha Dé Danann: 156
tynghed: 158, 173

U
Ulysses: 154
uncanny, the: 24, 134-139
unheimlich: 133-139
Unicorn: 15, 73, 81-84, 154
unicorns, as phallic symbols
Ural Mountains: 54
Urðr: 41
Ursa Major: 55
utilitarianism: 21-22
Uzume: 167

V
vaccines: 106-111
VeggieTales: 220
Venerable Order of St. Hubertus: 79; 98
venison: 44, 177
Venus (goddess): 15, 67
Venus (planet): 55
Venus and Tannhäuser: 67
Villodo, Alberto: 141
violence, settler: 98, 99, 170
violence, sexual (see rape)
Virgin Mary: 82
virtue, tests of: 40

virus, Zika: 111
virus, zoonotic: 102-105
Vita Gildae: 172
von Uexkill, Jakob: 23
vulture: 229

W
Walden: 204
Warner, Marina: 20, 27, 86, 142
Warriors of the Wasteland: 74
wasteland: 14, 40, 90, 159, 213, 222-223, 228; 243
weaver: 29, 41-42
Weddynge of Sir Gawen and Dame Ragnell: 159-164
Wengrew, David: 98, 119
weregild: 76
Westminster Abbey: 63
Whit Tuesday: 155
White, Gordon: 7-9, 99
Whiteboys: 157
Wife of Bath's Tale: 153, 159, 177,
wild hunt: 64
Wilson, Edward O.: 142, 205
Windling, Terri: 51
Wledig, Macsen; 154
wolf: 32, 85; 93, 100, 132, 239
Wonder Tales: 86, 142
World Tree: 56, 59
wound, thigh: 28, 69, 83
Wrangham, Richard: 113
Wuhan: 103
Wyckhuys, Kris: 127
wyrd: 29, 41, 249

X
Xerxes: 185

Y
Yakama: 233
Yakama National Correctional and Rehabilitation Facility: 208
Yamna (Pit Grave) culture: 167
Yeats, W.B.: 92, 240
yoga: 203, 215, 235, 242
Yule: 29, 32

Z
Zeno of Citium: 196
Zeus: 28, 58, 60, 166
Zhang, Sarah: 107-108
Ziglar, Zig: 142

Melinda Reidinger

    Melinda Reidinger lives in a rural part of the Czech Republic with her family and two wolfdogs. She's a former academic, and now a writer and translator.

    Her personal practice is best described as eclectic hedgewitchery with elements of classical and fayerie cults.

RITONA

Ritona is a not-for-profit publishing and educational organisation advocating for pluralism, tolerance, and respect for pagan, indigenous, and non-industrial ways of being in the world.

Find out more about our work at ABEAUTIFULRESISTANCE.COM

www.ingramcontent.com/pod-product-compliance
Ingram Content Group UK Ltd.
Pitfield, Milton Keynes, MK11 3LW, UK
UKHW020248240426
12048UKWH00027B/1661